Early Praise for *Effective Remote Work*

Jim has done an outstanding job of distilling years of remote-working experience into a helpful guide for those preparing to orient toward remote work as well as for those who manage a remote workforce.

➤ **Mike Riley**
   Author, *Portable Python Projects*

I've been a remote worker for over a decade. So many of the stories James describes are photographic memories for me. This is the missing manual for turning your team into a remote powerhouse.

➤ **John Athayde**
   Author, *The Rails View*

Working in a partial or fully remote world requires new skills combined with a different mindset. *Effective Remote Work* showcases this mindset through applying practical tools teams can use to build remote-working skills. This book is a must-read for any modern-day development team where anyone at any time might be remote.

➤ **Patrick Kua**
   Founder, patkua.com

Equitable opportunities for all workers regardless of their physical location is one of the most important issues tech companies will face with our new reality of a hybrid workplace. James Stanier provides an actionable blueprint on inclusive practices for remote teams that will make the workplace better for everyone.

➤ **Nik Bhattacharya**
  Senior Engineering Manager, Google

COVID-19 forced us to be remote. James shares the ways we should be doing remote work the right way.

➤ **Jesse Anderson**
  CEO, Big Data Institute

Effective Remote Work

For Yourself, Your Team, and Your Company

James Stanier

The Pragmatic Bookshelf

Raleigh, North Carolina

Many of the designations used by manufacturers and sellers to distinguish their products are claimed as trademarks. Where those designations appear in this book, and The Pragmatic Programmers, LLC was aware of a trademark claim, the designations have been printed in initial capital letters or in all capitals. The Pragmatic Starter Kit, The Pragmatic Programmer, Pragmatic Programming, Pragmatic Bookshelf, PragProg and the linking *g* device are trademarks of The Pragmatic Programmers, LLC.

Every precaution was taken in the preparation of this book. However, the publisher assumes no responsibility for errors or omissions, or for damages that may result from the use of information (including program listings) contained herein.

For our complete catalog of hands-on, practical, and Pragmatic content for software developers, please visit *https://pragprog.com*.

The team that produced this book includes:

CEO: Dave Rankin
COO: Janet Furlow
Managing Editor: Tammy Coron
Development Editor: Adaobi Obi Tulton
Copy Editor: Jennifer Whipple
Indexing: Potomac Indexing, LLC
Layout: Gilson Graphics
Founders: Andy Hunt and Dave Thomas

For sales, volume licensing, and support, please contact *support@pragprog.com*.

For international rights, please contact *rights@pragprog.com*.

Contents

Part III — Creating a World-Class Remote Culture

Acknowledgments

When I finished my first book—*Become an Effective Software Engineering Manager*—at the beginning of 2020, I said to myself, tired from writing more than 300 pages, that I wasn't going to be doing *that* again anytime soon. However, 18 months later I find myself sitting here writing the "Acknowledgements" section of my second book.

Well, what happened? As you may know, *a lot* happened in that year. And much of it was challenging. We found ourselves stuck at home, away from our families, in a place that we'd settled in primarily due to the location of an office.

As the months unfolded, the pandemic made us completely rethink our life choices. Remote work developed from a novelty into an essential part of our lives. We sold our house and relocated across the country so that we could be near our families and the Cumbrian coasts, lakes, and mountains that we love. We quit our old jobs and took the plunge into something new. I got my dream job working for Shopify, a fully remote company. Rebecca, my partner, started her own business. We've never been busier, happier, and more connected to others. A new chapter in our lives has begun thanks to working remotely.

In fact, remote working has had such an impact on us that the possibility of writing about everything that we've learned from transitioning ourselves and our teams to remote seemed almost too good to be true. I'm thankful that The Pragmatic Bookshelf has yet again given me the opportunity to write about a subject that is tangential from all of the fantastic technical books that make up the majority of its canon. It's been a pleasure to work in partnership again with Adaobi Obi Tulton, a true superstar of an editor who has made this book so much better than I could have done by myself.

The ideas in this book didn't emerge in isolation. I'd like to thank all of my previous colleagues at Brandwatch for having countless invaluable discussions and debates as we dealt with the transition to remote work in the pandemic.

Many of those core ideas have been developed into topics in this book. I'd also like to thank my colleagues at Shopify for being so incredibly welcoming, inspirational, and supportive and for being a world-class company for remote workers to be.

As this book was being written, I was thankful to receive in-depth reviews and critiques along the way from a wide network of smart people. Thank you to Dave Copeland, James Da Costa, Jesse Anderson, Mike Riley, Nik Bhattacharya, Pat Kua, Stephen Bussey, John Athayde, and Yanick Nedderhoff for your time and your feedback. You've improved the finished work by an order of magnitude.

Last but not least, I'd like to thank Rebecca Harrison for once again being there every day in every way. Not only have you been my partner, my friend, and my confidant throughout this entire process, you've created the most beautiful illustrations, which adorn many of these pages. I couldn't have done it without you. Once again, thank you to Finch, our Welsh Terrier, for all of the beach walks and chaos that have helped clear my fuzzy brain. You've been acknowledged in *two* books now, but don't let that go to your furry little canine head.

And let's not forget the most important thank-you of them all: you. I hope that this book takes you to wherever you want to go, near or far. The possibilities are truly endless if you have a computer and an Internet connection. Go and do what you want to do. You can.

Even though the future seems far away, it is actually beginning right now.

   Mattie Stepanek

Introduction

Ah, it's you! I'm so glad you're here. We're about to go on a wonderful journey together. But before we get started, I'd like you to think about why you picked up this book. Maybe you are already a remote worker and you're looking to refine and improve your skills. Perhaps your role is now allowing you more flexibility in where you work and you're curious as to how to set yourself up for success. Maybe you're even dreaming of making a big move out of the city and into the country and you want to get an idea of what remote working might mean for you. Whatever your situation, this book is here to show you the way.

There's a considerable cultural shift that's continuing to unfold in the technology industry. Open-plan offices and daily commutes used to be seen as an accepted part of our work lives, with changes in our careers sometimes requiring us to move our homes and our families to faraway cities, or even other countries. However, the times are changing. Technology companies and workers are now seeing the many benefits of allowing remote work to be the norm, not the exception. You, too, can be part of this movement.

But here's the snag: we haven't had much guidance in how to *effectively* work remotely. We have spent decades operating in our offices, interacting predominantly synchronously and face to face with our colleagues. We have gotten used to the amenities of the office, from meeting rooms and whiteboards to communal areas and free coffee. Working remotely isn't just doing your work away from the office. The way in which we work needs to significantly adapt for us to be happy, healthy, and effective while remote. But don't worry: this book will take you on that journey, and *you can do it.*

The Biggest Remote-Working Experiment in History

One of the most significant global events of the twenty-first century so far has been the coronavirus pandemic.[1] The outbreak of the highly infectious

---

1.   https://en.wikipedia.org/wiki/COVID-19

respiratory disease, which began at the end of 2019 and spread worldwide through 2020, caused governments to put whole countries into lockdown, with citizens only allowed to leave their homes to perform essential tasks, such as buying groceries and exercising. If you could work from home, you had to do so. Those who did took part in the biggest remote-working experiment in history, with millions of workers stationed at home for many months.

Few companies were prepared for the reality of their entire workforce working from home. Workers struggled with isolation. They tussled with the difficulty of balancing their home lives and their work lives; the lack of physical space and equipment for a comfortable and ergonomic work space; and the shift from impromptu, synchronous, in-person interactions to scheduled video calls and asynchronous messages. It was a lot to adjust to in such a short space of time.

People experienced Zoom fatigue from spending all day in front of their computers on video calls and then struggled to get their work done effectively in the space in-between. Many people, from individual contributors to CEOs, based on this initial experience, deemed that remote working was impossible to sustain for long periods of time or that it was a fad that would never catch on. The most skeptical even viewed working from home as a way for workers to slack off in private, away from the prying eyes of their managers.

However, despite all of the initial struggle, some workers and companies embraced the change. They recognized that people could be more effective by working flexible hours that suited their home lives. They saw the value in not needing to spend several hours of each day commuting to and from the office. They understood that working remotely created more time that they could spend with family, friends, and loved ones. Those who welcomed a new way of working could begin to see a future where they could have more choices in *where* they wanted to live and *how* they wanted to live their lives.

As the pandemic eased, many companies were changing—or had already changed—to support remote work permanently. To succeed, these companies understood that there had to be adaptations made in the way that people worked together when they were distributed and also that remote culture had to be established from the top down. It couldn't be one rule for the executives and another rule for everyone else.

These companies that embraced remote work spent more time writing to each other and less time on video calls. They allowed people to have more autonomy over when they began and ended their days. They focused on the output of employees rather than the time spent at the computer. These companies realized that you can't work remotely the same way that you did in the office. You had to work differently. You had to adapt. This adaptation process is what this book is about.

Where You're Headed

You may be at different stages on your journey. You might be interested in seeing whether remote working is for you and what it might entail if you were to do it. You may already be a remote worker and are curious about how you can better formalize your remote-working practice to be happier and more effective. You may be a company CEO who is researching whether you should allow your company to be remote and what that might mean for existing and new employees. Regardless of where you are—from individual contributor, to manager, to executive—we've got you covered.

And even if you never work remotely yourself, it's highly likely that you already have colleagues who are remote to you. They may be at home, or they may be in different offices. All of the tools and techniques in this book will give you a better understanding of the challenges that they face when interacting across geographies and time zones. You will learn about many habits, techniques, and tools that may just make you rethink the way in which you currently do things, for the benefit of yourself and others. If you bring a little curiosity, we're sure that the journey we're going to take together will be compelling and worthwhile for you and those you work with.

This book is split into three parts, starting small and specific and then expanding outward into broader and deeper topics. It begins with the basics in a prescriptive manner, such as setting up your home space and managing your workload. Then, as the book progresses, you'll notice that the topics become more abstract and nuanced, where there is no definitive right answer or process. However, we'll always explore topics in such a way that you will have a lot to mull over with regard to how something affects you, your team, and your company.

There's no need to read the book from beginning to end, although we do build upon topics from previous chapters as we progress. And once you're done, we hope that this book can become a reference guide that you dip in and out of long after you've reached the final page.

The Outline of This Book

In the first part of the book, *Getting Oriented for Remote Work*, you're going to start out with the fundamentals. In *A Remote Future*, we're going to explore the possibilities that remote work can offer for you both in your work life and your personal life. Then, in *Getting Set Up*, we'll get hands-on by building your work space, both physical and mental. You'll finish this chapter ready to get your routine and habits in order.

We'll then move on to the second part of the book, *Building Effective Remote Teams*. This is packed full of tools and techniques for how both you and your team can function effectively remotely. This begins with *Treat Everyone as Remote*, an important mantra that will be present throughout the whole book. With this in mind, we'll explore the many facets of synchronous and asynchronous communication in *The Spectrum of Synchronousness*, so you know what to use and when. Then, using the previous two chapters, we'll see how a typical day plays out in the office and see how that compares to successful— and unsuccessful—days spent remotely in *The Same but Different*.

The key to remote communication is the production of documents, diagrams, designs, and video recordings. We'll explore how you can use these to your advantage in *Artifacts for a Better Future*. Building up a library of these artifacts allows you to be prepared for *Onboarding and Orientation*, which needs careful consideration in the remote world. We'll follow this by learning *Effective Communication Techniques* for yourself and your team. Then we'll finish this part of the book by exploring management. This covers both *Managing Yourself* and *Managing Teams* remotely. You'll learn a whole host of ways in which you'll need to adapt your style to be effective.

The third part of the book considers the wider picture: *Creating a World-Class Remote Culture*. We'll consider what factors make a company's remote-working experience great in *The Remote Working Test*. You can apply these to your own company to see what needs improvement or use them if you are interviewing elsewhere. Then, we'll consider *Creating a Handbook*, which can be the central repository of information for your department. In *Becoming Fully Remote*, we'll explore what it means to make remote work the norm for workers rather than the exception, and what effect that has on culture and day-to-day life.

We'll conclude with two chapters focusing on our health and on society. First, we'll focus inward in *The Hard Parts*. Remote working is not all roses; many experience isolation, burnout, and other mental-health issues. We'll explore these so you can look out for yourself and others. Then we'll conclude by taking a forward-thinking look at how we might be able to tackle some of our industry's deep systemic problems in *The Path to Equality Is Remote*.

What's Next?

Before we get going, I'd just like to thank you for picking up this book and embarking on this journey with me. This book is for everyone in the technology industry. No matter your experience or your position, we are all in this together. Remote working is always going to be a part of our work lives from this point onward, so we should treat it as another skill that we all need to continually hone, much like our writing and our programming.

This book contains everything that I wish I knew when I began working remotely, and I hope that it has a positive impact on your life. Maybe you'll find working with others who are not in your office that much easier and more enjoyable after you finish reading it. Perhaps you'll start working from home for a few days a week to spend more time with your family. Maybe you'll even be looking to relocate to a simpler and quieter life while still being able to do the work you love. *So much more* is possible now that we can work remotely. We can all embrace it together. And this is just the beginning. Think about how much innovation we have seen in the last thirty years. Remote working is only going to get better and better.

Now it's time to get started. Let's consider a remote future.

Part I

Getting Oriented for Remote Work

First up, let's get oriented. We'll start out with the basics.

We're going to explore the shift to remote working and what it could mean for all of us in the future. Yes, that includes you.

Then, before we start becoming an effective remote worker, we need to get ourselves prepared. You'll work on the remote setup that you need, which includes your work space and also your habits and mindset.

CHAPTER 1

A Remote Future

```
[09:15] ben: so how are we doing stand-up now?
[09:15] you: video call, the link is on the invite
[09:15] lara: grr, i haven't installed it yet
[09:16] ben: just click "join from browser"
[09:16] lara: cool, joining now
```

Ding-dong!

One by one, familiar faces pop up on your screen. Ben's mouth is moving, but no sound is coming out.

"Ben, you're muted," you say.

He raises his eyebrows and finds the mute button. "Can you hear me now?"

"Loud and clear," says Lara.

"This is weird, isn't it?" you remark.

"Yeah, we haven't got the whiteboard with all of our sticky notes anymore," says Ben.

"Good point," you say. "Did anyone take a picture of it recently?"

"Hmm, no."

"OK, we'll just have to keep track of what we're doing from memory."

Lara has an idea. "How about we use Jira?"

Ben seems unhappy. "Oh man, not Jira. We should use GitHub issues to track our work instead."

"Not everyone has access to our GitHub organization though," you say. "Not enough seats. The product team wouldn't be able to see what we're doing."

"Hmm," says Lara. "Perhaps we could use Trello."

Ben makes a sour face.

You interject. "I wouldn't worry so much for now. We can't go into the office for a while, and this is all a little weird. So let's just carry on the best that we can. We'll work out ticket-tracking software later."

"Just please don't let it be Jira," says Ben.

You hold up both hands. "It's fine, it's fine. What are you all working on today? Let's go around clockwise like we usually do."

Ben and Lara start talking at the same time.

"But I thought I was on the right," says Lara.

"Not on my screen," Ben replies.

"Ben, you can go first," you say.

"OK. First up, finish yesterday's performance bug. But I noticed that none of the build system works from home because we're not on the office network."

"Huh, that sounds bad," says Lara. "Let's all find a solution for that first. We should talk to IT."

Ding-dong!

Emma joins the call, ten minutes late.

"I'm so sorry," she says. "My dog isn't used to me being at home, and she won't stop barking to go outside."

Meanwhile, Ben's connection has frozen and his video feed shows a smudged, pixelated face with its mouth open.

"I have a feeling we're all going to be barking to go outside pretty soon," says Lara.

When humans are beginning to explore new concepts, they tend to use metaphors to aid their understanding. Using metaphors allows other humans to make a link between prior knowledge and a new domain. For example, in more recent history, we have frequently used the term *cloud computing* to refer to using machines that are not our own to run our applications. *Cloud* in this metaphor means *out in the ether somewhere*, rather than computers floating around in the sky. It's easier to explain and allows people who aren't familiar with the concept to more quickly get a feel for what it means.

Metaphors like these were rife in the early days of the World Wide Web. Television programs pondered the effect of the *information superhighway* on society, where everybody would have access to a *global information library*, allowing users to research topics and partake in group discussions from a personal computer.[1] Illustrations on the front covers of magazines depicted roads twisting through outer space, surrounded in a vortex of ones and zeros.

Popular science publications in the '90s wondered whether the Internet revolution could hold the key to a major step change in the way that we worked. If we all had access to the information superhighway, we could simply *telecommute* to work in the morning. Instead of driving our cars or riding the train, we could just *surf the web* from the comfort of our own homes to do our jobs.

As is often the case, the human imagination is able to dream far beyond what is possible at the current time. Significant changes have been required in both technology and culture to transform the concept of telecommuting into the modern-day reality of what we call *remote work*.

The good news is that we now find ourselves at a juncture where those early dreams of telecommuting on the information superhighway can be a reality for each and every one of us.

In this chapter, we are going to consider the impact of our remote future:

- We'll begin by *seeing how technology has progressed* to the point where remote work is now a reality for many—if not all—of us in technology. We'll consider some notable step changes in the history of the Internet that got us here.

- We'll observe how these decades of innovation have now been met with *an event of historical significance that has fast-forwarded societal change.*

- We'll touch upon how *remote working is here to stay and what that means for you.* The skills needed for remote working are now essential for any modern software engineer, whether they decide to work remotely or not.

A Brief History of the Future

Remote working has been a long time coming.

---

1.   https://www.sciencedirect.com/science/article/abs/pii/S0140366497001503

Although we may take our current situation for granted, giant leaps have occurred over decades that have in turn inspired their own subsequent giant leaps. Each consecutive innovation has stood upon the shoulders of the giants that came before it.

The Intergalactic Network

In the 1960s, various early computing experiments were taking place. At the Massachusetts Institute of Technology (MIT), J.C.R. Licklider penned memos about the concept of an *Intergalactic Computer Network*, where everyone on the planet is interconnected and can access the same data and programs wherever they are.[2] Later, as head of the computer research program at the Advanced Research Projects Agency (ARPA), Licklider and colleagues worked on the fundamental building blocks of data communication networks. Concurrently, similar research was taking place at RAND Corporation and the National Physical Laboratory in the United Kingdom.

By 1965, with the brand-new PDP-8 computer, which was small enough to sit on a desktop, researchers turned their attention to the application of computer networks theory to solve a real problem: staff in different locations wanted access to each other's research sites to collaborate together.

By 1968, ARPA spawned the Advanced Research Projects Agency Network (ARPANET) project, the grandparent of the modern Internet. In 1969, four research sites in the United States were selected to build the software that would drive early networking hardware and allow for remote communication, which also required inventing the first network protocols. In September of that year, the first host-to-host communication was made, which, in classic computing fashion, crashed the receiving computer. However, as it often does, the second try worked.

The scientists and researchers were connected, and new ground had been broken.

The World Wide Web

By the time we reached 1989, the global backbones of the Internet were in place, but they were a long way away from the daily life of the everyperson. But a software engineer at CERN, the European Organization for Nuclear Research, Sir Tim Berners-Lee, was getting frustrated at how difficult it was to share information with other researchers.[3]

---

2.   https://www.computerhistory.org/internethistory/1960s/

3.   https://webfoundation.org/about/vision/history-of-the-web/

Sir Tim noted that it was easier to go and ask people a question in person than it was to work out how to log on to a remote machine and then learn a new custom software program on that computer to find what you wanted. However, he had an idea: a technology called *hypertext* could be used to describe information so that it was easily readable, linkable, and discoverable. By 1990, he had written the initial versions of software that enabled HTML, URLs, and HTTP retrieval to work. The World Wide Web was born.

In 1993, it was decided that the technology that powered the web should be available for free, forever. Soon, the first Internet browsers followed, and the rest is history. The popularization of the web fast-forwarded it into the homes of those who could afford it via dial-up modem. It seemed that every computer magazine had a free trial for an Internet provider on a compact disc attached to the front of it.

The early adopters were now connected.

Everything, Everywhere

Home Internet connections were transformed with the introduction of broadband and wireless Internet in the early 2000s. This always-on, high-speed connection, which has been getting increasingly faster and more reasonably priced with time, became as fundamental to the utilities of the modern home as heat and water-main connections.

As the new millennium unfolded, technology progressed at a rapid pace. Cellular networks could achieve the data speeds of broadband. The capabilities of phones advanced to fully fledged, Internet-connected pocket computers that, importantly, most people could afford to own. Anyone could concurrently create documents and spreadsheets, manage codebases, take group video calls in high definition, and record and edit video from wherever they were in the world, often using free software to do so.

Just like that, everyone was connected.

The foundations were all in place, but remote work didn't follow as a natural consequence. Technologists mostly commuted into offices. Shifting the cultural status quo to remote was another matter entirely, requiring a different catalyst for change.

And it came.

Lockdown

On January 9, 2020, the World Health Organization announced that a novel strain of coronavirus had been identified in a hospitalized patient with pneumonia in Wuhan, China.[4] By February 2, travel restrictions began as the recorded fatalities from the novel coronavirus, now known as COVID-19, surpassed those seen in the entire 2002 SARS pandemic.

By March, governments worldwide had declared national health emergencies with cases and hospitalizations rising rapidly across the world. In unprecedented measures, many countries forced all nonessential workers to stay at home in lockdown.

The world began to change with fewer people moving around. Many companies that relied on footfall such as cafés, bars, and restaurants were unable to survive. Shops closed, city centers became ghost towns, and many, regrettably, lost their jobs. But many workers and companies began to discover that those decades of innovation that connected the world together might allow businesses to survive, and even thrive.

Those in the technology industry, and those in other industries who could, began working from home in what was the biggest remote-working experiment in history. The foundations for distributed working—the result of decades of innovation—were already in place. But now they were being put to the test.

Work-from-home guidance continued through most of 2020 and 2021. We tried our best to make it work, despite the difficulties. Early on in the pandemic, when schools and childcare were closed and parenting also included teaching and nursery duties while juggling our jobs, we struggled, all while worrying that those close to us were going to catch the virus. It was a challenging time. But we rose to the challenge.

As time passed, and as restrictions lifted, we saw adaptation. With life becoming a little more normal, and with children returning to school, many people realized that working from home wasn't so bad after all. Many even began to prefer it. They were reaping the benefits of not needing to commute long distances every day, being able to see their families and pets more, and being able to control their work environment in a way that they never could in open-plan offices.

---

4. https://www.who.int/china/news/detail/09-01-2020-who-statement-regarding-cluster-of-pneumonia-cases-in-wuhan-china

Some companies had already decided early on in the pandemic to stay remote when it was over.[5] Others that kept pushing out their potential return-to-office dates were made to think again after surveying their staff. They found that many wanted to be remote all or some of the time in the future.

Even the biggest technology companies that had significant investments in office space found that their employees were less excited about coming back to their campuses than they originally thought. Even in light of the beautiful architecture, free food, and the inimitable presence of their colleagues, the flexibility of remote work was more attractive. Thus, some tech leaders began to change their minds about staff returning to the office. Facebook and Microsoft announced that remote work was now a permanent option for their employees, despite previously not entertaining the idea.[6,7]

The catalyst for change had arrived, and the world of work was likely never to be the same again.

Remote Is Here to Stay

Significant events have a habit of fast-forwarding cultural progress to the point that it becomes almost impossible to reverse. The COVID-19 pandemic was one of those events.

So many workers were now used to the flexibility of working from home that they simply couldn't imagine being without it. For example, staff at the *Washingtonian* magazine walked out when their CEO wrote an op-ed piece that appeared to discourage remote work.[8] Similarly, a U.S. poll from January 2021 showed that 44 percent of people working from home wanted to continue indefinitely.[9] Who would have predicted that response ten years earlier?

When such a significant proportion of the workforce wants something, it becomes a table-stakes factor in hiring and retaining talent. In 2021, it was reported that millions of knowledge workers were quitting their jobs because the pandemic had made them rethink the role of work in their lives altogether.

News outlets called this phenomenon The Great Resignation.[10] A sign of the times was apparent: an analysis of the percentage of job postings on the Y Combinator–run website Hacker News showed that the pandemic generated

5.   https://twitter.com/tobi/status/1263483496087064579
6.   https://www.bbc.co.uk/news/technology-57425636
7.   https://blogs.microsoft.com/blog/2021/03/22/the-philosophy-and-practice-of-our-hybrid-workplace/
8.   https://www.bbc.com/worklife/article/20210618-the-workers-pushing-back-on-the-return-to-the-office
9.   https://news.gallup.com/poll/329501/majority-workers-continue-punch-virtually.aspx
10. https://www.newyorker.com/culture/office-space/why-are-so-many-knowledge-workers-quitting

a shift from 30 percent to 75 percent in jobs that allowed remote work. However, as the pandemic eased during 2021, that percentage was still increasing, to nearly 80 percent of all jobs posted.[11] It seemed that the workforce had spoken, even on a website that had such close ties to Silicon Valley startup culture.

Another Arrow for Your Quiver

So much has changed in so few years. The time that we need to learn the skills to effectively work remotely is now. And that's why this book is here. It's because fully remote collaboration and communication is now no longer solely in the domain of the eccentric, outspoken few; it's what all of us are going to be expected to know as a core facet of our jobs going forward.

This is because even if you like working in an office, it's likely that many of your colleagues are going to be *remote to you*. They may be at home, in coworking spaces, or in other offices distributed around the world. We need to accept that remote workers are always going to be part of our teams and our companies and ensure that we are working together in more effective, efficient, and inclusive ways. We need to change our mindset from optimizing for synchronous physical presence to optimizing for asynchronous global distribution.

Not only will this make your work easier, it will be a force multiplier in how impactful you can be in your role. With remote work, there are far fewer limits to who you can access, who you can talk to, and who you can team up with to bring your ideas to life. Because even though everyone may be far away, we're all just as close to each other as our computer screens. The possibilities are endless.

And the upsides aren't all limited to our work. The possibilities that remote work brings can affect all of our lives in so many ways. That daily 6 a.m. train journey need no longer exist. Parents can see more of their children and make fewer sacrifices in their own careers to raise a family. We can be there for our parents as they get older. We can live somewhere that we choose, rather than somewhere near an office. We can lower the barrier of entry for so many people worldwide who did not have the fortune of being born in particular countries or cities or near prestigious universities.

Like the early packet-switching network experiments in the 1960s, and like the explosion of the World Wide Web in the 1990s, our technology can enable

---

11. https://rinzewind.org/blog-en/2021/percentage-of-hacker-news-job-postings-that-mention-a-remote-option.html

possibilities that we may have never dreamed of. And now those possibilities are for a more diverse, inclusive, and global workplace, wherever we happen to be.

It all starts here. We can learn to thrive, and not just survive, remotely.

Let's get started on this journey together.

Time to Get Set Up

Here's what we covered in this chapter:

- We saw how *technology has progressed to the point where the possibility of remote work is now real* for most of us. We have the machines, connectivity, and tools required to do our jobs wherever we are.

- We needed to combine the tools with an *event that fast-forwarded cultural change in our society.* That shift happened during the COVID-19 pandemic, which enabled the biggest remote-working experiment in human history. It seems that the experiment was successful.

- We now find ourselves at a point where *remote working is here to stay.* We saw that knowing how to work remotely is now an essential skill that you need to work effectively in our industry. Because even if you're not remote, it's likely that many of your colleagues will be.

Given that we're feeling suitably motivated, let's get the practicalities sorted out first. Come with us into the next chapter where we're going to get you set up to succeed.

CHAPTER 2

Getting Set Up

Click.

You join the meeting as the familiar ding-dong sound plays out of your speakers. Abigail has already joined the call.

"Hey!"

"Hello," you reply, increasingly sheepishly.

You begin to notice the drastic difference between your surroundings. There you are, perched in the kitchen, a pile of dishes to your left and some peeling wallpaper to the right.

There Abigail is in what looks like a professional streamer's gaming den. On either side of the frame, you can see how her desk is truly gigantic; it forms a semicircle around her like the command deck of a starship. On her walls neon lights emit a warm, colorful glow. There's even a framed poster of the company logo. Where did she get that?

"Wow," you say. "Your room is amazing. Where are you in your house?"

"I'm in my home office," says Abigail. "It's up here on the top floor, and it looks out over the mountains. Check it out!"

She swings her webcam around and you see one of the most beautiful views that you've ever seen. You don't know what to say.

"Neat, huh? I love being able to work from home."

You glance out your window at the cars on the busy main road below. A pigeon pecks at some litter.

"That's great! I didn't know you lived in such a nice place."

"I'm very lucky. My partner has his studio in the basement, which gives us plenty of space for our nanny to tend to the children on the ground floor."

"Sounds amazing," you say, watching your toddler tugging at the curtains. "Hold on a second." You mute yourself and turn around to shout, "Stop that! Get down! Now!"

You turn on a virtual background. It's a mountain range.

"OK, so can we talk through this design document?"

When we talk about people who are working remotely, it's likely that most of them are working from home. Sure, some remote workers may be living a nomadic lifestyle, traveling the country and working from coffee shops, but the reality is that most of us remote workers are just here at home. Plain and simple.

For those of us who worked in offices for many years, working from home originally seemed like quite a novelty. In fact, the occasional day of working from home because of a doctor's appointment or a child home sick from school may have stirred up nostalgia from childhood memories when we, too, were home from school, complete with awful daytime television and an air of breaking the rules. How naughty.

But the fact of the matter is that working from home isn't a particularly new concept. For example, in England during the Middle Ages, it was common for peasant dwellings and workplaces to be combined under one roof in what has been retrospectively called a *workhome*.[1] Animals would live at one end, and people lived at the other end in an open-plan arrangement. You would see spinning, weaving, butchery, and tanning taking place alongside sleeping and dining. Sometimes a shop front would open onto the street where goods were traded.

At the turn of the nineteenth century, these workhomes became less popular. Sometimes there were practical reasons, such as health and hygiene. But more predominantly, there was a desire to *zone* property so that there were places people worked and places people lived. Social reformers of the time began to rally against the concept of workhomes, destroying the buildings

---

1. http://www.theworkhome.com/history-workhome/

and replacing them with dwellings that were not suitable for both working and living. Working at home was sometimes forbidden in tenancy agreements.

Later, the Industrial Revolution saw the erecting of large factories that workers traveled to daily, clocking in and clocking out at set hours. Workers often lived within small terraced properties that sprung up in the towns that the factories were located within. The mass commute was born.

By the middle of the twentieth century, the only home workers remaining were those in professions such as baking or shopkeeping, or those who had other community roles such as the clergy. From that point onward, most blue- and white-collar workers would accept commuting as a core part of their working life, with some spending many hours a day on trains and in cars going to and from their workplaces and homes. Well-dressed commuters— typically in suits and polished shoes—arriving at the train station at the crack of dawn could be seen as a symbol of success at the time.

Those working in technology may have at some point moved to cities to get jobs. This meant they made numerous compromises around the size of their homes. Those who were at the beginning of their careers may have counted themselves lucky to have a separate bedroom let alone a dedicated space for home working or even a garden for some fresh air.

Before the 2020 pandemic, many people working in technology did not have dedicated office space at the top of their priority list when choosing a place to live. After all, why would they? The company provided all of those things for them. But the extended period of working from home to slow the spread of the coronavirus showed us all just how difficult it can be to configure our homes so that we can do full-time computer work comfortably and safely. After all, we'd have to go back to the Middle Ages for it to be a default consideration of the very architecture of our residences.

In this chapter, we look at getting set up for remote working:

- We look at the *typical provisions of the office* and see which ones we should be aiming to replicate at home.

- We go through the *basic setup*. We cover what you need and some tips for getting your work space sorted.

- Unfortunately, *since we all live in the real world*, we discuss all of the common compromises and difficulties of putting together your home work space and what you can do about them.

- We conclude by *considering the mental scaffolding that you'll need* as part of setting up your work space. It's not all about equipment after all. It's also about your habits and behaviors.

The Office: What We Want and What We Don't

If you're trying to replicate a working environment at home, you should think about what you want. Let's think about the offices that many of us have worked in as a starting point for getting some inspiration. What do we think about when we imagine the office of a technology company? Perhaps it's one or more of the following things:

- Open-plan seating arrangement, maybe even with hot desking so that people can sit where they want

- Plenty of communal areas where staff can intermingle, such as kitchens and sofa spaces

- Meeting rooms and collaborative spaces with whiteboards and screens

- Table tennis, foosball, and other fun group activities

- Buzz of noise and chatter as people meet, greet, enter, and exit

OK, hang on a second.

It seems that most of these features aren't the sort of things that we need to concentrate on replicating in our remote setup. Modern offices are optimized to be an impressive place for visitors, to encourage the presence of staff, and to facilitate in-person collaboration. That's all well and good for when a client is being shown around; but when we begin to think about what we want from our *remote* setup, we realize that our goals are quite different. We need to get right back to basics about what we need to do our jobs well.

We also are inevitably going to have to make compromises because we are providing our own space to work in. That space will likely be limited. We don't have anywhere near the budget that a company would to create our work space. We need to focus on the most important factors and do the best we can with the resources we have.

So what are we going to be doing? If we are working remotely, our interactions with our colleagues will either be written digitally, such as via email or chat, or they will be made via video or voice calls. When we're not interacting with our colleagues, we'll be trying to concentrate on getting our individual work done. On top of all of this, we will likely be spending a lot of the day stationed in the same physical space.

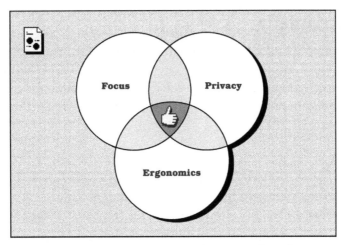

As depicted in the previous diagram, workers need to focus on creating a setup that allows them, to the best of their ability, to meet these three criteria:

- *Focus*. We need to be able to work and minimize our distractions.

- *Ergonomics*. We need to take the proper steps to ensure that we're not putting unnecessary strain on our bodies.

- *Privacy*. We need to be able to have conversations that could be considered sensitive, where the parties involved know that they're not being overheard.

You might not always be able to achieve the perfect setup located in the center of this Venn diagram, but you can use these criteria as a guide to make trade-offs about your work space and also use it to think about how to continually improve your setup with time.

Your Turn: Rate Your Setup

If you've already been working remotely, especially at home, take some time to think about your current setup:

- See how it ranks with the three previous criteria of focus, ergonomics, and privacy. What would you rate it out of ten in each of those areas and why?

- Imagine having a video call with your manager where they are unhappy with your performance. Does that make privacy more important to you than when you first rated your setup?

- Are there any immediate changes that you could make to improve these rankings?

- If you had to compromise among focus, ergonomics, and privacy, what would you choose and why? Do you think it's the right compromise for the long term? If not, why?

The Basics, Briefly

If you're reading this book, you probably already know the basics. So we're not going to bore you to tears about how to do really simple things because you likely already know a lot about setting up computers, for example. But there are some nuances that are worth exploring with regard to your home setup.

Broadband

Unsurprisingly, for the best remote-working experience, you'll want to ensure that you have the best possible Internet broadband connection that you can get. And that Internet connection will need to support *everyone* who is online at any given time in your household to keep conflicts to a minimum. If in doubt, get the bigger package. It's worth it.

Many households use Wi-Fi routers to distribute connectivity around the home. This is certainly easier than wiring Ethernet cables into every room so you can plug in your devices directly. However, depending on the layout of your home and the materials that it's constructed from, you may find that there are areas with poor connectivity. Go into all of the different areas of your home that you may expect to be in with a laptop or similar device and see whether the signal-strength indicator dips or whether videos still play with no issues.

If you do have dead spots, think about how bad the problem could be. If you live alone and you're likely to be spending most of your time at the desk, there might not be a problem. But if you have a busy family life and may need to share space with others or dip in and out of rooms to take calls, poor connectivity is a bind. There are solutions that you can look into for extending your Wi-Fi signal, such as home mesh-network products or power-line adapters. They're well worth it for avoiding frustration.

One important point worth noting: if you are reading this book because you are dreaming about the potential for remote working to allow you to move away from your current location and live somewhere more rural, *always* check broadband speeds before moving. That beautiful house by the lake may be currently unable to get fast enough broadband to have reliable video calls; and if you want it, it may just cost you a small fortune to have engineers run fiber several miles over (or through) a mountain. Always plan for the worst-case scenario.

Laptops and Ergonomics

Unless you work for yourself, it's likely that your computer is provided to you by your employer. It's also likely that it's a laptop rather than a desktop, even if you predominantly work in an office. Laptops make it easier to go from desks to meeting rooms to sofas, allowing you to work from anywhere with minimal context switching. This also has benefits when working remotely because you can perch at a place of your choosing in your home, or you can take your computer to the local coffee shop if you fancy a change of scenery.

With big increases in battery life and computing power, laptops have become our primary machines. Yet this isn't good for your body. Because laptops are primarily designed for portability rather than comfort and for occasional rather than permanent use, there are trade-offs that over time may be harmful for your body.

You need to think about ergonomics. More specifically, you need to make sure your work environment at home is such that you are spending as much time as possible in positions that are comfortable for your body—especially your hands and wrists—and that you're doing so by making conscious choices about where you work and what equipment you use. Otherwise, conditions like repetitive strain injury (RSI) and carpal tunnel syndrome can develop and prevent you from doing your job altogether. Maybe forever. Yes, it really is that serious.

Let's have a look at advice from the Mayo Clinic about setting up a safe work space.[2]

You'll need to do the following:

- *Get a good computer chair* that supports the curve of your back. It needs to be adjustable so that you can ensure that your feet rest flat on the floor and your thighs are parallel to the floor. It should also have armrests that keep your shoulders relaxed while typing. If you can't get your feet flat on the floor, you should use a footrest.

- *Get a desk* that has suitable clearance for your knees to support the proper chair posture. It should be sturdy and not too high. If it has a sharp edge, you should use a wrist rest or pad to dull it.

- *Use an external keyboard and mouse* rather than the ones that are built in to the laptop. This ensures that you can place them in the most comfortable

2. https://www.mayoclinic.org/healthy-lifestyle/adult-health/in-depth/office-ergonomics/art-20046169

position. Laptop keyboards and track pads can force your hands and wrists into positions that could be damaging to them over time.

- *Set up your monitor at the right height* so that it's directly in front of you, at about an arm's length away. The top of the monitor should be at or slightly below eye level. It should be directly in front of your keyboard so that you keep your neck straight. The brightest light source in the room should be to your side. If you don't have a separate monitor, you should put your laptop on a stand with the screen in the previously described position.

As you can see, there may be a lot more equipment required for an ergonomic setup than your employer may be offering to you. Your comfort and safety is paramount; so if your employer is not offering to purchase a chair, desk, keyboard, mouse, and monitor, we highly recommend going into your own pocket to do so. Your hands, wrists, and neck will thank you later.

This doesn't mean that you can't occasionally take your laptop elsewhere in your home or outside to work. In fact, it's encouraged. But you should do long stints of work at a place that's ergonomically correct so that you aren't doing any long-term harm to your body. It might not feel like there are any problems now, but issues can creep up slowly. Prevention here is better than a cure because often there's no cure for issues such as RSI. There's only mitigation.

Webcams and Microphones

In the same way that our laptops aren't primarily designed for ergonomics, they're also not primarily designed for video and voice communication. Sure, they facilitate it, but they do a decent job at it rather than a great job.

Even if you've spent hundreds of hours using your laptop for video calls, how much do you know about what it's like to be on the other end when you're talking? Have a look in the settings of your videoconferencing software and see whether it lets you record a test video that simulates what it's like to be on a call with you. If your videoconferencing software doesn't have that functionality, you can find alternative software, sometimes even built into your operating system, that can do the same job. It's likely that you'll discover the following:

- *The video quality isn't as good as you expected*, especially if you're used to watching high-definition videos online.

- *The audio is way worse than you expected*, possibly with it sounding like you're in an echoey room, or just far away from the computer.

If you want to improve this situation, you'll need to get additional equipment. You'll need a separate webcam and microphone. In terms of complexity, webcams are fairly straightforward. You'll be able to find plenty of webcams that can stream video in high definition, and some of the higher-end models enable you to change optical zoom and field of view to make sure that you're framed correctly and positioned well in the shot so that you and your viewers feel comfortable. Webcams typically connect via standard interfaces such as USB and, as such, are easy to set up and use.

Typically, videoconferencing platforms limit the quality of the video that's being sent and received. This means at the top end of the fidelity spectrum, where you may encounter video makers recommending that you hook up an expensive digital single-lens reflex (SLR) camera, you're going to be spending a lot of money for diminishing returns. If you want the best bang for your buck, a good quality webcam will be a significant upgrade over anything built into your computer.

Microphones on the other hand can get really complicated. Bad audio can be incredibly distracting for participants, so you'll want to get your choice of microphone right. If you want the easiest option for better-quality audio, you can buy a headset that has both headphones and a microphone; although, the quality can vary, so make sure you check out some reviews. This will be immediately better than the laptop microphone. If you prefer an external microphone, you're entering into territory that can quickly get confusing and expensive. You'll soon find yourself wondering whether you want a dynamic, condenser, or ribbon microphone and whether you want it to be cardioid, bidirectional, or omnidirectional. And do you need a boom arm to hold it and a wind muff to cover it? What about a pop filter? Should you be using the auxiliary port (AUX) connection rather than USB?

If you're getting intimidated by these questions, a headset will probably be good enough. If you're intrigued, do your research, because not only can it get complicated, it can get expensive. Roughly speaking, cardioid microphones only pick up sounds that are directly in front of them. They look like the ones that singers use on stage. They mask out other sounds in the room. Bidirectional and omnidirectional microphones pick up sounds from elsewhere, which isn't good if you have a lot of background noise.

Some microphones sit on the table, but you'll need to be mindful of knocking it over or tapping the desk while it's on. Boom arms can attach to the desk and let you bring the microphone closer to your face, like a radio-show host. The choice is yours for what suits you best. A headset is better than the microphone that's built into your laptop, for sure. A $1,000 microphone setup is probably even better, but do consider what is good enough for your situation before you get pulled down the rabbit hole of gear reviews and recommendations. It's probably less than you think you need. The more you spend, the more you get into the law of diminishing returns.

And remember: a good Internet connection is the most important asset that you have. In terms of quality, this is the order of importance: Internet connection, microphone, and camera.

If you have any disabilities, especially physical, there may be additional considerations for workstation ergonomics and video and voice communication beyond what we have just mentioned. These may require more involved and expensive solutions for you to be able to work comfortably and safely while remote, so we would recommend talking to your employer for financial assistance if you haven't already.

In the Real World

You must remember that regardless of how wonderful you want your ideal setup to be, the reality of your home situation is always going to throw a wrench into the works. Let's have a look at some areas where issues can arise and then see what you can possibly do about them.

Lack of Space

The biggest issue with working from home is space. There are many reasons that you may not have a dedicated private-office area in your house. You may live in a city where the price of properties and rent is expensive, meaning that you can't afford it. You may be sharing a house with other housemates and every part of the house, other than your bedroom, is a communal area. It may be early in your career and you haven't had the opportunity to save for a home of your own that you can configure exactly to your needs. You may even own a home but there's no clear area for an office, given that you may not have taken that into consideration when purchasing it many years ago.

This means that we have to compromise. Remember that the perfect home-office space is one that allows you to have *privacy, ergonomics, and focus.* You may not be able to achieve all three, so perhaps you'll have to decide which two to have instead. This may mean putting a desk in the living room to achieve ergonomics, using headphones to focus, but knowing others at home will be able to see your screen. And you may have to take your laptop elsewhere in the house for video calls. The exact compromise will be something that only you can decide.

Depending on your living arrangement, compromises over space can also mean that others in your home need to be mindful of what you need to do your work, and you need to be mindful of what they need to be at home. For example, if the only place that you can achieve an ergonomic computer setup is the kitchen table, it follows that your partner may need to find somewhere else to feed your daughter lunch each day; or perhaps you can find a compromise that works for you both. Maybe if you're both working from home, you can time-share particular areas so that you both get a fair deal.

Either way, any compromise over space, especially when it makes a home space into a multipurpose work and home area, will also require conversations about what it means for people living in the house. It's always recommended to have explicit conversations about the effect on all parties. If these issues are not talked about, they can inevitably bubble up with time and create arguments about one person inconveniencing another.

Poor Connection

Even though broadband connections at home are common, they can sometimes be unreliable. Your connection to the Internet becomes even more critical when working from home because you need it to take part in meetings as well as doing your individual work. There's nothing more frustrating than trying to lead an important meeting only for your connection to be lagging or disconnecting, making you frustrated at something that's entirely out of your control.

We mentioned earlier that you should try and get the best broadband connection that you can, taking into account other Internet usage occurring in your household while you're working. We also mentioned that you should be aware of any areas of your house where the Wi-Fi signal is poor. However, there will be times when despite your best efforts to be on the best broadband plan, and despite your homewide perfect Wi-Fi coverage through your clever router placement and signal extenders, your connection is just going to be bad. Maybe there's a fault on the network, or maybe a vehicle has accidentally backed into the junction box at the end of your street. It happens.

In these situations, you need to think like an engineer and have options that give your connection some backup and resiliency. This could be, for example, checking to see what the quality and data usage is like for a video call on your smartphone via the cellular network. Is that an option that could work for you in a pinch? What about dialing in via phone call? Is that something that your workplace's videoconferencing allows? Could you perhaps get a USB dongle that gives your computer a connection via the cellular network so you can switch out quickly if needed? Or could you use a Wi-Fi hotspot on your phone? You should think about having a number of solutions on hand for when a day of connection doom inevitably happens.

Being prepared can be the difference between losing your connection for fifteen seconds and then continuing as normal via your backup option, or wading through a day of stress and frustration as you continually disconnect with no viable alternatives available to you.

Lack of Privacy

If you aren't a manager, you may think that your privacy isn't all that important when you're at home. The amount of privacy that you need is up to you. However, there are some other people you need to think about:

- *Those you're on video calls with.* Even if you feel comfortable sitting in your living room with the rest of your family in the background, the people on the other end of your video calls may feel uncomfortable being seen by others and also having everything that they're saying potentially broadcast to strangers within earshot.

- *Those in your home.* If *you* have no problem mixing your work life and home life, remember that the others in your household may find it more difficult. For example, if your partner is taking a day off, seeing you working might cause them to think about their own work and feel stressed. Your presence working in a particular space may make others in that space unable to relax or focus.

Consider giving yourself privacy for the benefit of others as well as for yourself. For example, you could take video calls in a quiet space behind a closed door, such as in your bedroom. This minimizes the residual impact of you working around others in your household. It also means that those you are speaking to on video calls will have less hesitation about saying what they really think because they'll feel less observed by people they don't know. Remember that your videoconferencing software may allow you to blur your background or set a background image to increase privacy.

Noise

Noise pollution is a real problem. Working from home may mean that your closest allies in this world may become your closest enemies because of them chewing gum, tapping their fingers, or bouncing their restless legs. Putting headphones on can be a remedy to unwanted noises, but not everyone wants to have to drown out their surroundings with music. Additionally, when wearing headphones, you may end up typing or breathing more loudly, inflicting the pain back on those who were originally annoying you!

Even if you aren't on many video calls during the day, continual hammering on your keyboard may drive others in the room to despair. Multiple people working from home in the same household with no separation from each other's typing, speaking, coughing, and fidgeting can cause a normally happy relationship to turn painful. Did you know that your partner sniffed so much while they were on the computer? Did they *always* eat that loudly?

Have a conversation with those you share your space with about noise. Would you each prefer that calls are taken in a private space? Is it time to stop using that clicky mechanical keyboard until you have a separate office in a bigger house? Would you prefer if you each ate in the kitchen and not in front of each other when you're working? Are the washing machine and vacuum cleaner out of bounds during the workday?

An inconspicuous everyday noise such as a fork tapping on a plate can be a stress trigger for another person. Work out what you and others at home are OK with, and especially what you're *not* OK with, and then all agree to make a best effort attempt at minimizing the noise stress on each other via simple adjustments and allowances.

Installing Mental Scaffolding

There's another part of your setup that's potentially even more important than the physical location that you're working in, and that's your *mental setup*. Even if you've got the most perfect home-office space, your own relationship with it and the boundaries that you set with the rest of your household are going to be what determines your happiness in a remote environment.

Bookends and Checkpoints

One neat part about working in an office is that you don't live there. (At least, you shouldn't be living there.) At the beginning of the day, you travel to the office, and at the end of the day you travel home. This provides you with natural *bookends* to the beginning and the end of your workday, where you bring that physical and mental working environment into your life and then you let it go again when you get home.

There are also various *checkpoints* that are established when you work in an office. Perhaps many people take their lunch break at the same time, which encourages you to do the same. Perhaps your team used to have a routine of taking turns to make a round of tea and coffee for everyone at 11 a.m. These checkpoints provide a natural cadence to the workday that makes it seem less like an eight-hour slog at the computer.

When you're at home, you need to provide these bookends and checkpoints for yourself, even if it seems unnatural. After all, purposefully distracting yourself away from your work seems counterproductive and self-sabotaging. But it's critically important for your mental health to do so. It's also important for those you live with so you can be present for them when you're not working.

Think about a way in which you can create a routine that switches you into work mode at the beginning of the day and then switches you out of work mode at the end of it. These are your bookend activities. They don't need to be grandiose or difficult; you don't have to go running for an hour each morning. However, ensuring that you get up, wash, get dressed, and go for a short walk, for example, mimics the behavior of the morning commute and installs a mental bookend between home life and work life. At the end of the day, shutting down your computer, putting away your laptop, getting changed into more relaxed clothing, exercising, or picking up some groceries, for example, mimics the journey home from work and again installs a mental bookend.

You should also look to weave various checkpoints into the day that you can work toward and then allow yourself to take breaks. Perhaps you could always ensure that you make yourself a nice lunch by blocking out an hour in your calendar to do so. Maybe thirty minutes of exercise each day at a set time would be something to look forward to that again would refresh your mental state. One household chore a day gets you away from the computer and helps you stay on top of everything.

Think about it. What are your bookends and checkpoints going to be? Aim for at least one bookend activity each at the beginning and end of the day and three checkpoints throughout the day, such as coffee breaks, walks, and lunch. Oh, and if you're one of those people who prefers to seamlessly blend home and work all day, without any bookends at all, that's cool too. Whatever works for you.

Staying Healthy

One of the ways in which you can help decide on your bookends and checkpoints is to think about how to stay healthy. This isn't where the book is about to encourage you to take up weightlifting. However, do think about the following questions, which are essential for your physical and mental health:

- *Are you going to be getting enough physical activity?* This can be as simple as a few short walks a day, which can form your bookend or checkpoint activities. Exercise helps you control your weight, reduces the risk of disease, and improves your mental health and mood by producing endorphins. It's so beneficial, you can't ignore it.

- *Are you eating well and staying hydrated?* Being at home and away from all of the nice lunch spots near the office means that eating well can require more effort in the form of grocery shopping, food preparation, and cooking. However, being curious about food and seeing it as a skill to improve can be fun. You can hunt down some quick and healthy recipes and try them out for breakfast, lunch, and dinner. It can form part of your bookends and checkpoints, and it tastes good too.

- *Are you getting outside and among different surroundings?* Even if you're lucky enough to have a large home that caters to all of your needs, it can be detrimental to your mental health to not go anywhere else. It's also surprisingly easy to get into the habit of not leaving the house if there are no real reasons to do so. And we don't mean just doing the school run. Try to make sure that you're visiting different places during the week. Go for a walk and check out that park you've never been to; visit a different grocery store; or switch up your running route regularly so you're experiencing different areas.

- *Are you taking ample time off?* Even though you're working remotely, you need to ensure that you're taking enough vacation. And when you take that vacation, ensure that you actually do something that you can classify as a vacation activity, such as a day trip rather than just staying at home and sitting at the computer. It's vital for your health to do so.

Context Switching and Focus

Think about the cadence, routine, and rhythm of your home life. Is there a possibility that when your work life plays out at home, you're going to be continually bombarded by chaos? After all, perhaps one of the attractions of being able to work from home was that you're able to get away from all of the frustrations that you faced while working in an open-plan office. But did you factor in your partner, children, pets, and neighbors being equally distracting?

Working on this problem involves installing boundaries and making compromises depending on your home situation. For example, if you and your partner both work from home, discuss with each other how you can both have periods of the day to find focus. Perhaps one of you could be uninterruptible in the morning and the other can have that luxury in the afternoon. During a focus period, one of you can wear headphones while the other is there for the doorbell, your dog, or your daughter.

If you're able to come to a predictable arrangement where you have periods of the day in which you can focus, you can begin to arrange your work life around it. You can let your team know that every day your focus time is in the afternoon, for example, so that receiving calls is better for you in the morning when you're more interruptible.

During your focus periods, do whatever you can to ensure that you don't distract yourself. Close any non-work-related applications, put your phone on do-not-disturb mode, and ensure that you make the most of your focus time. That instant message from your friend can wait a couple of hours, and you'll feel better if it does. You can even get creative: if you get a lot of deliveries, you could install a lockable parcel drop box outside your front door so you don't get interrupted. There's always a way to optimize for less distraction. Be curious and try out some ideas.

If you find it hard to force yourself to focus at periods of the day, you can use some techniques to help. The Pomodoro Technique,[3] named after a tomato-shaped kitchen timer, is a time-management method that uses a timer to break down work into twenty-five-minute intervals with five- to ten-minute breaks in-between. You start the timer, do your work, and then make a note of what you've done at the end of each interval. Then you take a break and start on the next *pomodoro*. If you don't want to use a real timer, there are plenty of free websites and applications that you can use. Just search for it.

Work Imprints Itself

That commute to and from the office not only allowed you to switch on and off from work, it allowed you to leave those frustrating days in the place where they happened, far away from your home. That difficult person who made your blood boil could be compartmentalized until the next day when you go back through that office door.

Working remotely means that you're inviting all of the negative parts of work into your home. Frustrating situations, impossible clients, that pull-request argument: they're all now happening in your house. This used to be your safe place where you could shut out the world, but now all of those horrible things are right there with you.

3.　https://en.wikipedia.org/wiki/Pomodoro_Technique

Practicing bookending the day and installing checkpoints where you proactively do something else can help here. However, depending on how much you like your job, you can soon begin to feel that tension and stress imprinting itself on the area of your home that you work from. As you sit at your kitchen table with a coffee on the weekend, you feel your shoulders tensing up from when you sat there yesterday with all of that deadline pressure.

Think about whether you can design your home-working setup so that you can physically, mentally, and visually step away from it at the end of each day. If you are lucky and have plenty of space in your home, you could achieve this by closing your home-office door. But if you're in the more likely scenario of needing to share space, think about ways in which you could work in an area you can close off once you're done with it.

For example, if your desk is positioned in the corner of your living room, could you get a room divider to put in front of it when you aren't using it? Perhaps you could even cover it with a blanket. If your setup shares space with other functions of your household such as where you eat, always tidy everything away at the end of the workday so that it is out of sight and out of mind, ensuring that symbolically you are done until the next morning.

If you find that with time a particular area of your house just feels stressful, switch it up. Move your desk elsewhere if possible, or even just work less ergonomically for a couple of days from your laptop to reset how you feel about that area.

The Golden Rule

We hope that you're now feeling like you've got all of the information that you need to get your remote-working setup configured to the best of your ability, taking into account all of the compromises.

Here's what we covered:

- We enumerated the *typical provisions that you'll have when working in an office* and then thought about which ones you might want and might not want in your remote-working setup. We saw how you'll want to optimize as best as you can for *focus, ergonomics, and privacy* and considered some of the trade-offs that you might have to make to get there.

- We went through *the basics* for your work space and what you'll need.

- We thought about *what happens in the real world* when it comes to your work space and covered some strategies for dealing with the inevitable compromises of not quite having the perfect home office.

- We touched upon what you'll need to do to have the right *mental scaffolding* to ensure that you're setting yourself up for success.

We're going to be digging more into how your working habits and daily routines can play out in Chapter 5, The Same but Different, on page 79. But before we do that, we need to learn the Golden Rule of remote working. Let's look at that next.

Part II

Building Effective Remote Teams

Now that we've got everything set up and ready to go, it's time to start learning and refining all of the new skills that we need to succeed in the remote world.

We'll be covering everything from the mindset of treating everyone as remote, to synchronous and asynchronous communication, comparing life before and after remote working, onboarding new staff, and managing yourself and others.

With all of these tools at your disposal, you'll feel efficient, effective, and productive.

Let's start exploring together.

Equality is the soul of liberty; there is, in fact, no liberty without it.

> Frances Wright

CHAPTER 3

Treat Everyone as Remote

Ding-dong!

With that familiar sound, another video call gets underway. Just how many of these have you had this week? Ten? Fifteen? It's only Tuesday afternoon.

"Hey, everyone."

"Hey, Ben," you reply.

"MMMMFFFFFFFFFFFF BZZZZZZAAARRRRFFFF MMMFFFF!"

You jump out of your seat.

"I think there's a problem with your microphone, Luke. You're really, really loud," says Ben.

There's a rustling sound. "Is that better?" asks Luke.

"Yep, we can hear you now."

You hear the familiar sound of somebody else joining. You switch the view to Gallery to see who it is. The video feed appears to show a table with three indistinguishable human shadows sitting around it. The participant's name is Downtown Coworking Meeting Room 7.

"Hey, is that you, Sarah?" you ask. A voice answers you so quietly that you have to move your head closer to the laptop to hear it.

"Yeah, it's me. I live near Tara and Steve, so we've come over to this coworking space to do our calls today."

"Where's the microphone in that room? I think you're all going to need to speak much louder," says Ben.

A tiny voice replies, "I think it's built into the table somewhere." Sarah starts tapping the table to locate the microphone.

"We'll speak up the best that we can," says one of the three human shadows, although it's not clear who said it. You turn your volume up.

"We came to this space so we could use the whiteboard in our meetings. Seeing as we need to work on how we're going to build the back end, I thought we could draw it out."

"Where's the whiteboard?" you ask.

"Oh, it's just behind us. We've already been thinking about the design before the meeting. Can we take you through it?"

You resize their video feed to full screen. Indeed, behind the human shadows is a whiteboard. However it's so blurry that you can't make out anything that's written on it.

"Is there any way you can bring it closer to the webcam?"

"Sure, we'll try," replies human shape two, wheeling it across the room.

"How's that?" says an even tinier voice.

You squint. "It's better. You'll need to write everything really big though. I think you're farther away from the microphone now as well. I can barely hear you."

You turn your volume up to maximum. Your phone displays a message saying that listening to music at this level for a long period of time may be damaging to your hearing.

Luke speaks.

"MMMMFFFFFFFFFFFF BZZZZZZAAARRRRFFFF MMMFFFF!"

You pick yourself up off the floor.

Have you ever tried to meditate?

In Western culture, interest has been building in what's called the *mindfulness* movement. In our busy lives, filled with increasingly more tasks, interruptions, and distractions, many people have been struggling with their mental health.

Being more mindful in our lives allows us to be more aware of the present moment and the world around us. It can contribute to an improvement in our mental well-being.[1]

Being more mindful is fundamentally simple, but it's not straightforward. You may try to purposefully pay attention in the present moment only to find that merely seconds later you're caught up in a thought or a reaction to an event that's happening around you.

The frenetic and attention-seeking nature of your mind is most noticeable when sitting down and trying to meditate. You find a quiet space and time, get comfortable on a chair or a cushion, and close your eyes to focus all of your attention on your breath.

The breath comes in and you can feel it in your nose, lungs, and movement of your diaphragm. The breath then gently goes out, and that interaction that you had with that person in line at the supermarket was just so incredibly frustrating. You can't believe that they put their basket so close to you! Wasn't that just so rude? How must their parents have raised them to act like that? Oh, hang on, where were you again?

Mindfulness is simple but not straightforward. It highlights the contradiction between your intention to be mindful and the default operating mode of the mind. With a lot of practice, you can get better at noticing when thoughts arise and subsequently label them as just that: thoughts. Then it's back to being mindful in the present moment.

There are parallels between the challenges of being mindful and the challenges of supporting a remote-work culture:

- *They make us push against our default-mode behaviors.* Our brains are continually dancing around and distracting us with thoughts and feelings. Mindfulness combats this. And as resourceful yet impatient humans, we often just want to get on with our work in the easiest and quickest way possible. We do this by forging ahead alone, just talking to the people who are easiest to contact, and not wasting our time with broadcasting what we're doing. However, this way of working is suboptimal for remote working, and we must be mindful of our default behavior, notice it, and make small changes.

---

1. https://www.nhs.uk/conditions/stress-anxiety-depression/mindfulness/

- *They require continual, habitual practice.* Nobody becomes an expert meditator overnight. Reversing a lifetime of letting your thoughts repeatedly grab your attention takes years—even a whole lifetime—of daily practice. The same is true of remote working. We need to make many small habit changes to how we work and practice them purposefully on a daily basis.

- *We have all of the tools that we need already.* Becoming an expert meditator just requires your brain and your attention. You don't need anything else. Becoming an effective remote worker only requires you, your brain, and a computer with an Internet connection, something that most people now have access to. However, like being mindful, we just haven't fully understood how to use these tools to the best of their ability.

This chapter is going to explore this topic by introducing the most useful principle that you can learn in this book. In fact, it's so simple, it's just one sentence:

Treat everyone as remote.

That's it. You can close the book now; you're finished.

Well, you could. But we're going to explore why this maxim is simple but not straightforward. This chapter is about understanding and instilling the mindset of this principle on our journey to become, and to enable, masterful remote workers. You'll want to stick around for that. So here's how we're going to do it:

- We're going to dive into *how office culture has evolved to favor synchronous, in-person communication* and how this has created default habits that make remote workers feel like they're second-class citizens. We'll make a case for why we should be trying to change these habits.

- We'll look at the principle of *treating everyone as remote*. This fundamental change to company culture requires communication and collaboration to function as if every single person in the company is remote, even if they aren't. We'll see how carrying this principle in your mind can bring about real change.

- We'll *learn an array of simple, impactful actions* that you can use to more closely adhere to this principle, which can improve your own experience if you're remote, or improve the experience of others if they are. You'll be able to start making change happen in your team.

You'll leave this chapter wanting to write your new favorite principle on a sticky note and then attach it above your monitor. It's that good. However, the author accepts no responsibility for any damage that you cause to your wallpaper or paintwork in the process.

Out of Sight, Out of Mind

One Apple Park Way, Cupertino. 1 Hacker Way, Menlo Park. 1600 Amphitheatre Parkway, Mountain View. Memorable addresses for some of the biggest technology companies in the world: Apple, Facebook, and Google.

At these locations, gigantic collegiate campuses offer employees an office experience that few can match. At Google's Mountain View campus, complementary breakfast, lunch, and dinner are served at canteens, and snacks and drinks can be picked up from coffee and juice bars. On-site technical support is available twenty-four hours a day, seven days a week. Forgot your charger? Grab another. There are free gyms and fitness classes, and bicycles and scooters are available for zipping around between buildings.[2]

Perks aside, the biggest and best offices in the world can also be objects of worldwide architectural significance. Apple Park, a 2,800,000-square-foot neo-futuristic ring resembling a spaceship, was designed by Norman Foster and is wider in diameter than the Pentagon.[3] It's no wonder that smart folks from all around the world are willing to relocate themselves and their families to pursue their dreams of working for these companies.

How could you not want to be a part of this?

Glass Walls, Ping-Pong, and Flat Whites

Office design in technology companies the world over has mirrored the concepts seen at Apple, Facebook, Google, and other tech giants, albeit on a smaller scale and more limited budget. Free drinks and snacks, ping-pong tables, and open-plan desk configurations are common occurrences when there are engineers writing Python and JavaScript nearby. But how did this happen? Let's take a little trip through time. Our first stop is California, just one year before World War II.

---

2.   https://www.inc.com/business-insider/best-google-benefits.html
3.   https://www.fosterandpartners.com/projects/apple-park/

Hewlett-Packard began in 1938 in a garage in Palo Alto. After a short stint in rented offices, the company constructed its first office in 1942 using an open-floor-plan design. This was initially intended for versatility in configuring the interior layout, but the company noted that it had a serendipitous effect of sparking creativity.[4] Additionally, it allowed senior staff in the organization to show that, culturally, they were *one of the gang*, too, by not hiding away in private offices behind closed doors.[5]

In the decades that followed, open-plan office layouts in technology companies were present but still conservative in comparison to today. Often, measures were taken to create some visual and auditory privacy. Yes, the dreaded cubicles. The comic strip *Dilbert* famously depicts the plight of a white-collar engineer in an open-plan space full of these dividers. The movie *Office Space* is filled with tales of stapler theft, test-procedure specification (TPS) reports, and slacking off at the cubicle-filled technology company Initech.

Then change came. During the 1990s technology boom, startups sought to differentiate themselves to prospective employees by having unique office spaces, sometimes driven by the need to find inexpensive and flexible space available at short notice, even if it happened to be inside a warehouse or a loft building.[6] Technology companies with quirky open-plan offices that symbolized their culture quickly became the norm, often citing the need to seat their staff closely together in fun environments to foster innovation and collaboration.

Does Open Plan Harm Productivity?

It's likely that you're a smart and creative person who does a complex job, and it's also likely that you've spent a lot of time working in an open-plan office.

The question is, do you really like this arrangement, or do you find it more distracting than working in private?

The strongest detractors of open-plan offices state that they're simply the cheapest option to seat staff and that they are more symbolic of a company's cultural intent than they're an implementation of a productive work environment.

---

4. https://www8.hp.com/us/en/hp-information/about-hp/history/hp-timeline/timeline.html
5. https://www.executivecentre.com/blog-article/open-plan-design-what-have-we-learned/
6. https://www.fastcompany.com/90285582/everyone-hates-open-plan-offices-heres-why-they-still-exist

Hello? Is Anybody There?

So given that since the '90s technology companies have provided flagship offices containing a bevy of perks and benefits to attract talent, is it any wonder that remote workers have had a difficult time feeling like they're a legitimate part of the company?

Let's imagine a situation where a technology company has recently allowed their employees to work remotely. Two engineers on the same team, Alice and Bob, have reacted to this news in different ways. Alice lives close to the office and enjoys going in every day. She finds it easy to put her headphones on and focus, regardless of what's going on around her. She decides to continue coming in each day.

On the other hand, Bob has a long commute and also has been finding it impossible to concentrate with all of the noise around his desk. He also can't focus when listening to music through his headphones, so he has been experiencing daily frustration and stress as the company hires more people, which means more noise. Bob decides to work from home so he can get the silent environment that he needs.

So what happens next? Alice continues to come into the office, actively discussing her work and ideas around her desk and the kitchen area. She chats with other colleagues in the subsidized canteen and over the free coffee. She leads the design of the new feature that the team is building by holding daily huddles around the whiteboard next to her desk. Nothing changes for her.

What about Bob? He feels like he is missing out. Often the team forgets to join the video call for stand-up, leaving him stranded on his own. He notices that sometimes he can go a whole day without interacting with anyone else in the company. He can't see the design for the new feature because he can't see the whiteboard. His grocery bill is higher because he has to buy his own food and coffee. He wishes he had his twenty-seven-inch monitor at home.

This is a common situation. Companies feel like they have taken a giant cultural leap by allowing employees to work remotely; however, they completely fail to adapt their ways of working to provide an equal experience for those who aren't in the office.

We must not let this happen.

Remote Workers Don't Feel Equal

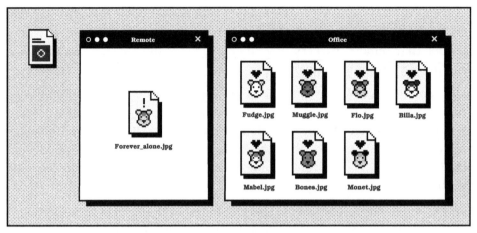

A survey of 2,000 remote employees from organizations with more than 250 employees in 2020 highlighted many of the issues that remote workers face in companies that still maintain office presences[7]:

- 60 percent of participants feel that they miss out on important information because it's only communicated in person.

- 80 percent of remote workers feel that working remotely presents additional challenges that in-office workers do not experience.

- 51 percent of participants have avoided sharing a document with a colleague because they were unable to find it or thought that it would be too difficult to find.

The 2019 edition of the same survey found similar trends in the participants' responses:

- Remote workers reported that they were often excluded from meetings and were unable to get access to important documents.

- Attempts by companies to organize digital information often fall short in their functionality, with issues around access and collaboration leading to wasted time and sometimes employees just giving up.

- A majority of remote workers felt that their challenges could be solved by better technology and a digital-centric work culture.

The heart of the issue that remote workers face is that companies are providing provisions for remote workers as an afterthought because remote working is

---

7.   https://www.igloosoftware.com/state-of-the-digital-workplace

the *additional, supplementary,* or *secondary* way of working, lower in precedence than the primary way of working, which is in an office.

These issues only begin to get solved when there's a shift in culture that forces all of the tools, technology, and processes to change. For good.

A Principle for Cultural Change

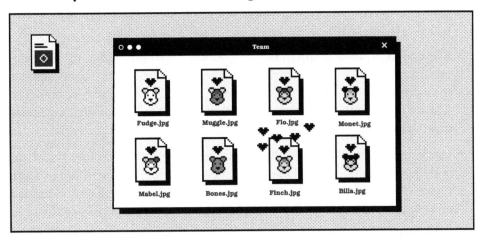

If you want to create permanent change, you have to start by changing the culture.

The only way to offer a first-class, remote-working experience is to change the culture of your team, department, or company to treat every worker as if they're remote, regardless of whether they're working in an office or not. It requires a mindset shift in every individual in the entire company.

Without a change in culture, you have little more than arbitrary rules for people to follow. "Oh, we have to do that every time we have a meeting? That's annoying." "When we're designing a feature, we have to do *what* now? How bureaucratic of leadership to give us all of these arbitrary procedures!"

Without cultural change, you just have checklists to enforce behavior. People don't follow arbitrary rules without a good reason. The cultural change provides that reason.

Treat everyone as remote.

And what's more, if you can create cultural change, you won't even need to write those checklists for best practice. Instead, better behavior will follow naturally as people will understand how to act in accordance to the new culture within your team, department, or company.

We repeatedly witness real-world examples of rules implemented without a neighboring cultural change have a diminished effect:

- Despite many countries having laws in place to make discrimination based on gender, race, and socioeconomic background illegal, we see the effect of a culture that allows this discrimination to still happen. The Black Lives Matter social movement is a protest against racially motivated violence against Black people, which is a systemic cultural problem worldwide.[8]

- Even though most companies are committed to championing diversity and inclusivity, by only allowing employees to work from flagship offices in global cities such as London and New York, they close the door on talent who can't afford to relocate to these locations or can't commute long hours away from their families each day.

- Many companies will cite equal opportunities for progression, but, conversely, their upper echelons of the org chart are predominantly white males who live within a short commute of the headquarters or are deemed so valuable that the rules of working in the office don't apply to them.

There has to be real cultural change to get the results that you want. Otherwise, the rules don't matter.

To properly facilitate remote workers, treating everyone as remote is the cultural change that's required. It's fundamentally about treating everyone equally by giving everyone access to the same information, people, tools, and opportunities to succeed, regardless of whether they're sitting in an office in Berlin or doing their work from a coffee shop in Jakarta or a bedroom in Tokyo. Treating everyone as remote declares that the headquarters of a company is the Internet and everyone works there.

For example, when a meeting happens, treating everyone as remote dictates that each participant should join a video call, each with an individual microphone and video camera, even if only one of the participants isn't in the office. It also suggests that using video calls to communicate naturally leads to creating a recording of the meeting and archiving it for watching later. It dictates that the drawing of the new software architecture should probably be done digitally using software that allows for screen sharing and real-time remote collaboration, rather than on a whiteboard in an office with a webcam pointed at it.

---

8. https://en.wikipedia.org/wiki/Black_Lives_Matter

Keeping the principle of *treat everyone as remote* in mind is similar to being reminded to check your posture. Are you sitting straight? A simple sentence can snap you out of your default mode, reminding you to pay attention to the periphery, making adjustments if necessary.

Although consisting of only four words, the principle paves the way for real change and democratization of the workplace. Gone are terms such as *satellite office* and *remote workers.* There's no need to categorize anyone as such anymore. They're just *workers,* regardless of where they're sitting with their computers and Internet connections. Gone are the days of wanting to be transferred to the head office to be closer to the company executives. All of them are just a video call or email away.

Treat everyone as remote is the mantra that changes the culture of your company for the better. And the best part is that you can do it regardless of your seniority in your company. It's truly a grassroots movement.

Taking Practical Action

So far, we've explored how the development of office design and company culture has made remote workers feel increasingly excluded and that cultural change is required to redress the balance. Now we're going to introduce practical actions that you can take to make that cultural change happen.

This section was written with the assumption that you currently don't run a team, department, or company. If you do, that's even better because you'll have more power to create an immediate impact. However, anyone can be a force for bottom-up change by championing the principle, following through with actions in their own work, leading discussions within their team or area of influence, and getting others onboard to repeat the same process.

You just treat everyone as remote. It's that simple. The rest will follow.

What we're going to work through in the following sections is just the beginning, and the upcoming chapters of the book dive deeper into the theory and practice as we start to unpack the core concepts. But let's get started right away. You'll leave this chapter with a plethora of techniques to try.

Start Subtle

Every journey begins with a single step. So let's take it. To begin with, you're going to be subtle. Sneaky. Like a small mouse in a trench coat with sunglasses on.

You're going to start embodying the principle of treating everyone as remote without telling anyone that you're doing it:

- *Write down the principle somewhere that you can see it.* A sticky note on your laptop or monitor works pretty well, or you could set it as your desktop background, or you could scrawl it across your wall with a marker, although that may make for an interesting conversation with whomever you share your living space with. Just tell yourself that you're now doing this, and make sure that you're able to continually remind yourself about it. Remember: it's like checking your posture.

- *Go about your day and be mindful of how your work unfolds.* Do you find that your team operates by private, individual conversations, or does the whole team have visibility into what's going on at any given time? Do you tend to send direct messages rather than use the group chat? Is information written on whiteboards as a reference point rather than in a shared document? How does this compare to the principle we want to follow?

- *Make small shifts.* If you have regular meetings, start a shared document with rolling minutes and ask people to contribute to the agenda. Have everyone join with individual microphones and webcams. Have them mute when not talking to avoid feedback. Take a picture of the whiteboard diagram and share it in the group chat; or even better, transcribe it to a shared document format that allows for remote collaboration. Fundamentally, look at each piece of work and every interaction that you do and question whether it contributes toward treating everyone as remote. If it actually inhibits remote workers from getting involved, make a subtle change.

- *See how others react.* As you continue to make small shifts to the way you work, what subsequent changes do you notice in other people you work with? Do you encounter any resistance, and, if so, why? Are others actually following your lead?

The side effect of making many subtle improvements is that humans have a natural tendency to mirror the behavior of others when they like what they see. And we guarantee that they will. So even though you're a proverbial mouse in a trench coat, it might just turn out that this simple step begins to start a whole movement within your team.

Audit Your Tools

In the survey we referenced earlier, one of the common reasons that remote workers felt that there was a barrier between them and the rest of the company was because of the poor quality of the tools that they had available. Your own situation may vary here. But just remember that if you're able to use the latest and greatest in chat apps, videoconferencing, office suites, and integrated development environments (IDEs), all with functionality that supports real-time remote collaboration, count yourself lucky; you're in a much better situation than many. Some organizations are slower moving, more old-fashioned, or simply lacking in the technical literacy to be on the cutting edge.

Regardless of the situation you're in, you can audit the tools that you're using in your team. What tools are you using for the following activities?

- *Chatting* to each other throughout the day via the Internet, for both work-related and fun reasons

- *Writing software*, from typing lines of code, to testing it, to reviewing changes and deploying to production

- *Having meetings*, both one to one and as a group

- *Writing and collaborating*, such as for documents, presentations, and spreadsheets?

Given that you have to treat everyone as remote, how well do your current tools serve this need? Are people able to collaborate together natively in these applications, or do you have to send email with attachments to work with people outside of the office?

You may be able to suggest to your team that there are better alternatives, depending on the amount of red tape at your organization. The Google Workspace suite,[9] which includes the usual office applications, also provides excellent collaborative functionality. Chat applications such as Slack[10] and Discord[11] have free tiers. Microsoft Visual Studio Code[12] is an IDE that has remote pair programming built in. Figma[13] and Miro[14] offer multiuser collaborative design and diagramming.

---

9. https://workspace.google.com/
10. https://www.slack.com
11. https://discord.com/
12. https://code.visualstudio.com/
13. https://www.figma.com/
14. https://miro.com/

Your Turn: Build Your Dream Tool Stack

There's a world of tools out there that can help you do your job better as well as support remote workers as a first-class citizens. Many of these tools are free or have free trials, so you should give them a go and see whether they would be helpful for you or your team to better embrace the principle:

- Spend some time putting together suggestions of what your dream tool stack would be for you to work on. Do you wish you could be using Slack, Microsoft Teams, or Discord? What about moving your codebase to GitHub and doing your reviews via pull requests and your continuous integration via Actions?

- For each of your tools in your dream stack, how many are free, or at least have free trials?

- If your workplace allows it, start subtly and begin using these tools for your own work. Write that new design in Google Docs and invite others in for commenting. Create that diagram in Miro. Give others a taste of what your dream tool stack is like, and see whether they'll want to join you on this adventure.

- If some of the tools in your dream stack start getting traction, talk to your manager to work out whether you could find some budget to start using them within your team for real.

Begin a Shift to Asynchronous Communication

We'll touch upon asynchronous communication in detail in Chapter 4, The Spectrum of Synchronousness, on page 53. However, in the same way that you're starting to subtly shift to treating everyone as remote, you can also subtly shift to using more asynchronous means of communication every single day. But what does *asynchronous* mean? Well, simply put, it means using methods of communication where all of the participants don't have to be there at the same time to take part.

Communicating in this way may come naturally to you, especially if you're introverted and prefer an exchange over chat rather than a face-to-face meeting. However, for many people this is hard, especially if they excel in bustling offices. But there's a good reason for everyone to change. Not only does it better support remote work, it's more respectful to the fact that we're all doing difficult work that requires deep concentration.

Walking over to a colleague's desk to get some information is a satisfying experience for the person needing their question answered. They get what they want while making a connection with another human being, and they do so on their own schedule.

However, the same isn't necessarily true for their colleague. They get interrupted from the task that they're concentrating on, and they have to context switch to answer the question. Additionally, the rest of the team who are either not listening because they have headphones on or because they're not physically present in the office, miss out on that interaction that may be beneficial for them. They could have learned something or been able to contribute to the discussion.

By mindfully shifting your synchronous interactions to asynchronous exchanges, you adhere to the principle of treating everyone as remote while being more respectful of the time of others. If you're extroverted or used to predominantly face-to-face interactions, you may have to reprogram your expectations. Using more asynchronous communication means that you might not get answers straightaway because people are busy. It means you may have to switch to working on something else for a while until your other task becomes unblocked.

Although this might sound inconvenient, it's beneficial in the long term. Not only does it mean that more people can thoughtfully get involved in a discussion regardless of their physical location, it sends a clear message that you are respectful of how other people spend their time.

Your Turn: Go Async for a Week

There's no better way to understand the benefits of asynchronous communication than by doing it yourself. Here are some ways that you can do so:

- Review all of the meetings that you have in your calendar this week. Could any of them be replaced with asynchronous exchanges instead, such as a short written update? Could that save time and increase the opportunity for longer periods of deep concentration for those involved in the meeting?

- When you have the immediate urge to ask a question in person or via a video call, think about whether you could achieve the same result by sending a written communication such as an email or chat message. This way, the other person can reply on a schedule that suits them.

- Consider the potential eyeballs that could see your communications if they were asynchronous instead of synchronous. How could you optimize to increase the number of potential eyeballs and therefore increase the number of people who could potentially be involved in the conversation? (If you're thinking this sounds a bit like Internet marketing, well, it is.)

- Try these techniques out for a week and see how it goes. Did it change the way you work for better or for worse? What were the benefits and drawbacks? Did you find yourself interacting with more or fewer people than you usually would?

Make Time and Participation Expectations Clear

Building on the shift to asynchronousness in the next chapter on page 53, something you can do that can make communication more precise is to set clear time and participation expectations:

- *You can state whether or not you'd like a reply.* Say that you're broadcasting some information for everyone's benefit but it doesn't need any action on their part. This reduces the mental load of the recipient.

- *If you want a response, you can set a respectful time frame for it.* Not everything needs to be answered immediately. Instead, be respectful of other people's time by stating that it's OK for them to reply by the end of the day, or even by next week. The longer the time frame, the more opportunity for people to get involved regardless of their schedule, location, and commitments, both inside and outside of work.

- *You can let people completely opt out of a communication if they don't need to read it.* Simply declare that you're sharing something in case people are interested but there's no required commitment. People love that. Conversely, if communication is critical, do state that you would like everyone to digest it.

This has a number of benefits. Not only will making your time and expectations clear let you get what you need out of any particular exchange, it's a gift to those who you're communicating with because they know exactly what to do without needing to waste brain cycles figuring it out.

Do Not Abuse Time and Commitment Expectations!

Even though it can be tempting, do not use the classic project-management tactic of setting unreasonable expectations for your communications. If a reply can wait a day, say it can. Don't be pushy and ask for a reply in an hour.

 Tricks like this are like special moves in a computer game. You can use them every now and then, but it completely depletes your energy bar and then you have to wait for it to recharge. If you keep trying it, it won't be effective because people will just stop listening to you.

Setting generous time frames is an act of respect that puts the gift of control in the hands of the recipient. It also shows how wonderfully organized you are.

Produce More Artifacts

Here's another idea that builds upon a shift toward more asynchronous communication: try to produce more artifacts. What do we mean by artifacts? We certainly don't mean dusty ancient tomes and golden masks hidden beneath the sand. What we mean is tangible, archival documents that will stick around for longer than the duration of a conversation.

If you're thinking of an idea, consider transforming that conversation you're having into a written document. There are a number of reasons that this can be beneficial:

- *You develop your ideas more effectively.* In technology, we're all working on complicated things, often to the extent that we can't solve all of the problems that we're facing just by thinking about them. Instead, by writing about them, we can better formulate our thought processes and reflect on them; and often we end up with much better ideas than we had in the first place.

- *You invite collaboration from others.* If you write your thoughts in software that allows for others to collaboratively comment and edit, you're not only able to increase the number of eyeballs that land on your document but you can increase the number of brains that wish to take part and make your ideas even better.

- *You leave an audit trail.* Have you ever come across a problem and felt sure that you thought about it awhile ago yet you're unable to remember what your conclusion was? Don't let that happen anymore! Get in the habit of writing your ideas in documents as they come to you and then archiving them somewhere searchable for the future. You can do this at a personal level by taking notes that you can share if needed, but you can even do this at a team and department level to document your collective discussions and designs.

Every time you have an idea, write it down. Not only will it make the idea better, it will allow others to participate regardless of where they are in the world. In a few years, you might even save yourself time by consulting your past self on a familiar-looking problem.

Broadcast at a Level Above

A simple way of increasing the potential participants in any interaction is to take it to the level above. Instead of having a conversation with one individual privately, why not do it in full view of the team in their chat channel so that more people can get involved? Think of the org chart and the groups that exist in your department, and try to elevate your communication to the level above, if possible, so that the number of potential participants increases.

You can achieve this by combining all of the principles that we just covered. Mindfully think about how you can involve people regardless of their location. Use tools that make it easy to work collaboratively. Use asynchronous communication where possible. Write and develop your ideas and share them. Make it clear when you want input and by when. Archive your ideas in a place where you and others can find them in the future.

By doing all of these things, it's easy to involve more people. Is your team getting a bit stuck designing that new feature? Well, all you'll need to do is send the link to the document around to the whole division. Simple. Just be diligent about not creating too much noise.

In addition to upholding the principle of treating everyone as remote and allowing opportunities for the wisdom of others to enhance your work with their own ideas, you'll gain another beneficial side effect: you increase your visibility as a diligent and proactive employee. This can only do good things for your career progression.

Your Turn: Hoisting

A common compiler optimization is to take loop-invariant code and move it outside of the loop so that it only executes once rather than every time the loop executes. You may have already noticed that unoptimized communication happens all of the time at your company, where you find yourself repeating yourself again and again and again. Here's what you can do:

- Think of communication that happens repeatedly at your company. Perhaps there are status updates that are requested and shared verbally over and over again. Maybe people are continually asking questions about the roadmap or milestone dates because they haven't been written down.

- Become an *optimizing compiler* for communication and think about how you can hoist that information to the level above. What would you need to do for this to happen? Perhaps you could broadcast a biweekly written update to the department on your team's progress, rather than having to continually answer questions from others in the organization about how your project is going.

- As you're thinking of hoisting repeated communications, are there any patterns that are emerging? Are other teams suffering from having to give repeating status updates all the time? Are pull requests turning into heated arguments over the correct way to lint the code because nobody has defined it? Hoist the information. Capture it in documented form, then broadcast it at the level above.

Now It's Showtime

Once you've been through a period of acting covertly and you're starting to feel comfortable making small changes to treat everyone as remote, it's time to more formally introduce the principle to your team.

You can do so the following ways:

- *Present it.* Let your team know that you've been learning about the principle of treating everyone as remote. You could prepare a short presentation, or you could write your findings in a document and share it with them. Outline what it means and how practicing it yourself has had a positive effect on the way in which you've been going about your work.

- *Chair a discussion.* Encourage a discussion among the team about how they collaborate. How does the team feel about the default way in which you all work together, and how far away from their ideal does everyone on the team feel? How does the ideal compare to the principle in this chapter? Is it closely aligned?

- *Collectively analyze how you work together.* Categorize the various interactions that you have into those that abide by the principle and those that don't. What have you personally learned by following the principle, and what did you change? If you were all able to work differently, would it bring benefits to the team, either through improving your processes or by creating a better work environment?

- *Agree to a period over which to enact change.* List all the changes that you would like to make. Remember that just being mindful of the principle can make many habits begin to improve. Then decide on a period of time over which to attempt and measure the change. Perhaps you could align it with whatever iterations you work on as a team, such as your sprints.

- *Do it!* Encourage each other to make adjustments. Remind each other in your daily stand-up. Set it as your team-chat channel's topic. Praise people who are making an effort to change their habits. Create a virtuous cycle.

- *Have a retrospective.* After the agreed-upon time period has passed, reflect on what it was like working in your team before this experiment started compared to now. What habits have you picked up that have made it easier to work together? What has been hardest to change? Do you think that the team is more or less efficient as a result of treating everyone as remote?

In the likely event that you have a positive experience as a result of this experiment, think about how you can share your findings even more widely. Are there regular technical talk slots in your department where you could give a presentation about what you've done? See if you can spread the message even farther by hoisting.

Let's Build a Model!

So there we have it. *Treat everyone as remote.* It's simple, but it isn't straightforward. Like existing mindfully in the present moment, changing our communication habits to yield benefits for ourselves and our colleagues regardless of where they are in the world is a difficult habit to form. The default mode of our brains is to try to get everything that we need immediately by any means possible, but this flies in the face of being a diligent remote colleague.

Here's what we've learned in this chapter:

- *Office culture has evolved over the past seventy years to favor synchronous, in-person communication.* This has created default habits in the way we work that make remote workers feel like they're out of sight and out of mind. We need to work on changing these habits to create a fair and inclusive environment for everyone.

- *We need to treat everyone as remote.* The way in which we create this cultural change is to communicate and collaborate as if every single person in the company is a remote worker regardless of where they are physically located. We should carry this principle in our minds during everything that we do at work.

- *There are many simple practical actions we can take to adhere to this principle.* We covered changing your behavior subtly, auditing the tools that you use, shifting to use more asynchronous communication, making your expectations on time and participation clear, producing more artifacts, and broadcasting your message at a higher level. We then encouraged you to introduce the principle, and collectively experiment with these changes within your team.

In the next chapter, we go deep into the subject of synchronous and asynchronous communication and build a model that allows you to work out the best way to communicate for yourself and your colleagues. We'll do so by using an example from the game *Dark Souls* because treating everyone as remote requires that we all engage in jolly cooperation.

The past, like the future, is indefinite and exists only as a spectrum of possibilities.

Stephen Hawking

CHAPTER 4

The Spectrum of Synchronousness

It's a beautiful frosty morning.

True to your word, you made sure that you got out of the house for a brisk walk before starting work. You even put coffee in a travel mug to take with you to the park. The new routine is coming together. As the frozen grass crunches beneath your feet, and as the remnants of the sunrise tint the edges of the clouds with light orange, you begin to think that working remotely might not be so bad after all.

You arrive back home. Closing the front door behind you, you take off your coat and scarf and sit down in front of your laptop, pressing the space bar to wake it. You enter your password when it comes to life.

And then you notice something strange.

There are forty-six chat notifications bouncing around in red. Twenty emails that were sent after 9 p.m. last night. You feel a cold flush in your face and neck. Those messages continue until 1 a.m. You scan the subject lines of the emails.

```
URGENT --  CLIENT ISSUES -- PLEASE REPLY
URGENT -- SYSTEM OUTAGE
CRITICAL -- System checks failed
Platform down, please help
```

OK, this doesn't look good.

You open your chat client and look at the unread messages. Right, this really doesn't look good at all. A big outage happened and it looks like none of the key people was responding. And even worse, you're one of those key people and you had no idea that it was happening.

But wait a minute. Oh no, … nobody was even responding to the CEO's frantic messages. She was doing a client pitch at the time. This is really bad. You scramble to respond.

```
[08:49] I'm here. Reading up and looking into this.
```

You open the system graphs. Ouch. That's a really big outage. Six hours. But hang on a second. Why didn't anybody get paged about it? There's an on-call roster and messaging system for a reason, isn't there? You scan through the channel dedicated to conversations about the live system, going back to last night. There's a message from one of the new members of the customer support team.

```
[21:12] hey all
[21:12] getting reports of the app not loading from clients
[21:12] i just tried myself and it doesn't work
[21:12] can someone check it out please
[21:19] hello? can anyone help?
[21:21] lots of tickets coming in now, is anyone there?
[21:35] hello???
```

You rest your head in your hands. I guess they didn't know that people aren't monitoring the chat channel outside of work hours. The same applies to email. People usually pick up their messages in the morning. When there's an emergency, it's meant to be raised using the pager system that sends the on-call engineer a text message so they can reply immediately.

You sigh, rubbing your eyes.

They're new, so it likely isn't their fault that they didn't know. However, that little mistake just caused many hours of downtime, and it's going to take most of the day to write the postmortem and smooth things over with the commercial team. And that's not even mentioning the meeting that the CEO has booked in!

So much for that beautiful morning.

We all know that communication is difficult at the best of times. Humans are complex creatures, and when they're communicating about complicated subjects such as programming or software architecture or trying to debug production issues, it can certainly get quite messy. It's tricky enough when these conversations are happening face to face in the same location. So it isn't any surprise that as we've introduced a plethora of new communication techniques and tools, we're finding it even harder to say the right things to the right people at the right time, especially when we're distributed across the planet.

As engineers, we have an innate desire to make ourselves more efficient. So consider this question: What's one of the most impactful skills that you could improve upon? Is it your programming? Could it be your debugging? Well, we'd like to make the case that it's your communication. After all, software isn't built in solitude. It's imagined, designed, and implemented by teams of people.

Being a better communicator will make you a better programmer. After all, you write code for other humans; the compiler lets the computer understand it. Communication skills will make you a better colleague, leader, and manager. They will ensure that you are better able to build consensus around your ideas, designs, and proposed architectures. Strong communication skills allow you to build rapport with your colleagues so you can develop your working relationships through constructive critique and feedback.

Now this has always been true, but it has never been truer in the remote-work world. Not only do you need excellent communication skills to amplify the impact of your work, you need to be able to pick the right tools and techniques to communicate the right way at the right time. After all, as we've just seen, choosing the wrong method to communicate, even with the best of intentions, may just cause many hours of downtime.

So this is where this chapter comes in. We're going to piece together a framework that categorizes the different ways in which we communicate with each other so that we can study them, make correlations between them, and improve our skills along the following spectrum:

- *Synchronousness.* We'll explore the difference between synchronous (real-time) and asynchronous (intermittent) communication. By using examples of the ways in which we communicate via meetings, chat, email, and written documents, we'll see how all of these mediums sit at different points along a spectrum between synchronousness and asynchronousness, and we'll discover how each of them carries varying etiquette and expectations. We'll show how remote work requires a mindful shift toward asynchronous communication.

- *Permanence.* Next, we'll see how synchronousness correlates with the permanence of that communication. Are long-lived artifacts being created, such as written documents or README files, or does information expire as soon as the communication is over? We'll show that remote work benefits from creating more artifacts to better support one another.

- *Humanity.* After building a strong case for becoming more asynchronous through creating more artifacts, we'll show that this does have one negative effect: a reduction in feeling like we've had meaningful interactions with other humans. We'll cover ways to make sure that we occasionally break the rules to make ourselves feel happier and more connected to each other.

Let's get going. We'll start by looking at synchronousness.

Synchronousness

There's a high likelihood that you've come across the words *synchronous* and *asynchronous* before. These terms are used frequently in programming. If you're a programmer, you've already got the upper hand because we'll be using the same concepts in how to most effectively communicate with one another.

Let's start with some definitions:

- *Synchronous* means existing or occurring at the same time. When you have a conversation with somebody face to face, the exchange of information is synchronous. In our preceding programming example, the thread of execution executes the first line synchronously: the text is printed to the console immediately.

- *Asynchronous* is the opposite of synchronous. When you send somebody an email and they read it and reply a few hours later, that communication is asynchronous. In our previous code, the doMath() function is executed asynchronously while the thread of execution proceeds to print the third line out to the console.

We can further describe various characteristics within these definitions. Typically, synchronous communication happens at the same time and location and in the same format:

- *Time.* This means that for the communication to take place, all parties must be interacting at the same time. This may occur without planning if two people meet in a corridor, or it may require scheduling a meeting.

- *Location.* For communication to happen at the same time, it will often be in the same location. This could be a physical room, but it could also be a video call.

- *Format.* To exchange information immediately, all parties will typically use the same format, such as their voice and body language or a chat client.

Given that asynchronous communication is the opposite, we might imagine that it could happen at a different time and location and in a different format:

- *Time.* One person could send an email in the morning to another person in a different time zone, and they can then reply at their own convenience.

- *Location.* You could write a message using a phone while on a bus in Berlin, and the recipient could reply via an email client on a laptop in New York.

- *Format.* That email could generate some thinking that's explored further with a written proposal for people to read and comment on over the coming days.

So we can see how synchronous communication allows an immediate resolution and exchange of information, but it requires constraints in the time, location, and format of the exchange. Asynchronous communication typically takes longer to resolve, but it has far fewer constraints on how it occurs.

This may already have you pondering the numerous trade-offs that need considering when communicating with other people, and we'll cover those shortly. However, there's an important distinction to be made first. The type of communication you choose isn't a binary selection between synchronous and asynchronous. Instead, the different ways in which we communicate form a continuum, and you must choose wisely.

The Spectrum of Synchronousness

On a typical workday, we communicate with each other in a dazzling variety of ways. We may use email, chat, video calls, pull requests, code, wikis, or recorded video. As you saw in our opening narrative, a particular format may carry with it certain expectations, advantages, limitations, and implications for the human being at the other end. No wonder it's easy to make mistakes and get frustrated while we work on complicated things.

What we really need to communicate better is a model, so we can make informed decisions about the time, location, and format that we use based on exactly what it is we're trying to communicate. This sounds complicated, but stick with us here; it's simpler than you think.

This is because our model is nothing more than a straight line with arrows at both ends. On the left of the line, is a label for synchronous communication.

On the right of the line is a label for asynchronous. Then we plot on the spectrum the different ways in which you may communicate in a given day, as shown in the following diagram.

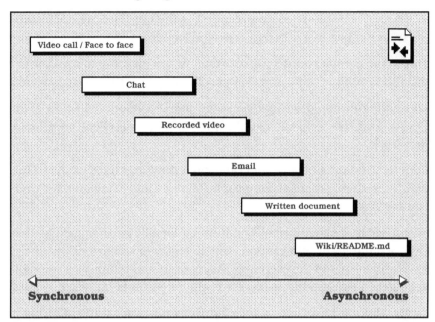

As you can see, one form of communication usually isn't uniquely synchronous or asynchronous. Often, it's somewhere in-between. Let's walk through each of the communication methods in the diagram:

- *Video calls or face-to-face chats* are completely synchronous. Everybody involved needs to be present at a specific time because the communication is typically happening via each individual's voice and body language.

- *Chat* is a written medium and is therefore less synchronous than a video call because it can be read later. However, information has a short half-life because a chat implicitly carries a temporal dependency. Are you catching up on a chat from a few hours ago? Sure, that probably makes sense. But are you reading through a chat from two months ago? It's probably now mostly irrelevant. You had to be there at the time.

- *Recorded video* can be viewed later and requires more preparation than a chat. But it usually serves as a mechanism to catch up on a missed meeting or as a way to more effectively present something visual rather than a long-term archival format. A recording of a meeting from a few weeks ago or a video updating everyone on the progress of an initiative probably won't be referred to repeatedly. Video also can't be indexed and searched.

- *Email* is where we start producing more permanent asynchronous artifacts. Email by nature is archival and searchable and is often used for important communications such as delivering an employment contract or confirming that a payment has been set up. Some people reply to email quickly, but some take many days to reply. However, that is to be expected.

- *Written documents* require some effort to produce and can be used as the cornerstone of a project or proposal. Typically, a well-written document can last forever. Most online document software allows collaborative editing and commenting, making this a compelling format for developing ideas.

- *Wikis and README files* are completely asynchronous and typically have no interaction between the author and the readers. If they are well-maintained, they can last, and be useful, indefinitely.

Now that we've listed them, you may be coming to terms with just how many choices we have to navigate when wishing to communicate. Briefly pause and reflect on your own experience in the following exercise. When you're done, we'll consider what approach to take to better support remote work.

Your Turn: Categorize Your Communications

You communicate in many different ways during a typical week. But it's likely that you do so mostly without thinking. So let's think about it:

- Using the different forms of communication in the previously described spectrum, work out what percentage of your time you spend on each of them during a typical week. Do you use specific methods for specific people or teams? If so, why?

- Which of the types of communication do you find the most fulfilling, and which do you find the most frustrating? Do you prefer speaking or writing to get your message across? Are you a strong speaker but a weak writer, or vice versa?

- For the mediums that you find frustrating, think about why that is. Is it because there's a mismatch between your preferred mediums and those of others? Or is it because you feel that those methods aren't being used correctly?

Shifting Right

When we work together in an office, convenience and habit typically mean that we spend a lot of time on the left side of the spectrum: synchronousness. After all, when your colleagues are just across the room from your desk, it's natural to stand up and walk over to have a conversation in the moment.

When working remotely, we lose the ability to do this. But should this be a cause for concern? After all, engineers know that it's a pain to be interrupted midthought because the complex internal representation of a computer program in their brain immediately evaporates into thin air when somebody asks, "Have you got a minute?"

Additionally, a bias toward in-person interaction leaves out anybody who isn't physically there. One could argue that it isn't suitable for any company that has multiple offices because it severely limits the collaboration that can take place across multiple locations. And if everybody is remote, you have as many locations as you have people.

If you've worked in a large company, you've probably already seen the effects of synchronous communication as the default:

- Individuals are typically physically seated with their teams in the same office.

- Teams that collaborate frequently are often located in the same physical location.

- The weakest bonds among different parts of the organization often occur when there is a geographical divide among them.

Colocation can have a tangible and inconvenient effect on the software being created. Conway's Law, as discussed in the book *The Mythical Man-Month* [Bro95], states that any organization that designs a system will produce a design whose structure mirrors the organization's communication structure. It follows that when companies expand into different locations that opening an office and hiring new engineers might be an implicit design choice in how that company architects its software.

They just might not know it yet.

Changing Your Mindset for Remote Work

To fully embrace remote work, we need to shift our mindset and habits to the right of the spectrum. Instead of choosing the convenient option, we need to choose to communicate in a way that enables an equal level of contribution from anyone, regardless of where they are located in the world.

We need to shift right.

That's the habit that you need to promote within yourself and with your colleagues. Every time you communicate, can you purposefully shift further right along the spectrum?

For example, could you

- Turn a *face-to-face conversation* into an exchange in the team's chat channel, or even create an ephemeral chat channel around the topic? This way, more people have the opportunity to overhear what's being said and contribute to the discussion.

- Record a *video call* so that those who are unable to make it, or those who didn't know it was happening, are able to watch it later?

- Decide to stop a long *chat* exchange so that it can be written more thoughtfully and purposefully in an email?

- Take an *email* thread that is proposing an idea and turn it into a more detailed written document so that it can be read more easily in its entirety and then circulated for comment and consensus?

- Extract an agreed-upon design in a *written document* and turn it into a permanent wiki page that serves as the cornerstone of a whole project?

Every single interaction could be an opportunity to shift right, and by doing so you are having much more of a dramatic impact than you may think. Why is that?

It's because you're making your workplace more remote friendly. No more invisible exchanges in the corridor. You're giving more people the opportunity to discover what's going on and then have a route to contribute to the conversation. You're breaking down geographical silos and fighting the tide against Conway's Law.

All it takes is a shift right.

Mediums Carry Expectations

One of the common frustrations when interacting at work, especially as you begin to shift more to the right, is that many people don't realize that a choice of communication medium always carries with it an implicit expectation of how the exchange should unfold. Some may know this already, and many others pick up on it naturally with time. But violations of these expectations can cause friction. It happens time and time again.

In our opening narrative, the support engineer didn't get a response in the chat room when an outage was occurring. This is because the implicit expectation of the chat room is that people aren't monitoring it all of the time. Therefore, chat shouldn't be the first choice of communication when there's a critical issue. Instead, the engineer should have used the after-hours pager system, which *does* have an expectation of an immediate reply. That's why the on-call rotation exists: mediums carry expectations.

In less extreme circumstances, you'll have experienced—and maybe even been frustrated by—situations where the wrong medium is being used for the expectation that the communicator has. For example, the executive who sends email with the words URGENT, PLEASE REPLY ASAP in the subject line is only going to get an immediate reply if someone happens to check their email. Instead, they should pick a medium with the correct expectation, such as using the phone, sending a text message, or scheduling a video call at the nearest possible time.

So what are the expectations of the mediums on this spectrum? The answer varies among companies and individuals, but it usually looks something like the following table.

Medium	Length	Reply Expected	Reply Time	After Hours
Phone call	Short	Yes	Immediate	Yes
SMS	Short	Typically	Hours	No
Chat	Short	Typically	Hours	No
Video call	Medium	Yes	Immediate	No
Email	Medium	Not always	Days	No
Recorded video	Medium	No	N/A	N/A
Written document	Long	No	N/A	N/A
Wiki/README	Long	N/A	N/A	N/A

Remember that frustration occurs when people have particular expectations but pick a medium that doesn't match them. This includes you too. So even though your blood may boil, it's not necessarily because your coworker is a buffoon. They just might not know about these expectations. Why not show them this grid? Perhaps you've even made the wrong choice yourself.

When it comes to choosing how you communicate, remember that it's your responsibility to pick the medium that matches the expectation that you have for the exchange. If you need to get in touch with someone after hours, consider sending them a text message. If you don't need them to reply immediately, send an email. A mindful choice benefits them as well as you.

If you find an exchange evolving into something that is no longer matching the expectations for the medium, take the bold step to shift it into another format that is better suited, ideally while also shifting right as you do so. You can practice thinking about this in the following exercise.

Your Turn: Revisit Your Communication

In the previous "Your Turn" exercise, we asked you to categorize your communication over a given week. Grab those notes right now:

- Are there any opportunities for any of your communications to shift right?
- Of the communications that you don't find fulfilling, how many are because there are repeated violations of the expectations that you have for that medium? For example, do you get a lot of urgent email after hours or have long-winded meetings that could easily be written in a few paragraphs of for everyone to read? What can you do to improve this situation in the future?

Strong and Eventual Consistency

Another factor to consider when choosing how to communicate is closely related to a concept from distributed systems. When designing distributed systems, you have to think about the balance between strong consistency and eventual consistency. If you have ever worked with large databases—especially distributed search indexes and key-value stores—you have probably encountered this concept, even if you didn't know what it was called.

Large storage systems can have deployments of hundreds of nodes, with data replicated and mirrored in multiple places. This increases the resilience of the database (i.e., it can continue to serve reads if a single node goes down) and can increase read throughput (i.e., if multiple copies of the data exist over many nodes, reads can be served from multiple places, spreading load throughout the system).

However, keeping the data consistent among all of the nodes at any given time can be quite a challenge. This is where the design trade-offs come in:

- *Strong consistency* means that every time a new value is written, modified, or deleted from the database, all nodes must agree on what the new value is before it's available to be read. This typically means that new operations will block until the system has updated all relevant nodes.

- *Eventual consistency* means that the constraints around update operations are loosened by allowing nodes to potentially have different data, which is then resolved later via some policy. This may mean that reads of that data could show stale values for a period of time. Assuming that's acceptable, not needing to stop the world with every update results in a system that can achieve much higher throughput.

A-ha! You may be beginning to see the parallels with communication of information and whether you choose synchronous or asynchronous methods to do so:

- When using *synchronous communication,* you're communicating in a way that implicitly has *strong consistency.* For example, in a video call, all parties have to stop what they're doing at a particular time to all exchange and receive the same information by the end of the call, assuming that they're all listening.

- Comparatively, when using *asynchronous communication,* you're communicating in a way that implicitly has *eventual consistency.* When you send an email or a written document, there's always the possibility that some recipients will only read some of it, or not read it at all, and you need to be comfortable with this fact.

Therefore, this factors into the choice of how you should choose to communicate. For example, is it critically important that everyone has this information? Then choose a synchronous method. That's why a company all-hands meeting to announce an upcoming merger is a good choice; everyone should be there so everyone can know. Conversely, is the information something people can learn if they're interested, but it's not critical that everyone know all the details? Then choose an asynchronous method to broadcast it. Simple.

Since you're a smart person, you probably have a lot of great ideas at work. It's likely you also love making a lot of progress on them. Due to the nature of strong consistency and eventual consistency, you'll need to think about the speed of information exchange and the amount of consensus needed:

- When you want to move fast while maintaining strong consensus, you'll want to work within a small group. This is because you'll need all parties to agree to allow progress, which is equivalent to all database nodes needing to block new updates to achieve strong consistency.

- When you want to maintain a strong consensus in a large group, you'll need to move slowly. This is because it requires input from everyone, which can be potentially impossible with a large number of participants.

- If consensus is less important, you can move fast in a large group by broadcasting what you're up to asynchronously and mirroring the behavior of eventual consistency. If anyone else needs to know what you're up to, they can read your latest update.

You may have heard of the project management triangle, which refers to how the quality of a project is constrained by cost, scope, and time. The dilemma

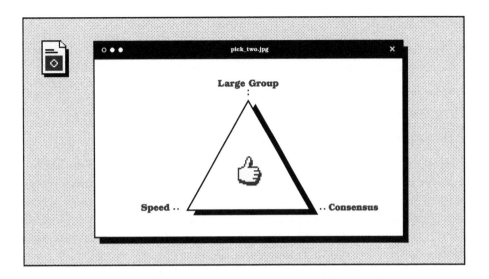

is that you can never have all three; you have to compromise on one of them. You can't have something cheap and fast that's high quality, nor can you have something fast and high quality that's cheap.

The same is true with group size, speed, and consensus, as shown in the previous diagram. You can only pick two. The art is in knowing which two to pick. Think through the scenarios in the following exercise.

Your Turn: Pick Two

Imagine that you have to do the following tasks. Which two ways of communicating would you choose for each one and why?

- Reviewing and merging a pull request
- Deciding the company strategy for the next year
- Designing a new feature within your team
- Proposing a new storage architecture rewrite for the whole platform

Permanence

Whenever you communicate, you create artifacts. These can range from a memory of a conversation in a colleague's brain to a detailed written proposal circulated to the entire department. Similar to the continuum between synchronous and asynchronous communication, there's a spectrum between impermanence and permanence. But what do we mean by that?

- An *impermanent* artifact only lasts for a limited period of time.
- A *permanent* artifact lasts or remains unchanged indefinitely.

There are several dimensions that determine permanence:

- How *relevant* is the artifact, both now and in the future? Would it accurately represent a decision, system, or process if somebody finds it?

- How *accurate* is it? Does it fully document its subject matter, or does it require additional information to fully describe it? Could it be out of date?

- How *useful* is it? Is it worth someone's time to read it?

We've all experienced permanent documentation that's misleading. Perhaps you've found an open source project and struggled to get it working because the README file isn't up to date. Maybe you found a document describing the architecture of part of a system you're going to work on, only to find later that it's the old version and you wasted your time understanding it. As humans, we're excellent at creating artifacts to address our current needs, but we don't always pay full attention to what will happen to those artifacts in the future.

When communicating, we need to be mindful of this. We need to think of the future. Are we making it better? Or are we setting a trap?

Look at the correlation between permanence and synchronousness in the following diagram.

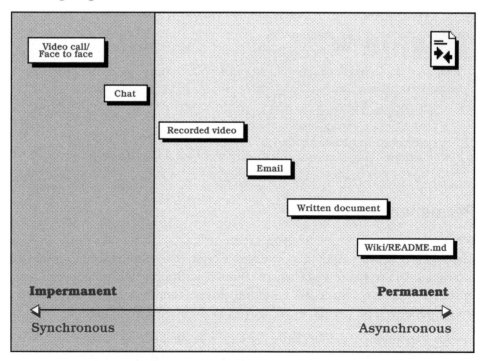

As you can see, synchronous communication generates few permanent arti-facts for the future. Asynchronous communication, on the other hand, can't occur without artifacts created to support it.

If a company is centered around physically colocated offices, a bias toward synchronous communication creates few artifacts. This is why remote workers often find it difficult to feel like part of the team. They simply don't see or hear what's being worked on because they're not there.

Decades of working in spaces designed for in-person communication, with Ping-Pong tables and canteen lunches, have left our skills for creating good artifacts severely underdeveloped. Perhaps your shared filesystems are full of out-of-date documents that are misleading and incomplete because they were used as a support mechanism to synchronous communication rather than for the core tenet of an asynchronous workplace.

We need to address this to build world-class, remote-work cultures. There are some key principles to follow to make this happen. You can apply these principles at the individual, team, department, or company level. Each of them builds upon the mindset of shifting right that we covered previously.

We need to do the following:

- *Leave an audit trail.* Every individual should think about an audit trail for their work so that others can find relevant information if they're interested.

- *Maintain an index.* Teams, departments, and even the whole company should think about how to create an index page that links to important documents, processes, and tools in a way that facilitates self-discovery.

- *Mark, file, tidy, and delete.* We're great at creating new documents but not so great at revisiting old ones and taking the required steps to make sure that they're still relevant.

Let's have a look at these areas individually.

Leave an Audit Trail

When students learn mathematics, they're typically asked to show their work as well as the solution. This isn't only to encourage them to think through the problems in clear steps. It also allows the teacher to understand the process that they used to solve the problems. We could benefit from adapting this approach more broadly in our work.

Some of the tools we use to develop software have evolved to create audit trails as a feature. For example, version-control systems like Git allow you to inspect —and even replay and change—the history of commits in a software project. You can often go back in time and understand what happened and why.

You should be thinking of applying the same principle of leaving an audit trail to your communication and decision making. Similar to the student tackling a math problem, we should pay attention to showing our work, often by applying the shift-right principle to whatever we're doing.

For example

- As you go about your day, you should keep your team *informed* about what you're working on by writing updates in a team chat channel. When you *make a decision* about something in a chat,you should broadcast it in written form, such as in the team chat or via email.

- At the end of the week, each person could write a brief *update* about what they've been working on and why and what is top of mind going into the next week.

- In *meetings*, you should maintain an agenda with notes that contain the history of what you talked about. Additionally, you should record each meeting and store it in a shared filesystem.

- When starting new *projects*, you should work on your ideas in design documents that anyone can view, ideally storing them in a central place so that anyone can discover them later.

- When you make a major *architectural decision* in a codebase, you should document exactly why you made the decision and how it affects the structure of the code going forward.

We will dive into more detail with practical examples and templates to follow in upcoming chapters. But you can get started right away in the activity on page 69.

Leaving an audit trail can seem like hard work if you're not used to doing it. However, once you start, you'll notice that it has numerous advantageous effects on the way that you do your work. Not only does it contribute toward making the future better by helping others revisit your progress and decisions regardless of their location, it encourages more opportunities for you to apply critical thinking to what you're doing and invites the same from others. Even if you're working alone, you gain more opportunities for interaction with your colleagues, which is especially important with remote working.

> ## Your Turn: Begin Your Audit Trail
>
> What better time to start a new habit than right now? As you go into your next workday, begin thinking about what kind of audit trail you typically leave. Do you currently work in the open or in a silo? Try to practice the following habits and see what kind of effect they have on you and your team:
>
> - Write a short update in your team channel about what you're going to be working on that day, with links to tickets, pull requests, and documents.
>
> - As you complete tasks, share with your team links to what you've done.
>
> - When you end the day, write an update about what went well, what you achieved, and what didn't go so well. State what you're going to do the next day.
>
> - Try to implement some of the shift-right behaviors previously outlined, such as emailing a decision that was agreed upon verbally, recording and archiving meetings, or writing to your team a bullet-point overview about how you feel about your week before winding down on Friday afternoon.
>
> How did it feel working this way, if you didn't before? Did you find that it affects your thinking or planning in a positive way? Did you notice an increase in interactions with your colleagues?

Maintain an Index

Regardless of whether you're an individual contributor or a manager of one team or a whole department, creating indexes to information is essential for keeping your house in order, increasing the discoverability of artifacts, and encouraging others to work this way.

Before search engines like Google made the discoverability of information on the Internet much simpler, websites like Yahoo! curated indexes of popular content by category, making it easier for people to find what they were interested in. You should be doing the same at work. The results can be transformative.

Search engines for documents at work are not as good as Google. No matter how hard you search, you can't always find that document that you're after. What was it called again? Was it *software projects* or *team allocations*? Did it have a typo in the title? Was it even stored here?

Given that you're not having to archive the whole Internet, maintaining indexes yourself can be a great way to make the important items discoverable for everyone. It could be as simple as a shared document with hyperlinks that anyone can edit.

For example, an index for a team could contain the following:

- Quick overview of what the team is called and what they're working on
- Members of the team and how to contact them individually
- Links to the team chat channels and email groups
- Links to the code repositories that they own and are working on
- Links to shared folders with design documents and architectural diagrams for current and past projects
- Rolling meeting agendas and recordings

The index could be linked to the staff directory, the team's chat channel, and the codebase documentation. It doesn't take long to create, but it can be the start of a movement. And what's more, humans have a habit of mirroring other behaviors that they like, so it won't be long before other individuals and teams start their own indexes as well.

Your Turn: Create Your Team Index

OK, it's time to create an index for your team:

- Pick the tool or software that your team is used to using for sharing documents, and create a new one that contains the information outlined previously and anything else that you can think of.

- Share the document with your team. What do they think? Is there anything that they think should be added to it? Link to it in your team's chat channel and anywhere else that your team has a digital presence.

- Share it with others in other teams and the wider department. What do they think about doing this for their own teams?

- Find someone influential in your department (e.g., the leader or senior member of the staff), and see whether this idea can gain traction across all of the teams. Promote the idea of having an index for the whole department too.

Mark, File, Tidy, and Delete

I'm sure we've all moved to a new home and have marveled at just how much cruft we've collected over the years: those duplicate pans you bought when you lost the other ones (only to find them again), that second bicycle pump, and those empty photo frames that you didn't even take out of the box from the last time you moved. All of this stuff that you forgot about makes it harder to reorganize everything. So you don't.

The digital artifacts we create are no different. A design document that assists a productive discussion and decision today may just waste an hour of someone's time in a year when they fail to realize that it's no longer relevant. It's your duty to ensure that you're keeping your proverbial closets tidy with good habits.

Looking back at the spectrum of synchronousness and permanence, we can observe the following:

- Artifacts that are produced from communication closer to the left side of the spectrum will typically have a *short shelf life.*

- Artifacts that are produced from the right side of the spectrum will typically have a *long shelf life.*

That makes sense: the video recording of a meeting probably isn't going to be an artifact that you'll want to come back to in several years, but it may be useful for people who missed the meeting to catch up in the coming days. Conversely, the README file for a software project should probably be *evergreen,* meaning that it's as relevant today as it will be in the future.

So what this means is that

- *Short-lived artifacts should be labeled as such.* This can happen implicitly (e.g., an old code commit is implicitly short-lived because there are commits after it in the same file) or explicitly (e.g., a written summary that's no longer useful is marked as old or is archived away or even deleted).

- *Long-lived artifacts should be kept up to date.* Any unmarked written document or wiki page should be occasionally revisited and updated to ensure that it's still relevant and useful.

Conflict occurs when there's a violation of these principles, which often happens toward the right side of the spectrum of synchronousness. Wikis or README files stagnate but it's not clear that they have. Written documents are no longer relevant, but they're not marked as such.

Always make it clear when you're creating a short-lived or long-lived artifact. You can forget about appropriately labeled short-lived artifacts because future readers will understand that they're no longer relevant when they stumble upon them. Long-lived documents need tending over time. If you link your long-lived documents from index pages, it's a neat reminder that you should occasionally go back and do some gardening on them.

Your Turn: Find That Cruft!

It's time for action. Just how much cruft can you find in your work filesystems that is breaking the fundamental rules of short-lived and long-lived documents?

- Take a look through artifacts that you've created or read within the last week. Is it clear which are meant to be short-lived and which are meant to be long-lived? Why? If not, why not?

- Make or suggest improvements to better identify those documents by their intended shelf life. This could be as simple as deleting, archiving, or just flagging a document as old in the title. It could mean refreshing a long-lived document so that it has up-to-date information.

- When you're done, show your team what you did and why. Make the suggestion that everyone should do this occasionally as a gift to your future selves.

- Now for some fun. Search in your work filesystem for words like *plan, outline, design,* and *goals,* and see what the oldest, most confusing document is that you can find. How did it end up in this state? What do you think you should do about it?

Restoring Your Humanity

Before we go any further, take a deep breath. We are about to make a case against everything that we've covered so far in this chapter.

But why?

Whether you like it or not, you're a human. (If you're reading this and you're not a human, science would be quite interested.) We're social creatures, regardless of whether you're having a day where you feel like you'd rather lock yourself in your home and never see another human ever again. Our strength as a species is built upon understanding one another, mirroring the behaviors of one another, and working together toward altruistic goals. We've evolved to be around one another because it brings us many positive benefits.

Humans working together can achieve great things, such as building society, innovating in science, and creating technology. For example, humans made the best video game ever: *Dark Souls.* (If you disagree, please return this book and ask for a refund.) Here, the protagonist is an *undead* in the mysterious city of Lordran. The undead are marked with the *darksign,* a burning ring that symbolizes their fate. They're warned that if they're not careful, they'll go *hollow*—a zombielike state—by losing their humanity. Players can restore their humanity by resting at the warmth of various bonfires dotted around Lordran.

Despite everything covered in this chapter, simply shifting right all of the time isn't the solution to all of our remote-work problems. Yes, it may make communication more concise and efficient. Yes, it may allow you to better think through problems. And yes, it may create better opportunities for people, regardless of their locations, to be a part of consensus and decision making. But this does come at a price. If you spend too much time away from interacting with other humans, it may have a detrimental effect on your mental health and happiness because you're fighting against our humanity, the core human trait that we've used over time to excel as a species.

At the start of the mass transition to working from home during the COVID-19 pandemic in 2020, it was reported that the replacement of in-person meetings with video calls was making many people suffer from a feeling of false intimacy that was leaving them grieving for face-to-face life.[1] Various theories speculated that our brains were finding it difficult to shift so suddenly from a physical world of connection through presence, voice, and body language to one that was a lower resolution and sometimes glitchy alternative.

Too much time spent away from humans, especially when the number of humans that you see in your personal life is small, can be detrimental to your mental health. So if this section of the book didn't exist, it might leave you with the impression that remote work would be best if you're able to efficiently exchange ideas and make progress entirely asynchronously. But as time goes on, you would feel less and less connected to other humans. And there's a high likelihood that you would feel less happy too.

We can add a final property to the spectrum on page 74, with a nod to *Dark Souls*. As brave warriors in our remote-working adventure, are we making ourselves feel *human* or *hollow?*

What you have to do to feel happier and more human is occasionally break the rules. Yes, you turn your back on everything you've learned in this chapter so far.

There's a balance to being efficient and also feeling like part of a community of other humans. You have to ask yourself each day whether you're feeling more or less connected to others. You need to check in with yourself regularly and make sure, dear adventurer, that you're not going to go hollow on us.

It turns out that you can rest in the warmth of the proverbial bonfire in a number of ways.

---

1.   https://www.bbc.com/worklife/article/20200421-why-zoom-video-chats-are-so-exhausting

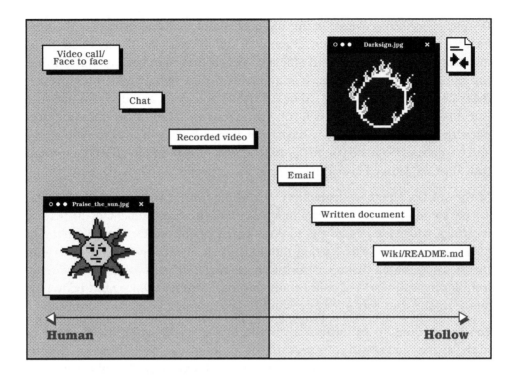

Encourage Goofing Off

Let's face it: not everyone spends all of their time in the office working solidly. Other activities that take place in the office include chatting with your colleagues in the kitchen, going out and grabbing a coffee, and maybe even playing a game of table tennis. So why should remote work be any different?

If you're a diligent and hardworking person, which you most likely are, it's easy to fall into the trap of overworking while you're at home. Because there are fewer opportunities to have ad hoc interactions with your colleagues, you can potentially end up grinding away even harder than you would if you were in the office.

So you need to goof off. But how? It turns out that there are a great number of ways, and they don't need any expensive setup or tools.

For example, you could

- *Openly encourage opportunities for fun conversation.* Creating chat channels or mailing lists that are for sharing pictures of your pets, family, or hobbies not only gives a welcome distraction from the day-to-day, it enables colleagues who work in different parts of the company to get to know each other better. You know, just like it happened when going into the office kitchen. Create channels around office locations, different types of pets, sports, or even the latest pop star. You can even keep an index of all these community channels and link to it in your onboarding documentation.

- *Book social time into the calendar.* Perhaps you could end your Fridays with a virtual happy hour that starts at 4:30 p.m. Maybe you could hang out with your colleagues at lunch, but virtually. No work talk, just fun talk. Perhaps you could end the day on Thursdays with a quick online game of chess or Rocket League, or whatever takes your fancy.

- *Collaborate for fun.* For example, every Friday you could all build a shared playlist around a theme using whichever music-streaming service you prefer. You could arrange a trivia game on a subject of your choice once a quarter. Or why not have your team watch a recorded conference talk or lecture together while discussing it in a chat channel?

Even though goofing off isn't actually *doing* work, it's still an integral part of your work. It's easy to default into execution-only mode when working remotely, but in the long run, it's going to drain your batteries and make you feel much less connected to others. After all, we work to make money, master particular skills, and serve our customers, but there's a lot of good in knowing and serving each other as well.

Shift Left on Purpose

Given that synchronous communication allows you more opportunity to feel connected to other humans, sometimes you've just got to shift left on the spectrum, even if it's more inefficient. (Yes, you need to be purposefully inefficient. I know that's hard.) Switch up the best practices that you've been learning about in this chapter now and again, but do tell your colleagues why you're doing so.

Here are some ideas for encouraging an occasional shift left:

- *Hold regular virtual office hours.* This works especially well if you're a senior engineer. Block out some of your focus time in the week to work openly on a video call that anyone can join. Less experienced engineers can learn a lot from watching you work, and they can ask you questions while you do so. Additionally, others can screen-share their own work and discuss it and get assistance if required.

- *Pair-program remotely.* Pick a ticket every iteration and pair up with someone else on your team. Many IDEs now offer remote pair-programming features.

- *Review a pull request synchronously.* Rather than sticking to the usual asynchronous method of reviewing a pull request, why not invite a couple of reviewers to come and look at it over a video call with you? This allows you to step through the code, discuss issues and solutions, and connect to others while doing so. If you can't arrange a live collaboration, a neat option is to record a video of your approach to the code changes and embed it in the description of the pull request.

- *Have a silent meeting about a written document.* If you have written a document with an idea or design for others to review, consider holding a silent meeting.[2] In a silent meeting, everyone joins and reads the document together, in silence, while on the call. Then, once everyone is done, the discussion can happen synchronously with one person taking notes. As well as connecting the group, this can stimulate more productive behavior because everyone is on the same page when the discussion begins.

If you want to inject a bit of positive chaos into proceedings, occasionally try to get people working together synchronously in real-time. For example, the whole team could use mob programming for some of their tasks,[3] or you could all try to write a design document together while on a call. At the very least, it'll be fun. Just don't tell them that we suggest that occasionally you should change the font color to white and say that there are strange technical issues occurring.

Meeting Up in Person

No matter how you try to simulate human interaction, it's impossible to replicate it. So if you can't beat them, join them in person. If you work remotely but in a location nearby some of your colleagues, try to find some time to meet up.

However, there are some rules that I would like to enforce:

- *Meet up on work time.* You would chat in the kitchen while people eat their lunch, so you can do this remotely as well. Forcing social activities into the early mornings or late evenings sets a bad example by principle, by saying that this is a social thing, and we don't do social things during the workday. Well, you would in an office. Building relationships and rapport with your colleagues is an important activity that should be taking place on work time as well.

---

2. https://medium.com/swlh/the-silent-meeting-manifesto-v1-189e9e3487eb
3. https://en.wikipedia.org/wiki/Mob_programming

- *Do something enjoyable.* You don't necessarily need to spend much money on eating out or paying for admission to somewhere, unless you want to. Instead, there are plenty of enjoyable free things that you can do such as going for a walk in nature, investigating a cool landmark in your city, or, if you're into it, going for a run or a bike ride together.

- *Try not to talk about work, unless it's useful.* Since you work together, it's probably natural that you're going to talk about work a little bit. However, try not to make it the main focus of meeting up; the choice of activity can have a real impact here. Instead, meeting up outside of work when you work remotely is primarily about getting to know each other as human beings, not just as analysts, engineers, or researchers. See if you can get to know your colleagues on a deeper and more human level. It'll make your interactions at work while remote better because it's harder to get frustrated at Steve the human being as opposed to Steve the chat handle who always manages to phrase things in a seemingly passive-aggressive manner.

If you happen to not live near any of your colleagues, you can do all of the previously mentioned activities with your family, friends, or pets. If that's not an option, make sure that you're regularly getting away from your computer during the workday and surrounding yourself with other people. This might mean working in a coffee shop or coworking space occasionally, or attending to meet-ups and talks in your local area.

Onward to Hyrule

OK, so we covered a lot of ground in this chapter. Let's recap:

- We looked at how there's a *spectrum of synchronousness* that spans between synchronous and asynchronous communication. It's not the case that the methods in which we communicate are simply one or the other because each has a place on the continuum. We plotted communication techniques and explored best practices for using them, including the need to shift right for remote working.

- We saw how there's a correlation between synchronousness and *permanence*, which dictates the type of artifacts that we create as gifts to ourselves in the future. We looked at the expected lifespan of these artifacts and how you can apply some simple habits to make them more future-proof.

- We overlaid what it means to feel *human* while striving for efficiency and saw how, paradoxically, being unwaveringly efficient and inclusive with your communication may just make you feel like the zombielike, hollow undead of Lordran. You have to break the rules occasionally and shift left to restore your humanity.

You should now be able to think more mindfully about the ways in which you communicate at work—whether you happen to be a remote worker or not—and be able to apply the models that we explored to ensure that you're communicating in the most suitable way for the work that you're doing and those you're communicating with. There's rarely a perfect way to communicate in any situation, but you can make significant improvements to your effectiveness by navigating the spectrum in this chapter.

Next up, we're going to explore a typical day in the physical office and then transform that into an equivalent day as a remote worker. You'll find that it isn't a straightforward case of doing everything you were already doing but over video call and chat instead. We'll incorporate the techniques that we learned in this chapter to see how your day should change. And get this: we'll do so by considering how Nintendo designed the land of Hyrule in 1992's video game classic, *The Legend of Zelda: A Link to the Past.*

Life is not shrinking for me; it's morphing into a whole new world of possibilities.

    ▷ Peyton Manning

CHAPTER 5

The Same but Different

It's the end of your sprint, and as per usual, you're having your retrospective, although this time, you're doing it remotely. Ben is leading the meeting this time around.

"OK, we'll keep it simple. We're going to use the stop-start-continue format. First, let's focus on the activities that we'd like to stop doing in the next sprint. I'll give everyone a couple of minutes to write down their thoughts, then we'll go around the room."

You see Ben's head dip as he beings to write. Lara has a question.

"Ben, how are we actually doing this? What are you writing on?"

"Sticky notes, just like we used to in the office," he replies.

"I haven't got any sticky notes," says Lara. "Me neither," you add. "Nor me," says Emma.

"Um, OK," says Ben. "How about you just use some paper and a pen?"

You look around your desk. No paper anywhere. You haven't even got a printer to steal it from. Hmm.

You have an idea. "I'm going to need to look in the other room, hang on."

"Me too," says Emma, leaving her seat. "Yep, me three," says Lara.

A few minutes pass. You can hear Ben's voice from the video call still running on your laptop. "Where is everyone?" he shouts. You run back to the call.

"Absolute nightmare," you say. "All I could find was this old bank statement, but I can write on the back."

"I found a notebook," says Emma. Lara still hasn't returned.

"OK, we need to get going or we'll run out of time," says Ben. "I've written mine down already."

Lara returns to the call. "The best I can do is some tissues and my daughter's crayons. I feel like a toddler," she says.

Emma has a question. "Ben, what are you planning to do with all of these notes we're writing?"

"I was going to put them up on the wall like we usually do."

"Right, but how are we going to stick our notes on your wall?"

"Um, good point. Thoughts?"

Lara holds up a shredded tissue covered in green wax.

"What do you think? Postmodern? Contemporary? I might frame it."

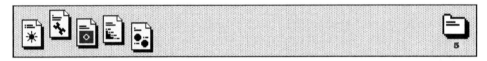

Remote working is like being in a parallel universe. So many things are the same as being in an office, but fundamentally, everything is different. You need to learn how to navigate through a new world that seems so familiar yet is filled with traps and pitfalls. This sounds like the plot to a particular classic video game.

In 1991, *The Legend of Zelda: A Link to the Past* came out on the Super Nintendo Entertainment System. It is considered to be one of the landmark games of its era and one of the greatest video games of all time.

The story of the game takes place in Hyrule, a land filled with dungeons, plains, a castle, deserts, and mountains. There's obviously evil afoot, and as the game progresses, a turn of events finds Link, our hero, teleported to the Dark World, which is a sinister mirror image of the sunny, grassy Light World. Green trees are replaced with hollow trunks, villagers with thieves, and deserts with swamps. Zelda's Hyrule Castle becomes the evil Ganon's Pyramid.

Link could teleport between worlds by using the Magic Mirror. However, he had to be careful. The Dark World is a dangerous place, and things aren't always what they seem. Teleporting between worlds on a bridge might just have you falling down a hole on the other side or stuck somewhere that you can't easily get out.

Fundamentally, you have to learn that the two worlds, even though they look familiar, require a different approach and way of thinking to proceed. And what's worse is that if you go wrong in the Dark World, the enemies are harder and it's often more challenging to find your way home. You have to adapt to conquer the game.

As we explored in Chapter 3, Treat Everyone as Remote, on page 33, the technology industry has spent decades optimizing toward working in open-plan statement offices. Moving to remote work without preparation is a bit like using the Magic Mirror to go from the Light World to the Dark World without forethought. You simply can't expect the terrain to be identical and for the same strategies that you used in the office to work for you when everyone is geographically distributed.

Instead, before looking into the Magic Mirror, the hero of the story needs to understand what lies through it, allowing them to change their approach to succeed in a more challenging world, but one where the ultimate reward lies. That's what this chapter is about.

Here's what we're going to cover:

- We're going to run through *a day in the life of a typical office-based engineer* at a software company, making note of the variety of activities and interactions that they have throughout the day.

- We're going to *go through the Magic Mirror with no preparation* to see why trying to replicate these activities remotely leads to a suboptimal experience. It's a bit like warping into the depths of a swamp.

- We'll see how we could *replay the day with better habits and techniques* that take into account what we've already learned about treating everyone as remote and shifting to more asynchronous interaction. This is how we change our strategy to win the game.

Right, we're going to start by running through a pretty normal day as a software engineer in a stereotypical open-plan office. Grab your sword and shield—I mean mouse and keyboard—and let's get going.

A Normal Day in the Office

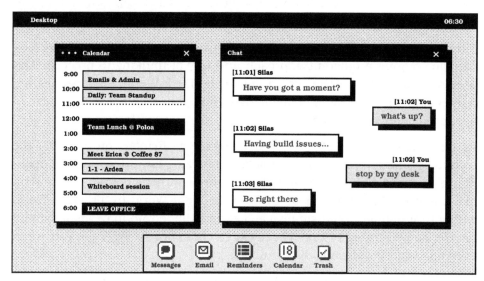

The alarm goes off at 6:30 a.m., and you hit snooze. Several times. By 6:50 a.m. you know that the train won't be waiting for you, so you leap out of bed, get dressed, put coffee in a travel mug, eat some cereal, brush your teeth, grab your bag, shout goodbye, and walk at double speed to the station.

Your train is on time and rolls up just as you arrive. You sit in the same seat as you do every day and pass the time on your forty-five-minute journey by reading the news on your phone and browsing the latest front-page articles on Hacker News. As the outside world begins to show signs of sunlight, it's time to exit the train.

Once you're past the barriers, it's a weave through a busy city center, passing coffee shops and the market toward downtown. You enter the building through the security gate, and go up the elevator to the fifth floor. You drop your bag on your desk by the window as your watch reads 9:11 a.m. It was a smooth journey today.

Stand-up commences at 9:15 a.m. Your team huddles around the whiteboard next to your desk and runs through the sticky-note tasks that are arranged into columns depending on their status. You discuss among yourselves what the plan of action is for today, then head to the kitchen to grab another coffee. You chat with a few of your colleagues about anything and everything, what they watched on television last night to what they've been working on over the past couple of days.

You've got a clear morning, so it's time to get your head down on your programming. You put on your headphones to drown out the noise and get cracking. An hour later, your colleague raises his hand and waves at you. You take off your headphones to speak. "What's up?"

"Have you got a minute? I'm struggling to understand how the parsing works here," he asks.

"Sure thing," you reply. You scoot your chair around to his desk and you look at the problem together, talking it through while running the debugger. Five minutes later you discover a bug. "Looks like a simple fix," he says. "I'll get a pull request up in a bit. Would you mind looking at it?" You're happy to.

Late morning brings a coffee refill, so you're back in the kitchen filling up and having a chat. Then it's back to programming for a while before your first meeting. One of the other teams is going to be redesigning a part of the codebase you often work with, so you get together in a room to draw out the changes on the whiteboard. Everyone seems happy with the approach, so the meeting ends quickly. The drawing is left on the board with a note: "Do not erase!"

Next up, it's the second meeting. Your team is refining the backlog ahead of the next sprint iteration. You huddle around your team's whiteboard again and collectively discuss which tasks are highest priority while your product manager drives the conversation. After some debate, it's clear to you that two of the tasks need to be broken down into smaller chunks. That's no problem for your product manager: "Gotcha. It makes sense to build this in two increments, so I'll go and rewrite these stories."

Some Terminology

If you're not familiar with terms such as *backlog refinement, sprint planning,* and *stories* from the world of Scrum, then worry not. A team's backlog is just its current list of prioritized tasks, and it usually gets reviewed and reordered if necessary on a regular basis. That's *backlog refinement.* The term *story* is sometimes used for tasks if they're written as user stories, for example, "As an analyst, I would like to export my data from the dashboard so I can add it to my report."

A *sprint* is a fixed period of time in which a team takes the highest priority chunk of their backlog and sets a goal to get that work done. The sprint planning session is where the team sits down to estimate the size of the stories in their backlog and thus work out how much they can do in the coming sprint. Simple!

It's lunch time. You walk around the corner to grab a sandwich from the deli, then you eat it in the break area near the kitchen. Once it's over, you spend some time hanging out with Chris, who leads the sales team. He's been sending you invaluable feedback on your new features as he demos them to prospects.

After lunch it's time for sprint planning. You're back at the whiteboard with the sticky notes, and you've got new green ones for the big task that was broken down into smaller ones. The backlog is in a good state. You collectively estimate the size of each task and then group together the ones that you believe you can get done in the coming sprint. Your product manager seems happy with this. "It looks like the goal is pretty clear: we're going to ship the first version of the new analytics graph to customers in two weeks. Do you all agree?" There are nods all around.

The afternoon is mostly clear of distractions, and you're coding away. Later in the day, your colleague lifts his head and hands again, and you take off your headphones. "The pull request of the bug fix is up if you wouldn't mind taking a look." You've no problem with that. You load the changes on your screen and you're joined at your desk.

"It was pretty simple in the end. This part of the code was ignoring one of the earlier fields on the schema for some reason. I've added it in, and there's a unit test to cover it." The change looks good. You click merge. "I'll go and deploy that to production now," he states, wheeling back to his desk. "No worries," you reply. A few minutes later you see a thumbs-up over your monitor, signifying it's live.

At the end of the day, your team is winding down. You use this opportunity to sketch out how you think your own code might need to change to take the other team's changes into consideration. You draw some boxes and arrows on the whiteboard while the others are packing up. Generally, there's consensus and you leave the drawing up for tomorrow to work on further.

You pack up your own bag, ensure you've got your train pass, and walk briskly back to the station so that you can get the 5:50 p.m. fast train home. You decompress from a busy day by watching the sunset's orange glow fade behind the city high-rises.

Observations

So what have we observed from this typical day in the office?

- *Synchronous interactions dominate.* The majority of interactions we described involve synchronous exchanges among people who are in the same office.

- *The physical space provides the main apparatus for interactions.* Little arrangement is required for various types of exchanges because the office provides them. Whiteboards, meeting rooms, and breakout spaces suggest the types of interactions that should be taking place.

- *There's an assumption everyone is physically colocated each day.* With the reliance on the physical space comes an assumption that it'll be occupied daily for it to work best.

- *Artifacts are limited and physical.* Drawings are left on whiteboards for later, and sticky notes contain tasks. To see them, you need to be there.

What Happens If You Don't Change When Working Remotely?

If you think back to Chapter 4, The Spectrum of Synchronousness, on page 53, you can see how so much time is spent on the synchronous left side of our communications model. It's the natural thing to do when the physical space implies that you should do so.

However, if we're aiming to adhere to the principle of treating everyone as remote on page 33, this reliance on synchronous and physically colocated humans becomes a hindrance. Practically speaking, why is that the case?

- When synchronous, verbal interactions dominate, *the only people who are able to take part are those who are there at a specific time and in that specific place.* This means that anybody who is busy, out sick, or working remotely is unable to be part of the conversation, which puts them in a position of inequality.

- When a physical space dictates interactions, *those who are not present in that space do not have the same opportunities to interact.* A remote worker sitting at their computer is unable to wander through the kitchen and have spontaneous conversations with others. This puts them at a disadvantage because they have fewer opportunities to interact than those in the office.

- When it's assumed that everyone is physically colocated by default, *effort isn't put into creating interaction points and artifacts that are accessible from anywhere.* Again, those who are remote will be at a disadvantage through reduced information discovery and accessibility.

- When artifacts are predominantly physical, *they're kept in a form that prevents input from remote workers and makes them feel like they need assistance to contribute.* It creates a hindrance. A physically colocated worker can edit the whiteboard, whereas the remote worker needs to ask to see it and also have someone edit it on their behalf.

Fundamentally, when the previous is true, the experience of being a remote worker when others are not totally sucks. It creates stress, frustration, and anxiety about not being able to perform at your best.

Let's relive the same day, except that some of the team is going to be working remotely and some of them will be in the office.

As for you? You're at home. Rewinding the clock, starting … now!

Through the Magic Mirror

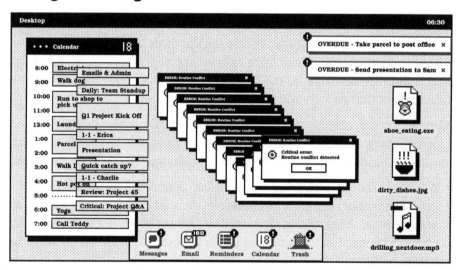

The alarm goes off at 7:30 a.m. You're working from home today, so there's no train that needs catching. You hit snooze. Then you hit it again. And again. Probably more times than you should. When you wake up later than you wanted to and see that your stand-up is in eight minutes, you roll out of bed, put on yesterday's T-shirt and jeans, run to make coffee in time, and then go sit by your laptop. You use the video-call preview to make sure your hair is presentable. It is, just.

After the familiar *ding-dong* sound as you join the video call, you say hello to your fellow remote-work colleagues today. "Where's the rest of the team?" you ask. "Have they forgotten to dial us in?" You send a message to your product manager on group chat. They're on their way. Another *ding-dong* later and you're waving at your colleagues who are in the office, standing in front of the whiteboard.

"Can you move the camera closer to the board?" you ask, because you can't see much more than the color of the sticky notes, let alone what's on them. Another *ding-dong* follows and there's now another camera that's closer to the board so you can better see what's going on, but it's quite disorienting. The conversation at stand-up is hard to follow because it's predominantly taking place among the group at the whiteboard, and you can't easily find moments to contribute. You decide to write your question about a parallel task needing to be unblocked into the group chat instead.

You go to the kitchen to get some breakfast, but forgot to defrost the bread. You settle with another coffee for now. You go and wash your face and brush your teeth and get back to your laptop after opening the curtains and windows. You have a clear morning, so you get on with your programming. You find a good few hours of focus, but you're hungry. You need to make a quick visit to the coffee shop to get some food.

You check the group chat before leaving. You see a message, "Has anyone got a second?" from thirty minutes ago, followed by some general conversation. You choose to ignore it while you get food. You pick up a croissant and juice from the corner and head back. You check the chat to see three unread direct messages.

```
[10:44] lara: ben's been stuck on this problem all morning, are you there?
[10:45] lara: please message him asap
[11:01] lara: you there?
```

You had no idea that he was stuck. You send a message to see what he needs help with.

```
[11:15] ben: i'm getting null pointer exceptions in the parser
[11:15] ben: line 282, input is the usual test file with the latest build
```

You stop what you're working on and check out his branch and build it and try to reproduce the error locally. What follows is forty-five minutes of back and forth via chat trying to locate the error. You're still in the middle of it when your calendar notifies you that you should be in a meeting about what another team is planning to do in the codebase. You tell Ben that you'll get back to him in a couple of hours.

You join via video call, and once again the action is happening on a whiteboard you can't see clearly and neither can Andy, who's also remote. After a frustrating twenty minutes, you're not sure whether you understand if the change is going to be a problem or not. "Can you please take a photo of the whiteboard and send it to me?"

You switch video calls to the backlog refinement meeting. Same deal as the last meeting. Most of the conversation is happening around a whiteboard that you can't see clearly. You find your attention drifting while trying to debug Ben's problem locally, and you just agree to the priority list that's there.

Back to chat. There are a bunch of messages from Ben.

```
[12:01] ben: any luck? i still don't know what's going on
[12:13] ben: lol, i can't even get it to compile now
[12:21] ben: tell me when you're free
```

You message him back, but you don't get a response. Perhaps he's gone to lunch. Speaking of which, you haven't thought about lunch. You look through the cupboards and find some noodles, which you cook. To say that they're disappointing is an understatement. You eat them in front of your laptop, while checking to see whether Ben has returned. No dice.

You join the video call for sprint planning, once again looking at a whiteboard from a long way away. But this time Ben has dialed into the call on his phone so he can have a camera closer to the board. "Where did you go?" you ask him. "Oh, we all went out for a walk," he says. "When I got back, Lara helped me fix my problem. It's sorted now." You can't help but feel frustrated that you wasted an hour of your time on it.

You begin estimating tasks in the sprint planning meeting, but two of the tasks seem way too big to take on. Your product manager sounds frustrated: "Didn't we just do backlog refinement a couple of hours ago?" You keep quiet because evidently you weren't listening when these tasks were discussed. They get put in the sprint anyway, and you'll have to work them out as you go. Patience is getting lost because they have to repeat everything multiple times to the remote participants.

The meeting is over, so it's back to programming. You try to pick up from where you got distracted with Ben's message earlier this morning. You settle into flow for around thirty minutes, but then your phone goes off. It's the pager system. The logs are filling up with errors in production.

You switch to the terminal and open the logs to see thousands of parsing errors: null pointer exceptions caused by a recent change. You go to the team channel.

```
[15:58] you: the live logs are full of errors. has anyone deployed?
[15:59] ben: it was me, i'm looking at it
```

```
[15:59] ben: i'll send you the commit hash
[15:59] ben: it's ca82a6dff817ec66f44342007202690a93763949
```

You check out the code locally and see that Ben pushed a change to production, and it doesn't have a unit test written alongside it. Ben says that Lara checked the change, but Lara is marked as Away on chat and isn't responding. You suggest rolling back to the last version and then writing a unit test out of the input that was causing the live system to fail.

After everyone knows what they're doing, you try to get back into programming flow, but it's challenging. You notice that the end of the day is approaching. You check the group chat.

```
[17:01] lara: see you all tomorrow
[17:01] lara: that architecture approach looks good, thanks for discussing it
```

What architecture approach?

You check the rest of the chat for an answer, but it seems everyone has gone home. You can't focus on your programming, so you decide to check Hacker News. It's cathartic and you lose track of time. You notice it's getting dark and check the clock. It's 6:30 p.m. and you should probably think about dinner, but you already know there's nothing in the fridge. You sigh.

Observations

Wow, that worked out pretty differently, didn't it? What happened?

- *Your routine suffered without the commute to define it.* When there's a train to catch and a place to be with other people, morning, lunch time, and evening follow naturally without much planning. When there was no place to be, you spent too much time in front of the computer, didn't get enough fresh air and exercise, and didn't ensure you had the food and drink you needed.

- *Without the office to define interactions, communication suffered.* The only people you spoke to were your team members, and even those interactions were patchy and frustrating.

- *The principle of treating everyone as remote was not followed.* You struggled as a remote participant in meetings and interactions in general. You didn't know when people were available, you wasted your time on something that was solved in person, and you didn't know about a meeting that happened at the end of the day without you. You felt like a second-class citizen.

- *The overall feeling was that of isolation and frustration rather than being part of a team.* Your attention was scattered and you were continually concerned that you were missing out on whatever was going on. You didn't make much progress on your own work, and you felt like you let the team down because bad code went live and you didn't spot the tasks that needed breaking down in backlog refinement.

Unfortunately, when companies do not follow the principle of treating everyone as remote and do not train their employees to carefully choose their interactions as per our spectrum of synchronousness, this is the everyday frustration of being a remote worker.

Practical Actions for a Better Day

Let's make some changes.

If we want remote workers to be equal contributors who suffer no hindrance, we need to take numerous actions to allow them to discover information, have conversations, and feel like they're as much a part of the team as anyone else. Here are the steps to take to do so:

- *All meetings should be done via video, with each participant using their own individual camera and microphone.* This gives every participant the same visual and auditory cues as everyone else and ensures that all asynchronous interactions can be attended by anyone who's available, regardless of where they actually are.

- *Shared collaborative documents should form the backbone of interactions, not whiteboards.* No sticky notes and no pen doodlings allowed. Instead, software needs to lead the way. Anything that requires organizing, understanding, or viewing before a meeting should be shared via collaborative software. Then, during the meeting, it can be screen-shared to the group, and everyone can edit and annotate it in real time.

- *Chat should be used to create spaces to have spontaneous interactions.* Because the physical office dictates interactions—such as bumping into people in the kitchen—similar spaces should exist in the digital world. We should use chat channels that represent physical locations, or even metaphorical ones such as #thewatercooler to signal that we want people to mingle, interact, and goof off.

- *All interactions should be mindful and forgiving of others.* We should remember when interacting with someone remotely that they may not be immediately available, even if their status says that they are. We should also remember basic manners that you would use in the office, such as politely asking for someone's time.

- *All interactions should ideally have some asynchronous element.* Either we default to writing to each other throughout the day via chat or by using collaborative documents if we're collaborating in real time via screen-sharing. This means that others who aren't present have an opportunity to view the information later if they wish.

- *All important interactions should ideally produce some artifact that can be viewed asynchronously, even if it's short-lived.* Creating an audit trail isn't only useful to yourself but useful to others who have an interest in what you're doing or who need to get up to speed with it for their own work. We should work in a way that produces notes, documents, chat messages, video recordings, and more so that we work in the open in a discoverable manner.

- *Synchronous interactions should still occur when urgency is key.* For example, if a bug needs checking, simply screen-sharing your IDE as if you're sitting next to the person is a powerful way to work together with speed.

Whew, that's a lot of changes! And in addition to this, as a remote worker, you'll need to take practical steps to look after yourself to be able to work at your best:

- *Use your commuting time to create a clear start and end of the day.* Instead of rolling out of bed and on to the computer because you no longer have a commute, you should create a fake *commute* that forces you to take time before and after work to move your body. This could be as simple as going for a quick walk or a more vigorous structured exercise of your choosing.

- *Ensure you're setting yourself up for success.* Without the office full of snacks and drinks, or the nearby city center with numerous cafes and lunch spots, make sure that you have what you need every day to fuel your body and mind. This means planning your meals, ensuring you have the ingredients, and making time to prepare and eat them.

- *Create ample time for breaks by mimicking what you would do in the office.* How many times in the office do you walk over to a colleague, go to the kitchen, visit the bathroom, exit the building to go into town, and so on? When you're at home, it's easy to do none of those things, either through bad habits or the guilt of not working. But this is bad for you. Think about how often you'd usually get away from your desk, and then do that same thing at home, even if it means a quick stroll around the block. It's absolutely essential.

So is there another way of bridging the gap between these two worlds while also staying mentally and physically healthy? Well, using the previous advice, it turns out that there is. Let's have a look at how this experience of remote working could have played out differently using what you just learned.

Conquering the Dark World

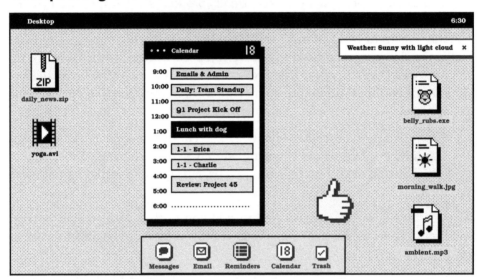

The alarm goes off at 6:30 a.m. You sit up, stretch, and get yourself out of bed. You throw on your clothes and eat breakfast while listening to the morning news. The coffee you make goes into a travel mug, and you get your jacket and shoes on and head out for a walk to start the day. You collect your thoughts as you head through the park and then back to your house. You go via the grocery store to pick up your food for the day.

Once you're back, you have a shower and brew more coffee. You tidy the kitchen and head into the other room to your desk and open your computer. It's now 9 a.m. You log on to chat and switch to the #usa channel. Someone has already started the "Good morning!" thread. You say hello to your colleagues and get involved in a chat about the latest Marvel movie.

At 9:15 a.m. you switch to your team's channel, where the automated prompt sends out the link to the video call for stand-up. You join. You hear that familiar *ding-dong* sound as you see the faces of all of your team members, each having individually joined the call. You can see from their backgrounds that some are at home and some are in the office. "Morning all," says your product manager. "Check this out," she says, rotating the camera to her toddler who has fallen asleep face first on the couch. "He's got the right idea, hasn't he?" You laugh. "OK, I'm sharing …"

The screen-share starts, and you can see the familiar columns of the team's ticket-tracking software. "OK, let's walk through the board. Who's first?" Your team talks through all the tickets that are being worked on, and some get dragged into different columns. "Looks good," you say.

Your product manager speaks. "We've got backlog refinement later, and I'm just finishing up the sheet. I'll share it in the channel in about fifteen minutes. Leave comments ahead of later." You all wave and the video call ends.

You set your chat status to Away with a note to send you a DM if it's urgent. You minimize the chat window and open your IDE to work on your programming since you have a clear morning. You find your flow and crack on. An hour later, you hear that familiar ping. It's a DM from your colleague.

```
[10:20] ben: really sorry to bother you
[10:20: ben: I'm totally stumped with this parser error
[10:20] ben: when you have a moment, can I screen-share where I've gotten to?
[10:21] you: no problem. lemme refill my coffee, then let's do it
```

You join a video call, and Ben shares his screen. He shows you how he's stepping through the code in the debugger. Five minutes later and you've both discovered the bug. "I'll get a pull request up shortly," he says. "I'll post it in the channel when it's done. Are you OK reviewing it?" You've got no problem with that. You say goodbye and end the call.

Before you get back into some more programming, you check your messages and continue the conversation in the #usa channel from earlier, chipping in some more of your thoughts about the casting of that movie. Then it's back to programming for a while. You make good progress. You remember that you were meant to check the shared document ahead of backlog refinement, so you open the link in your team chat to see the highest priority items for the next iteration. A couple of them look like they might be too big and need to be broken down, so you leave a comment on the items in question saying that you think this is the case.

Then it's the first meeting of the day. Another team is going to be redesigning a part of the codebase you often work with, so you join the call to find out what they're going to do. Julia, the lead engineer, walks everyone through the proposed changes by using some collaborative drawing software to show roughly how the structure will change. Everyone's happy with the approach, and the meeting ends quickly. She shares a link to her drawing by email afterward.

Next up, it's the second meeting: backlog refinement. Your team joins the call, and the screen-share of the document begins. "Thank you everyone for checking it over," says your product manager. She agrees that the two tasks that you commented on are too big, and you all debate the best way to break them down and simplify them. You reach consensus, and before you all leave the call, she says she's going to rewrite the tasks ahead of sprint planning later on.

Lunch is here, so you set your status appropriately. You close your laptop and go to the kitchen to cook an omelette using the groceries you bought earlier. You eat it, then remember that you need to post a letter, so you head outside for a short five-minute walk. Back at the house, you check the #lunchchat channel and hop on the video call to say hello. Among the faces is Chris, who leads the sales team. He's been sending you invaluable feedback about your features recently, so you decide to join a breakout room to catch up with him properly.

Sprint planning is next. Another video call and screen-share. Lara chimes in: "I know we've had a lot of meetings today, so let's keep this short." You all nod. The big tasks have been broken down and turned into tickets in the backlog of your ticket-tracking software. You take part in estimation by typing task sizes into the chat on cue, and you reach consensus about what you can achieve in the upcoming sprint. "It looks like the goal is pretty clear: we're going to ship the first version of the new analytics graph to customers in two weeks. Do you all agree?" Everyone nods and leaves the call.

You have a distraction-free afternoon, and you make good progress on programming. A ping sounds, as you've been tagged in a message on chat. It's a link from Ben for the pull request for the bug you fixed earlier. You say you'll take a look and open it up and review the code. The change looks good, and you merge it. You see the continuous integration pipeline start to build it, and thirty seconds later, an automated message in the group chat says that the change is ready to deploy.

```
[16:29] ben: is that OK to deploy?
[16:29] you: yep. just check the logs once it's out to be sure
```

Ben clicks the deploy button in chat, and a few minutes later, another automated prompt confirms that the changes have been pushed live, along with a link to the graphs for that service in the monitoring system. You open it out of curiosity and see that data is flowing without any errors.

```
[16:33] you: seems good to me
[16:33] ben: yep. thanks for helping me with it
[16:34] you: i was having some thoughts about the other team's redesign
```

```
[16:34] you: if anyone's free, can i take you through it?
[16:35] lara: sure, now?
[16:35] ben: i'll join in 5 minutes, need a tea
```

You start a video call and post the link. You screen-share the diagram that was sent to you earlier. You annotate it with some additional boxes and arrows that point out where your current features interface and how you plan to adapt your code. Generally, there's consensus, and you save the diagram and reshare the link in the team channel.

```
[16:57] you: if you couldn't make it, this is what i think we should do
[16:57] you: just leave a comment here, we can go through it tomorrow
[16:59] lara: no worries, gotta go - see you then
[17:00] ben: bye!
```

You close your laptop and head upstairs to get changed into your running gear. You end the day like you do every day: a run across the bridge and back, where you can see the sunset's orange glow fade behind the tall city high-rises in the distance.

Observations

Well, that was certainly different, wasn't it? What happened?

- *Having a set routine helped the day go smoothly.* Going outdoors at the beginning and the end of the day can serve as a *fake commute* and help reinforce a transition to starting work and then ending work, leading to a healthier mental separation between activities. Some simple forward planning, such as getting groceries and setting clear times for breaks and making lunch, go a long way.

- *Chat, video calls, and screen-sharing provided replacements for interactions that would depend on the physical office space.* Collaborative software formed the backbone of team interactions. This means that everyone was able to interact synchronously while also leaving artifacts that can be revisited later, such as shared documents, drawings, and the ticket tracking system. There were also plenty of opportunities to engage in nonwork conversations throughout the day.

- *Everyone on the team treated each other as remote.* They followed common courtesies such as joining video calls with their own cameras and micro-phones, giving opportunities for people to comment asynchronously on their own schedules, and respecting other people's time.

- *The overall feeling was one of equality and of being part of a team.* Even though the whole team wasn't present in a physical location, their shared use of good etiquette and digital tools made everyone feel respected and equal.

Do you see how many small changes can compound into an entirely different experience by using the tools and techniques we looked at in the previous two chapters? And guess what? We've only just scratched the surface.

Your Turn: Transform Your Day

Now it's time to use what you learned in this chapter and see how you can take immediate steps to change your own working practices:

- If you work in an office, how much of your normal workday is based around synchronous interactions that use the physical layout and objects present in the office to dictate how interactions occur?

  If you're a remote worker, how often do you face scenarios like those in the second scenario? To make these situations better, do you or your colleagues, or both, need to change how you work?

- Regardless of whether you're working remotely every day, implement some or all of the changes previously outlined. Put a focus on creating more opportunities to contribute asynchronously using collaborative documents, applying equalizing measures to interactions, and treating everyone as remote. How does it change the dynamic of your day?

- Ask a colleague or friend who works remotely to identify their top three most common frustrations in their jobs. Are they things that can be addressed by the methods laid out in this chapter?

Let's Discover Some Artifacts

We hope that you enjoyed the journey that we took together in this chapter. We saw how there can be perils that lurk if you expect remote working to naturally unfold outside of the physical office without clear habit and mindset changes.

Here's what we covered:

- We ran through *a day in the life of an engineer in a physical office.* If you've ever worked in an office, I'm sure this all looks very familiar: kitchens, meeting rooms, headphones, whiteboards, and all.

- We *spent a day remotely* in a team and company that had not shifted its working practices to properly support remote workers. As you saw, it was a bit of a nightmare.

- We *played back the same day* spent remotely as part of a team and company that treats everyone as remote and exhibits the tools, habits, and mindset that enable high-quality interactions regardless of physical location. Didn't this day go much better?

Next up, we're going to be thinking about the artifacts that we create and use as part of our work and why they're even more essential in the remote world.

We do not follow maps to buried treasure, and X never, ever marks the spot.

      Indiana Jones

CHAPTER 6

Artifacts for a Better Future

It's 9:20 a.m. You've just finished your daily stand-up meeting and you're winding down the video call.

"Oh, before we go, have you seen it?" asks Lara.

"Seen what?"

"The document."

"What document?" you ask.

"It's not just any document," says Ben. "It's *The Document.* Capital T, capital D."

You're confused. "Is that a movie?"

Ben speaks up. "Here, I'll share it with you." You see his eyes track across his screen. "There. It should be in your inbox now."

You open your email, and there it is. A shared document called "Why Our Software Won't Scale Beyond September." It looks intriguing. Dangerous. The title pulls you in. Hang on, is this workplace clickbait?

"Let's end the video call before you get lost in it," says Lara. "Let us know what you think about it later. I won't spoil the surprise."

With your coffee in one hand, you scroll through the document. It's compelling reading. In fact, it's quite beautiful. That choice of font. That line spacing. And those diagrams. Wow. How long did this take to produce?

It starts with an executive summary. "If we don't act now, our company is going to be in serious peril in six months. Our user growth is outpacing our ability to scale our dashboard storage, and everything is going to come to a crashing halt." You scroll to the introduction. You read the graph that shows data growth plotted against time, and the blue line forms a hockey stick that goes red as it shoots up at the end.

You take another sip of coffee without taking your eyes off of the screen. You peel through the tables of figures and then get to the proposal for what needs to be done. It's a migration project that includes a major database redesign. There's a link to a GitHub project that has some example schema definitions. There's even a detailed README file on how to install it on your own machine and some initial promising benchmark tests using dummy data.

This is brilliant. You look back at the document. It's absolutely covered in comments supporting the work. And, whoa, look who commented: it's the CEO! She wants to green-light the project! She actually reads documents from Engineering? This is incredible. Who wrote this? Who is this person? You scroll to the top.

—*Lara Martin*

Your coffee cup hits the desk. You immediately open your team chat.

```
[09:43] you: LARA. you wrote this document?
[09:43] lara: it's something i've been looking into recently ...
[09:44] you: THE CEO COMMENTED. AND THE ENTIRE DEPARTMENT.
[09:44] ben: looks like we've got a new project, huh?
```

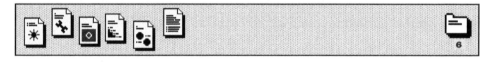

Artifacts are everywhere. From the legendary Master Sword to the Rosetta Stone, carefully crafted objects act as society's link to the past, giving us an insight into the wisdom of our predecessors who we can learn from and then carry it forward into the present day.

Imagine a world where humanity created no artifacts for future generations. No art, no carvings, no drawings, no written words. Where would we be? We would only have word of mouth to carry our knowledge into the future, an unreliable way of ensuring that our best ideas not only last for generations to come but are improved, extended, and generalized.

Now imagine an open-plan office, not unlike one you may have worked in. It's an office where no artifacts are created for future employees. No README files, no wikis, no design documents, no onboarding material. Where would you find yourself? With only word of mouth to spread institutional knowledge, mistakes get repeated, engineers getting sick or leaving the company bring whole projects to a halt, and new staff have a challenging and painful journey of asking for favors so they can ramp up into new roles.

If society as a whole has learned that the careful creation of artifacts is the backbone of our progress, the technology industry's recent history of open-plan office culture has encouraged the opposite. Stone tools found in Kenya date back 3.3 million years, yet the tools that your colleagues wrote last month may have already been forgotten about, never to be found again. And even if they were found, would anyone know how to compile and run them?

In addition to transcending time, artifacts transcend locations and cultures. Even if we haven't been to Egypt, we know that King Tutankhamun's burial mask is a world famous object that unlocks the door to knowledge of the ancient cultures and customs of that country. Just how many school children have stared at the gold and blue mask and were transported in their minds to another time?

Great artifacts spread knowledge, generate ideas, and inspire. In the opening story, we saw how one well-written document can transcend an individual, a team, and even a department. Artifacts can start a movement, connect people, encourage conversations, and even start a new project. They can lift a name to veneration. Or maybe to senior engineer.

Artifacts are the backbone of remote working. Creating effective ones is an art, just like programming. We've never before had such widespread access to the incredible collaborative tools that we can use, often for free, in our lives and work. You can type in a spreadsheet simultaneously in real time with colleagues in London, Tokyo, and New York, assuming that at least one of you is working at a peculiar time of the day.

In fact, not since the invention of the Gutenberg printing press have we had such an incredible step change in our ability to create and distribute knowledge around the world. So why are we settling with conversations around a whiteboard in an office with glass partitions? Let's think bigger and embrace the tools for what they were created for. The potential audience for your codebase, idea, or decision doesn't have to be your team or those in the vicinity of your desk. It can potentially be the whole world.

In this chapter, we're going to cover a whole host of ideas for creating fantastic artifacts that you can use immediately in your daily work.

Comparing Artifacts

When it comes to the creation and consumption of different types of artifacts, we are going to concern ourselves with three categories. If we were being picky, there would only be two, but because we are creating software, it is worth having a third category to describe special types of communication around producing code.

These are the three categories:

- *Written artifacts.* The most powerful tool in the remote-work arsenal is the written word. We'll cover different ways of using writing to document meetings, formulate and spread your designs and ideas, broadcast news, and store permanent useful information.

- *Codebase artifacts.* Because we're creating software, we'll cover everything to do with checking into your codebases, from commits to pull requests to README files and architecture decision records.

- *Recorded artifacts.* When we treat everyone as remote, we also encounter new opportunities to create recordings of audio and video. We'll cover recording and archiving meetings, creating asynchronous presentations and updates, and using video to annotate written communication.

Before we dive into each of these categories, we should cover something first. Given that we're engineers and we're interested in being efficient in our communication as well as our programming, what's the best way to create and consume information? Is it writing, listening, or watching? Well, like most things in life, the answer is always "it depends."

Consumption Considerations

What's the best medium to use if you want to consume information? According to research, it's reading. A study published in *Human Factors [Zie98]* showed that while proofreading, people are able to read English at 200 words per minute (wpm) on paper and 180 wpm on a computer monitor.

In comparison, in a paper published in *Proceedings of the Human Factors and Ergonomics Society Annual Meeting [Wil98]*, audiobooks are recommended to be listened to at 150–160 wpm, and the same figure is given for the average conversation rate in the United States.[1] If you're watching a lecture or presentation that has slides, the recommended rate is 100–125 wpm, according to

---

1.   http://www.ncvs.org/ncvs/tutorials/voiceprod/tutorial/quality.html

Linda Wong in her book *Essential Study Skills [Won14]*. So reading is faster than listening.

In addition to speed of consumption, another factor is even more important: retention. If you're spending your time consuming some piece of information, the longer you can retain it in your memory, the better. A study in the *Journal of Advanced Student Science [UXBB13]* showed that visual stimulation is more effective than audio stimuli at achieving higher memory retention and recall. It's also worth mentioning that it's easier to get distracted while listening to audio or watching videos in comparison to reading.[2]

So when it comes to consuming information, both for speed of input and retention, the written word wins. But what about producing information?

Production Pondering

Empirical measurement of the production of artifacts via writing or speaking is somewhat more difficult to quantify. Although an average professional typist types at around 50–80 wpm, and some highly skilled typists achieve speeds above 120 wpm (as noted in *On the Reappraisal of Microeconomics: Economic Growth and Change in a Material World [Ayr05]*), this doesn't really help us answer the question of whether it's faster and more efficient to capture our ideas as written or recorded artifacts.

Some people struggle with writing. Others are able to write coherent sentences at the same speed that they're able to think of them. Conversely, some people are fantastic at articulating themselves clearly while speaking in an improvised manner, while others shudder at the thought of speaking in front of a large group. They're fundamentally different skills to be mastered independently.[3]

Regardless of whether a piece of writing or a recorded talk is being worked on, both require preparation to be effective. In fact, if you're working on a suffi-ciently complex idea—which is likely, given that you're working in technology—the act of producing the artifact is a key part of developing the idea in the first place. You can't get there by thinking alone. How often have you written up your thoughts on how to design a new feature only to realize while doing it that your original solution is suboptimal and needs some improvements? Likewise, how often have you made an outline of a presentation only to com-pletely change the narrative by the time you write it and practice it several times?

---

2.   https://news.ycombinator.com/item?id=16603454
3.   https://scottberkun.com/2012/on-writing-vs-speaking/

This process is entirely natural and, in fact, should be fully embraced to make better artifacts. Those who aren't aware of this process produce ineffective artifacts. How many times have you read a design document at work only to be put off by what seems like a jumble of ideas that don't fit together as one narrative? How many presentations have left you confused? It's not your fault. The author just hasn't finished their work. The University of Chicago Writing Program uses the following diagram to explain this process.[4]

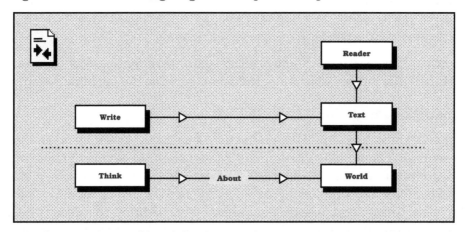

To think about the world and develop an idea, you need to write about it. This is true of a written artifact or presentation. You can't work through the entire design in your head. The writing process allows you to reflect on the idea as it materializes and then further improve upon it. This produces an artifact as a side effect of you developing your thinking process.

However, this same artifact you create to develop your idea is going to be the same thing your audience is going to consume to understand it. It's the barrier between your view of the world and the reader. The problem is that the artifact you produce to develop your idea will use language and structuring that primarily supports your idea generation rather than readability.

This means that to ensure your audience is going to understand it, you need to further refine it, often by simplifying, rephrasing, and reordering the information so that they're able to see the idea in the same way you imagined it in your head. You need to turn the artifact into a narrative that makes sense to the reader the first time they come across it. Many people are unaware of this second phase, and their readers are left confused as a result. If you've been left bewildered by a written document or presentation, it likely isn't your fault. The artifact has just gotten in the way of the author's idea.

---

4.   https://www.youtube.com/watch?v=vtIzMaLkCaM

Your Turn: Inspecting a Bad Artifact

Can you remember the last time you interacted with an artifact at work that was thoroughly confusing? Perhaps it was a design document that made no sense, or a newsletter that was so long and boring that you never finished reading it. If you can, find it.

- What is it about this artifact that makes it bad for the reader? Was it written with you in mind, or does it look like it primarily serves as a way for the author to organize their own thoughts?

- Think about how the artifact needs to change to make it more impactful to you as the reader. Does it need to be structured differently, or does it need different language and terminology so it's clearer?

- If you had to write this artifact again, how would you do it?

We've established that regardless of whether you're creating a high-quality written artifact or a recorded artifact, it's probably going to take an equal amount of effort to produce. So neither format wins for speed of production. In the case of a tie, you should do whatever is generally most suitable for your audience, who we know can consume written artifacts faster and retain them in memory for longer. And it turns out that there are additional benefits to doing this.

Searchability Scrutiny

What good is speed of reading and rate of retention if nobody can find your artifact in the first place? Search engines are excellent at indexing written documents so that users can find them based on keywords. The same is not true for audio and video. It's likely that the system that you use for hosting your shared documents at work has search functionality that does a decent job if you're looking for keywords in the title or the body of a written document; but it may be harder to find that video you vaguely remember that contains the reference to that database table.

If you do create many non-written artifacts, ensure that they're easy to find. It's highly likely that your colleagues would be unable to find your video presentation from three months ago unless it had an explicit link or was stored in a predictable filesystem location.

In addition to being easier to discover, written artifacts have excellent searchability within them. If you were looking for the part of the document that mentions the production database, you could just search for it by name. Conversely, even if you managed to find the video that contained the information about the production database, you'd have to skip around the content manually until you stumbled across the right part in the timeline. It's likely that you'd give up and try to ask the author directly, defeating the purpose of the artifact existing.

There are other usability factors to consider when choosing writing or recording for your artifacts. Remote working allows people from all over the planet to collaborate, and often you won't have the same native language. Written documents allow those with different native languages to use translation tools to help them understand complex sentences. This isn't possible with recorded video. More importantly, written artifacts provide solutions to visually impaired colleagues via the use of screen readers, but recorded artifacts offer no reliable equivalent for deaf colleagues. Even if you have access to software that automatically produces text transcripts, it can be inaccurate and frustrating to the user.

So when it comes to technological assistance, written artifacts also come out on top. This means they're faster to read, better for retaining information, equal in preparation time to recorded artifacts, and have better tools available to help non-native speakers and those with visual impairments. Surely then, we should only produce written artifacts and ignore everything else? Well, not quite.

Convenience and Humanity

There are three main scenarios where recorded artifacts are worthwhile:

- *When they take almost zero effort to produce.* Recording a meeting requires little more effort than clicking a button and then uploading the video file at the end. This can provide an archive of your regular meetings to anyone who was unable to make it that day. This supports those who work flexible hours or different time zones with little extra cost. Imagine, for example, how much time it would take to write a detailed summary of the meeting instead.

- *When they supplement another artifact.* As we'll see later in the chapter, a recorded artifact can be an excellent guide to longer and more complex written artifacts. A detailed written design of a new piece of architecture could be overwhelming to many readers; however, an accompanying five-minute video that walks through the main points can greatly reduce the barrier to entry.

- *When they give an opportunity to feel connected to other humans.* As we saw in Chapter 4, The Spectrum of Synchronousness, on page 53, there are occasional times and places to forget about efficiency or the right way to do things and instead break the rules to feel more connected to others. The same applies here. Creating a recorded artifact allows someone to hear and see another human being, which can be beneficial when talking through an exciting announcement or giving a monthly update. So, from time to time, substitute a written artifact for a recording to remind people that they are still working with other humans, and not robots.

When you're remote working, we highly recommend creating written artifacts as your first choice. Use recorded artifacts as supplements or archives of synchronous events, or use them sparingly for occasions where the positive effects of feeling connected to other humans outweigh the negatives of the format.

Written Artifacts

Now, without further ado, let's have a look at a number of written artifacts that you can use as part of your remote-working tool belt. Some of these may be new to you, and you should try them out. Some may not be so new, but you may come away with a renewed conviction that they could make your work life a whole lot better.

Meeting Minutes

Hang on, meeting minutes? That's a bit boring, isn't it? Well, not quite. When done well, meeting minutes can ensure that your meetings are better prepared, are more timely and structured, and have clearly captured actions. Minutes also are a rolling archive of everything you've ever discussed in case somebody misses a meeting.

Effective minutes do not require much effort to get right. The figure on page 108 shows a format that could work for you:

- *Each meeting is a separate section* as indicated by the date heading.

- *Bullet points list the agenda items* and each starts with the initials of the person who added it to the agenda.

- *Additional information is added as sub-bullets* during the meeting to capture what's being said.

- *Actions are written in bold* and specifically mention what has to be done and by whom.

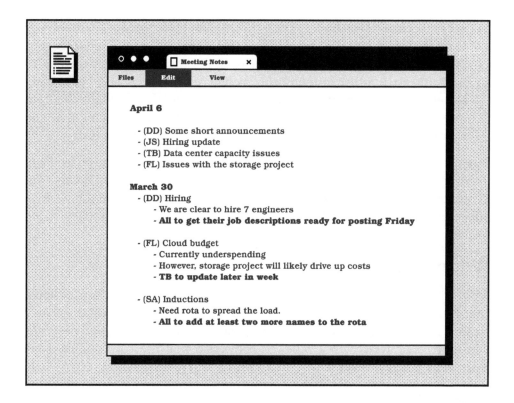

With this simple format in mind, here's what you should do:

- *Create a shared document for the minutes of every meeting.* You can use the format shown previously. It's simple enough for people to understand without much explanation.

- *Attach the shared document to the calendar invite.* This is the simplest way for people to find the minutes for a meeting—they're right there!

- *Remind the participants to add their agenda items well ahead of time.* A simple reminder a few hours before, or even a day before, will allow participants to include the items they want to cover. They also help the chair of the meeting allocate time by dividing the length of the meeting by the number of agenda items.

- *Screen share the minutes during the meeting.* Even though it's nice to see everyone's faces nice and big, screen sharing the minutes keeps the conversation on track. Everyone is able to annotate the minutes themselves while it's screen shared.

- *Have one person act as the chair.* A meeting chair is a fun responsibility. They need to ensure the meeting goes smoothly. This can be as simple as making sure all the agenda items are covered or as complex as putting the brakes on off-topic conversations to bring everyone back to the agenda. We'll cover more on the topic of chairing meetings later in the book.

- *Assign actions where needed.* As actions are identified, get them written in bold if you're using the previous format. Some collaborative-document software will even allow you to assign them to people, generating an email notification.

- *Roll over unfinished agenda items to the next meeting.* If items aren't covered, create a new section for the date of the next meeting, then hoist the uncovered items to the front of the queue for next time.

Using meeting minutes is a high-impact activity because it helps meetings go so much better. If you're feeling adventurous, you can even add a link to the video recording of each meeting in the minutes as well.

Your Turn: Use Minutes to Improve Your Worst Meeting

Find the worst-run meeting in your calendar. Go on, you know which one we're talking about. Let's make it better:

- Using the preceding format, create a shared meeting-minutes document for the meeting and attach it to the invite.

- Follow the preceding instructions before, during, and after the meeting to bring some structure to it. You can be the chair, or you can nominate someone else.

- Try this out in the meeting for a few weeks and then reflect on whether it improves. We bet it will. Maybe it won't be your worst meeting anymore.

Design Documents

The best features and architectures at software companies don't usually come from somebody opening their editor and then just hacking away in solitude until it's done. Usually it helps to do a few things before embarking on a big, new change to the codebase:

- *You'll want to think about it more.* As we touched upon earlier, all complex ideas will require writing to fully develop them.

- *You'll want to get others to check your thinking.* It's likely you work with other smart people who can confirm that you're approaching a new piece of work in the right way, and they'll also be able to point out things you haven't thought about or incorrect assumptions you made.

- *You'll want to get consensus that it's a good idea.* Once you've knocked your idea into shape, it would be handy for you to circulate it wider so others know what you're doing, both inside and outside of your team.

- *You'll want to create an artifact that outlines what happened on that project at that moment in time.* Sometimes you need to work on an old feature and you wish you knew more about why it was designed a certain way. It would be awesome if you could create an artifact that others could find in the future.

Well, it turns out that you're in luck! This is exactly what design documents are for. Although they can often be viewed as a chore, or even a hurdle that needs to be jumped over before the *real* work begins, making the creation of design documents an institutional habit allows for more carefully considered ideas with a higher chance of success and early identification of problems. It allows senior engineers to contribute regardless of where they're located, allows for achievement of consensus and for identification of dependencies among teams and systems, and allows for the addition of a summary artifact to the organization's knowledge base.

You're encouraged to check out the detailed article about how design documents are structured at Google.[5] In summary, a good design document will cover the following:

- *Context and scope.* This includes a short (think three paragraphs) section that outlines what's being built and the surrounding system that it'll exist within.

- *Goals and nongoals.* Bullet points show what goals the new system will achieve (e.g., allow users to quickly find their documents by title) and what it won't achieve (e.g., allow users to search within documents).

- *Design.* Beginning with a brief overview, outline the system and then break it down to describe the following constituent parts.

- *Application programming interface (API).* If the new system will have an API, include a sketch of what endpoints it'll have and what they'll do.

- *Data storage.* Cover what data will need to be stored and where, the volume of the data, and the access patterns.

---

5. https://www.industrialempathy.com/posts/design-docs-at-google/

- *Degree of constraint.* What's constraining this design? Is it legacy code, time, the programming language of the system it exists within, or something else? Focus on the choice being made with these questions in mind.

- *Alternatives considered.* Briefly list alternative designs that could have worked but ultimately weren't chosen and the reasons why.

- *Cross-cutting concerns.* How are issues such as security, monitoring, service-level agreements (SLAs), and privacy being considered?

- *System context diagram.* The simple box-and-arrow visual that follows places the new system into context with the other systems around it that it interacts with.

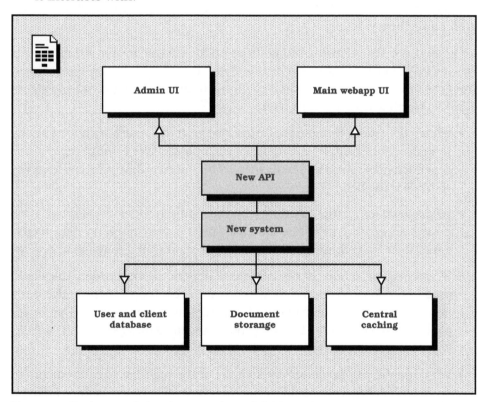

You may find it useful to have a shared folder where your team can archive all of their design documents over time. You can even link to them in the codebase.

The next time you need to get your thoughts together about a major new feature, write a design document. Then anyone at your company, all across the globe, can review, critique, and share for consensus that one idea in your head. Magic.

Idea Papers

Not every thought needs a full-blown design document. The detail that the format requires would make the barrier of entry far too high for sketching ideas. There are often times that you have a valuable idea about something that you or your team should be doing in the future and you'd like to start sharing that idea so you can build consensus.

That's exactly where an *idea paper* comes in. Think of it as a high-level design document without the need to go into the details of the implementation. An idea paper is the perfect way to write up your thoughts in a concise way that allows them to be shared for others to give their input. It has just enough of a structure to help you better formulate your thinking but won't burden you with all the heavy details.

You could use the following template as an idea-paper format for proposing new technical ideas. But it can be adapted for pretty much any type of idea, from the direction of your product roadmap to how you might want to structure the North American sales team:

- *What's your idea?* In a nutshell, describe your idea using a short, punchy sentence. For example, it could be as simple as, "We need to remove our dependency on Apache ZooKeeper." The shorter that you can express your idea, the better.

- *Why should we do this?* Outline why you think this idea is valuable. Does it solve an existing problem, increase speed or resiliency, or allow a customer to do something new? What goal are you trying to reach and why?

- *What effect will it have on the business?* Depending on the idea, this could range from less downtime to faster search results, to more active daily users or less time spent manually maintaining your system. Use bullet points to list what you're thinking about, and keep them short and concise. Where possible, use data to reinforce your ideas.

- *What are the requirements?* Make a list of the high-level requirements to execute the idea. This could mean commissioning or decommissioning a database, refactoring and extending some code, or changing the way that you do things entirely. Also, be explicit about what's out of scope. If there are any constraints or dependencies, you should call them out here too.

- *How will you know if this idea is a success?* Write down how you would measure whether the idea has worked or not. For example, it may be a measurement of user-interface speed, or data retrieval speed, or even a reduction in the number of clicks that a user takes to perform a common task. There's always some way to measure what you're intending.

A good idea paper doesn't need to be much longer than a few pages, if that. However, it enables you to develop your thinking through writing, spread that idea globally and asynchronously, and get crucial feedback as you work toward building consensus about it. The best idea papers can turn a whole business around. There's a lot of power in those few pages.

Your Turn: Write an Idea Paper

Over the next few weeks, take an idea that you've got in your head and turn it into an idea paper:

- Use the previous format to document your idea. Work through each of the sections and scrutinize them as you're writing. When you're done, does the idea feel stronger? Has it changed?

- If you're happy with it, share the idea paper with your team and invite them to comment on it. Tell them that you're experimenting with a new format and ask their opinion on it. You may find you want to adapt some of the sections to your specific purpose.

- See how your idea develops as others comment on it. Does it still stand? Would it benefit from sharing outside of your team to gain more input?

Newsletters

Even if you've spent most of your working life in open-plan offices and sitting next to other teams, it's likely that you've often wondered what everyone else around you is working on. When there's so much information to keep on top of in your own team, the effort it requires to stay connected to others and keep track of their progress becomes prohibitive.

However, a solution to this is surprisingly simple, easy to implement, entirely asynchronous, and something we all are already familiar with. That solution is newsletters. You can write a regular briefing from your team. All you need to do is pick a cadence that makes sense and ensure that they're archived. Again, like everything else in this section, an internally accessible folder containing shared documents is perfect.

But what should you put in them? Well, it's up to you:

- *Important updates.* Are you going to be incrementing to the next major version of your API? Deprecating a part of the codebase? Have you just shipped a new feature? A newsletter is the perfect place to let everyone know.

- *What you've been up to since the last newsletter.* This doesn't have to be a dry update. Tell a story. What have you been working on? Do you have any links to pull requests, a feature you shipped in the product, or information that you've learned? Think about what you would find interesting to read in someone else's newsletter and emulate it.

- *Requests for reviewers or commenters on your design documents or idea papers.* If you've been using the document formats we've presented so far in this chapter, your newsletter is a perfect way to widen their exposure to the rest of the department.

- *Milestones or goals that your team is working toward.* What is your team aiming to release next, and why is it important? Where can people find out more, and where can they come and talk to you if they have anymore questions?

A good newsletter is usually one to two pages long. Depending on your company and the size of your department, there may be an obvious outlet for newsletters already. Perhaps there's a pre-existing mailing list that you can use to send them around. Or perhaps there are particular chat channels where you can post them. Aim wide and far. The best part about sending newsletters is that if people don't want to read them, they'll simply skip over them. Those who are interested will dive right in. Ensure that others are allowed to comment when you send them out. You might even find the CEO in there!

And, hey, remember one thing: newsletters are more engaging if they have a little bit of fun weaved into proceedings. Perhaps people could take turns including photographs of their pets or some bizarre and interesting facts that they've found. This draws in eyeballs and increases the impact of what you're sending out.

Wikis

Where do you go when you want to look up some information about Edward V? Or perhaps find out what the four fundamental forces of nature are? Well, you probably end up on Wikipedia.

It's an evergreen portal into the known universe. You never know exactly who wrote each page, but the style remains consistent throughout. It's like an old

Your Turn: Create Your First Team Newsletter

See if you can kick-start a culture of writing newsletters by leading with action. It's time to create your first newsletter:

- First, lobby the rest of your team to convince them that it's a good idea. Choose an outlet for your shared newsletter document that makes sense, such as email or chat.

- Pick a cadence. You could aim for monthly to begin with because it gives time for the team to achieve enough to write about. Depending on how the newsletter is received, you can make it more or less frequent.

- Write it! Use the advice here to gather together all of the pertinent information about what your team is working on, including links to code, designs, and ideas.

- Send the newsletter and see how it's received. If you're unable to track open rates, pick a handful of people at random from other teams and ask them for their opinions on it. Are they interested in creating their own newsletter too?

friend: reliable, always there, and inevitably has the information that you need to solve a problem or even just to find out something new and interesting.

Given that we're so used to having this resource for *all of human knowledge*, why do so few companies have an equivalent for their internal knowledge? It's certainly a smaller subset of knowledge than the known universe. What gives?

Permanent, evergreen information that's kept up to date is a godsend. It can save a thousand questions and confusions. It can be the breadcrumb trail that lets other adventurers find their way among the department. You may or may not have access to an internal wiki or similar, but that doesn't mean that you can't get going by creating your own pages for important information. You can start by (guess what?) a shared document.

Record the important information for your team, but write it in such a way that would make it useful to an outside observer too. For example, you could create a page that contains the following information. If you don't know how to answer some of these questions yet, working them out can be the subject of some interesting discussions:

- *Brief description of what your team does.* This can cover your name and where in the department and the world you're located. Include a high-level description of what you work on.

- *Names and contact details of everyone on your team.* A list of names, job titles, and contact details should go here.

- *Your mission and outcomes.* Take some time to outline the mission of your team. Why do you exist and what kinds of problems are you trying to solve? Are you trying to build features for particular use cases, or are you maintaining and scaling the storage infrastructure? How do you measure your success?

- *Your responsibilities.* What parts of the codebase do you look after? Are you part of issue triage from the customer support team? Are you building the next-generation document store?

- *Where to find you.* Link to any chat channels or mailing lists where others can interact with you.

- *Links to shared folders of supplementary information.* If you've shared folders of design documents, idea papers, newsletters, or similar, link to them here.

Whenever you communicate, make a habit of linking to your team's wiki page in everything that you do. If you've made a good one, and especially if you keep it up to date, you'll notice that other people will begin to copy the idea. If you don't already have access to an internal wiki system, you'll notice that the momentum will begin to build around getting one installed. If you already have one, you might find a willing crew to revamp it.

Your Turn: Be a Wiki Influencer

Go ahead and create a wiki page for your team. You can then begin to spread the word:

- Find the right place to start a discussion about the usefulness of wiki pages in the organization. Mention how they could exist for teams, products, and common processes. See how many people think that this is a good idea.

- If you get support, start a new chat channel dedicated to wiki pages and publicize it. Show people yours and how you built it. Encourage them to make their own pages for their teams or include any other knowledge that would benefit from being captured.

- Whenever anyone updates the wiki pages, they should link to them in the wiki chat channel with a short description of what has changed. Once people see that there's a lot of activity going on around wikis, they'll want to get involved too.

Codebase Artifacts

In addition to reading and writing text to communicate and share ideas, there's something else you spend a lot of time writing: code. There are a number of good habits that you can adopt when writing code in shared codebases that'll not only make your life easier but will vastly improve the experience for those you collaborate with.

Let's get into it.

Commits

Regardless of which versioning system you use, the units of work that you contribute to the codebase are *commits*. Not only do they serve you as a way in which to structure your work so you can make changes to the codebase in steps, they form an audit trail: What changed, when, why, and who changed it?

You often don't appreciate well-structured and detailed commits until you have to do some codebase archeology to work out where a bug may have come from. Imagine that you're doing that right now, and consider the following two commit messages.

Here's the first:

```
Change type of ID to match provider change.

Upstream upgrades from our data provider have now changed
the size of the field required to store IDs.

- Changes ID field from int to long.

- Corresponding schema change is in schema codebase.

- Warning: not backward compatible.

Fixes #4557
See also: #4558, #5001
```

And here's the second:

```
change int to long
```

If you were trying to hunt down a gnarly bug with the parsing of this ID field, which would you rather read? Commit messages are artifacts, much like written documents. They require careful crafting so the next interaction with your code—which may be in a different time zone, tomorrow, next year, or maybe in a decade—lets the next person understand what happened at that moment in time and why.

If you want to be helpful to colleagues asynchronously, especially at times of stress, you can use the following rules:[6]

- *Start with a short (fifty characters or less) summary.* Make it clear what's changed in one sentence, and capitalize the first letter of the first word. This greatly helps the reader scan through a list of commits when working.

- *Follow with more explanatory text if needed, around seventy-two characters.* If you need more detail than will fit in the subject, expand underneath. Make sure you wrap the lines so that it can fit in a small terminal window.

- *Write the commit message in the imperative.* Say, "Fix bug" rather than "Fixed bug." If you use Git, this matches the automated messages that it generates.

- *Use bullet points to make your text clearer.* Think of the reader wanting to digest information quickly. Use bullets if they assist you in keeping your communication concise.

- *Focus on what changed and why, not how.* The commit itself will show how the code changed, so use the message to explain what changed and why. Consider the difference between the two previous example commit messages. The first focuses on what and why, and the second focuses on how.

- *Reference the tickets that cover the work being done.* This allows the audit trail to be followed further if necessary.

Remember: every single commit message is a miniature artifact. Make sure you're leaving high-quality information for others to consume asynchronously in the future.

Your Turn: Good Commits, Bad Commits

- Browse through the commit logs in some of the codebases that you work with. What's the quality of commit messages like? Do they follow the preceding rules? Would you be able to understand ever single atomic unit of change?

- Step up your commit message game over the coming week. Stop and mindfully think about each message you're writing, remembering that each is a miniature artifact.

- Search your favorite codebases for swear words—either at work or on open source projects. Can you identify when the developers were having a particularly bad day?

---

6.   https://git-scm.com/book/en/v2/Distributed-Git-Contributing-to-a-Project

Pull Requests

Pull requests group together one or more commits from an author for review as a submission to a codebase. If commits are paragraphs in a book, a pull request is the whole short story. Both writers and reviewers should take care to communicate clearly about the change because the pull request finishes the narrative that a ticket begins. It's also a highly visible place where you all set the standard for how professional developers discuss and debate changes, leaving footprints of your engineering culture with every comment. So no pressure, right?

Make sure that pull requests are not too big. A couple hundred lines of code will take a reasonable amount of time to understand and review. Break up large changes to the codebase into multiple pull requests.

You can create a pull request template to help guide others on writing better descriptions. Here is a good starter template:[7]

- *What has changed?* Simple. Just explain what the commits have changed. You should reference a ticket if one is available. Use a few concise sentences to explain what has happened at a high level. Anyone could be reading this, so make sure that anyone could understand.

- *Why?* What business or engineering goal is this pull request addressing? Is it adding a new feature, fixing a bug, or speeding up an API call?

- *How?* Draw attention to any significant design decisions that may not be obvious to the reviewer. Is some dependent work being done elsewhere, such as a migration or a change upstream?

- *What testing considerations are there?* In addition to writing unit tests, call out any risk of edge cases or particular things to watch out for when checking the code and testing the change.

- *Are there visual aids?* Include any diagrams, screenshots, animated GIFs, or video recordings that make the changes clearer to the reviewer.

- *Anything else?* If something else is worth calling out that doesn't fit into the previous categories, then do so.

Etiquette is also important[8] when reviewing a pull request and offering your feedback:

---

7. https://www.pullrequest.com/blog/writing-a-great-pull-request-description/
8. https://github.blog/2015-01-21-how-to-write-the-perfect-pull-request/

- *Take your time to understand the context first.* Read the description. Then read it again. Get into the mind of the author, the context of the change, and the surrounding code. Everything else flows from there.

- *Think before you react.* It's easy to see red and make an incorrect or unfounded comment, especially if you don't agree with the change. (One challenging colleague once immediately closed a significant pull request into the codebase he owned with the comment *no*. That was an interesting follow-up argument.) Take your time and collate all of your thoughts before replying.

- *Explain your suggestions clearly.* If you want changes to be made, don't just say what you want changed. Offer your explanations as well. Why are you making them? Will your own suggestions offer a neater or safer solution? Is it a simple matter of the author not following the style guide? Be explicit.

- *Ask rather than tell.* Use questions like, "What do you think about X?" rather than "Do X."

- *Be humble.* Remember that you're supporting a colleague. If you know more than them, it's your duty to coach them and set an example for others.

- *Avoid derogatory terms and be aware of bias.* Don't call someone stupid. Also, when discourse is neutral, it can come across as negative. Be positive.

If you're the author of the pull request and are responding to feedback, do the following:

- *Lead with appreciation.* Other people have taken their time to review your code, so be appreciative.

- *Ask for clarification if needed.* If you don't understand a suggestion, ask for more information.

- *Explain your reasoning.* If you don't agree with a reviewer's changes, explain why you decided to make the changes the way that you did, then ask whether it satisfies their concern.

- *Respond to each comment in a timely manner.* Although pull requests are asynchronous, replying quickly shows appreciation and respect for the reviewer.

- *Link to supporting documentation.* If there's a design document that can help reviewers understand the context of the change, make sure you link to it. The more context you can give the reviewer the better.

- *Use synchronous communication if confusion or debate keeps growing.* If it seems that the discussion is going nowhere or is even getting heated, suggest moving it to a video call at the convenience of the reviewers. Often it's a simple misunderstanding that you can resolve quickly.

Who'd have thought that pull requests are so nuanced? However, they're worth dedicating the time to. A culture of healthy asynchronous code review enables global engineering organizations to ship high-quality work, regardless of where engineers are located.

README Files

Earlier in this book, we mentioned that README files are artifacts that are on the rightmost part of the spectrum of synchronousness and also the spectrum of permanence. Not only does this mean that they need to be understood with no interaction with the original author, it means that they're evergreen. Like any good Wikipedia page, they need to be continually reviewed and updated. You could set an automated reminder for doing this, perhaps quarterly.

Any software project is difficult to understand the first time. Even if the code isn't complicated, bad documentation can waste hours if the instructions are not clear as to how to understand, install, and contribute to it. Therefore, a README file should always be included in the top level of your project's directory so that it's the first thing that anyone reads. So many subtle and implicit decisions are made when creating a software project, such as the programming language, frameworks and libraries, formatting of command-line arguments, the build system, and so on. The quicker you can get others up to speed with everything, the more likely others are going to feel encouraged to contribute.

Given that README files are high-impact artifacts, it helps to have a template to follow when creating them. Here's one that can help:[9]

- *Name.* This part is simple. Give the project a name that needs no explanation. As cool as it is to name your projects after Greek mythological figures, you might find that nobody knows how to pronounce them. (We realized after several years that nobody was pronouncing one of our own database projects—Mnemosyne—correctly. Even the creator was getting it wrong. We now call it MNDB.)

---

9.   https://www.makeareadme.com/

- *Description.* Use simple language to explain what this piece of software does. This could be a list of features or a link to the live application so people can look for themselves.

- *Visuals.* If it helps to include any screenshots, diagrams, or videos, do so here. Not only is this helpful, it looks nice.

- *Installation.* Provide clear, concise steps on how to install the project locally. Make sure that you've tried them yourself as well, preferably in different environments.

- *Usage.* Use a lot of examples to show how to run and use the software. This could be terminal commands that the reader can copy and paste, or links to further explanatory documentation like videos.

- *Support.* If the reader is having an issue, who should they talk to? Direct them to a chat channel or to particular individuals who can help them out.

- *Contributing.* If someone wants to contribute, what should they do? Should they just raise a pull request, or should they speak to the author first? Is there a particular process to follow, or a style guide to adhere to?

- *Authors and acknowledgements.* List the authors and give credit to anyone who helped build the system.

- *License.* If it's an open source project, include a license.

Lead by example and create high-quality README files in your software projects. Share the preceding template with others to help them do the same; or even better, contribute your own high-quality README files into your colleague's projects.

Documentation is incredibly important in software development: for ourselves, our colleagues, and our customers if we have public-facing APIs. If you want to dive deeper into writing high-quality documentation, the Write the Docs community is well worth checking out.[10] As you can probably imagine, its website is a well-organized treasure trove of articles, podcasts, videos, and conferences about the subject.

Architecture Decision Records

We've all experienced that feeling: we're looking at a codebase and we can't for the life of us fathom why it's been structured in such an esoteric manner. Some of us may have even experienced this when looking at our own code

---

10. https://www.writethedocs.org/

from many years ago. How are you meant to extend this, and just what on earth was the original developer thinking? Were they playing design pattern roulette? To prevent this issue from happening in the future, you can use an architecture decision record (ADR).[11]

As you work on your own projects and reach a decision point—a design choice, whether it be stylistic, framework-related, or how to build some infrastructure—you can capture it in an ADR. Broadly speaking, an ADR should capture the following:

- *Point in time* in which the decision was made
- *Status* of the ADR (proposed, accepted, rejected, etc.)
- *Current context* and business priorities that led to the decision
- *Decision* itself we made as a result
- *Consequences* of making the change, such as what is now easier or more difficult as a result

You can check your ADRs into a top-level folder in that particular codebase. Proposing a new architectural direction is then achieved by writing an ADR and raising a pull request into that codebase, where all parties who regularly commit to that codebase can see it. It also serves as an audit trail for how the code has changed over time. The context is not lost even if people leave the company.

You can begin a culture of creating ADRs in your team and then sharing them more widely with other colleagues in the department if you find them to be a success.

Recorded Artifacts

The last category we'll look at is recorded artifacts. We mentioned earlier in the chapter that in most cases, reading and writing are the most efficient means of communication when participants are distributed around the world. However, video can serve some important purposes, especially when there are situations where it can be created with little effort or when used as a supplement to other artifacts.

Meeting Archives

Most videoconferencing software allows the host to create a video recording of the meeting with little more effort than clicking a button. When the meeting is over, the video file is written to the host's computer. This isn't always

---

11. https://adr.github.io/

appropriate—recording one-to-one meetings doesn't seem right—but there are certain types of meetings that are definitely worth recording:

- Regular all-hands meetings where updates are given to a whole team, department, or company

- Technical talks and training sessions

- Regular group meetings such as sprint retrospectives and demos

When there are many invited participants, there is a greater likelihood of scheduling conflicts, vacations, or illness. Recording these meetings and archiving them in a shared folder that all participants can access is a great way for them to be able to catch up with the meeting if they were unable to make it the first time. There's no worse feeling than logging on after your day off to see a buzz of conversation generated around the latest departmental all-hands meeting. That doesn't need to happen anymore when recordings are being produced.

Additionally, for any meeting that covers material that might be useful to others, clicking that button and saving the recording can dramatically increase the potential number of people who could benefit from the material in the future. They can just watch the recording if they're interested in the topic.

If you have wiki pages for your team, department, guild, or committee, you can link to your archive of meetings if the content is not confidential. There's no better way of signifying that you work in an open and inclusive culture than publishing what you talk about.

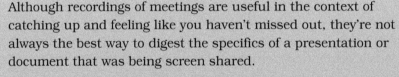

Always Link to Artifacts Covered in a Recorded Meeting

Although recordings of meetings are useful in the context of catching up and feeling like you haven't missed out, they're not always the best way to digest the specifics of a presentation or document that was being screen shared.

When uploading video recordings of meetings that used an artifact to drive the presentation, always complement it with a link to the artifact itself, such as slides. Often a viewer will want to read the material later or alongside at their own pace. Don't make them skip back and forth through the video to do so.

Presentations and Updates

Sometimes you want to reach a large audience with a presentation or series of updates. This could cover multiple teams, a whole department, or even the whole company. However, you already know how difficult it is to schedule a meeting with just one team, let alone hundreds of people.

You can reach this audience asynchronously by recording a video instead of creating a meeting. This works really well if you run any function, from a team to a guild or a committee.

However, there are some rules to follow to ensure that it's an efficient process for both you and your audience:

- *Keep it short.* Unless the material is incredibly deep and complex, don't go over five minutes in length. Much like YouTube videos that take too long to get to the point, you'll find that your colleagues won't engage if the content is too long. It'll end up in their *watch later* pile, where *later* converges on *never.*

- *Link to the artifact if there is one.* If you're running through a presentation or document, link to it when you send out your recorded video. If people are strapped for time, they can skim the artifact rather than watch the video, increasing the impact of your message.

- *Be natural.* Even though we've been taught that real-world presentations need to be rehearsed over and over and honed to perfection, this works against you in recorded video presentations. Not only does it dramatically increase the amount of time that it takes to produce the content in the first place, it can require more concentration for your audience to engage with it. Even worse, your message can come across as wooden. Instead, speak and act as naturally as you can, as if you're talking to someone across your desk. Don't worry about making mistakes; just correct yourself and carry on as if you're having a regular conversation.

Your Turn: Start an Async Talks Channel

Here's something neat that you can do. Why not start a series of asynchronous technical talks in your department?

- Start a chat channel and let everyone know that it exists.

- Get together a list of three to five people who can be your first speakers. One of those people should be you.

- Set a time limit of five to ten minutes for talks, and record one every two weeks.

- Encourage people to cover whatever is interesting to them. It could be their favorite IDE tips and tricks, what they're currently working on in their team, or an overview of part of the system architecture.

Supplemental Explainers

Another excellent use for video is for supplementing other artifacts. A short one-minute recording can help orient readers so they're able to understand the context of another artifact, reducing potential misunderstanding and confusion and bringing the content to life.

When producing an artifact that's long, complex, or particularly meaningful, consider whether a video might help:

- *Design documents* can benefit from a video to help orient readers. The more engaged readers you get, the better the feedback. You might be working on lesser-understood parts of the system that could turn away potential readers because they feel like they can't contribute. Recording a short introductory video as a supplement can help introduce new readers to the pages ahead, giving them vital context that helps them understand the problem and learn more about solving it.

- *Pull requests* can be a great place for a video supplement. A short recording taking reviewers through the changes, especially if they're nuanced or complex, can reduce the amount of effort and time to review. A recorded video can also be a great place to do a demo of the changes, again providing context and increasing engagement.

- *Wiki pages* can be brought to life with recorded video. For example, if you have your department's mission or values written in a wiki, an accompanying short video presentation embedded at the top of the page is an excellent way of walking them through the material.

It's never been quicker or easier to produce short videos, so make sure you're using them to the advantage of yourself and your colleagues. Just use them sparingly.

Getting on Board with Onboarding

So there you have it: a chapter stuffed full of tools and techniques that you can implement right away, regardless of whether you're working remotely or not. If you do, you might just notice that colleagues who aren't on your team start interacting with you more and that those who work flexible hours or are in different time zones have more opportunity to contribute and remain informed.

Here's what we covered:

- We explored the *different ways in which you can create and consume artifacts,* from writing and reading to recording and watching. We learned that it is usually most efficient to read and write, but as we saw in the The Spectrum of Synchronousness on page 53, sometimes it's good to break the rules to feel connected to fellow humans.

- We covered a whole host of *written artifacts* that you can use in your day-to-day work to record, ideate, and share information with others.

- We considered *codebase artifacts,* from the simple commit to the architecture decision record. Taking your code artifacts seriously can be a massive help to yourself and your colleagues, both now and in the future.

- We concluded by looking at *recorded artifacts.* We saw how there are low-effort ways to use recordings to form archives of series of meetings, for giving short presentations and updates, and for supplementing written documents.

In the next chapter, we turn our attention to onboarding and orientation of new colleagues. We'll see how this is a real challenge in the remote-working world. But guess what? You've now learned all of the tools to make that process a success. We'll explore how applying a lens of onboarding to everything you do can give you insights that will help everyone you work with, not just new starters.

We're all pilgrims on the same journey—but some pilgrims have better road maps.

> ⤳ Nelson DeMille

CHAPTER 7

Onboarding and Orientation

Monday, 9:15 a.m. You open your laptop, take a sip of your coffee, and log on to chat. Unread messages. A lot of them, from a lot of people. This is strange. One is from your manager. It's from late Friday evening. You click it.

```
[19:54] susan: Forgot to ask. is everything OK for Kevin starting on Monday?
```

Hang on. That's today. Uh-oh.

```
[08:45] mike: Did Kevin get his laptop delivered OK? I haven't heard from him.
```

You feel the wave of embarrassment. You forgot to check in with Kevin last week, ahead of him starting today. In fact, you completely forgot that he was joining the company altogether. He was on a three-month-notice period at his previous employer, and it's been so long since the interview happened that everything to do with Kevin had completely slipped your mind.

You immediately open your email and search your inbox for *Kevin.* You can't find his address or mobile number—only his personal email address. You fire off a quick email.

```
Hey Kevin,

It's me. I'm so sorry that I didn't check in last week.
Is everything OK? Did you get your laptop?

Please call me on 07700 900796 and I'll get this sorted for you right away.
```

You're now late for stand-up. You join the video call. Lara waves.

"There you are! Where's Kevin? We're excited to meet him!"

You sigh. "I dropped the ball last week and I forgot to check in with him ahead of today. I'm just getting in touch with him now, and I'll get him all set up when he gets back to me. We can do a welcome call later. Sound good?"

Your phone vibrates.

"Hello, this is Kevin. I just got your email."

You breathe a sigh of relief.

"I'm so sorry that I didn't check in at the end of last week. Shall we get your laptop set up so you can say hello to the team?"

"What laptop?"

"The laptop that we sent you via courier."

"I haven't received anything here. Did your recruitment team get my email about my change of address?"

Uh-oh.

Another message from the IT manager pops up on your screen.

```
[09:28] mike: looks like Kevin's set up his password and logged in
[09:29] you: I don't think that's Kevin ... calling you right now
```

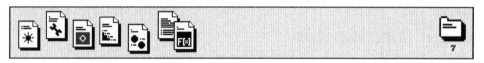

Cast your mind back to the last time you started a new job in an office. Was there excitement as you walked into the building for the first time and collected your ID card? Bewilderment as you saw the other new employees sitting in the breakout area as you entered? Were there friendly smiles while shaking hands with new colleagues? What was it like being shown around the office and to your desk? Meeting your teammates? Perhaps you all went to lunch together on your first day. Maybe you even got the Grand Tour of the Fire Escapes.

Starting a new job in a physical office is a daunting experience. It's a bit like transferring school halfway through the academic year. You're the new kid, and you're busy surveying the environment to work out where you fit in and who all of the new people are.

To address this initially overwhelming period of newness, companies typically employ numerous strategies to help employees find their feet. They may be hired as part of a batch to make them feel less alone during the orientation period. Perhaps they get assigned a mentor or buddy for their first few months. There may be lunches or socials arranged to help connect them to others in the company. They may be encouraged to never eat alone at lunch time by joining tables with other employees they haven't yet met.

All of these are opportunities for new starters to immerse themselves in the culture of a company by being immersed within the *physical* environment. They interact with a wide array of other employees and see how others work and collaborate with each other first hand, by example.

But what does this experience mean for a remote employee? Unfortunately, at many hybrid companies, remote onboarding is often an afterthought. This is especially true if the bulk of employees still work in offices. It's easy to feel like a second-class citizen if you aren't there in person. This chapter is about giving you the framework to change that experience.

In this chapter we're going to spend some time thinking about remote onboarding. But instead of talking about it like a *process* that all employees go through *once*, we're going to see how onboarding is a *lens* that we can continually apply to everything that we do, *all the time*. This is because in technology we're always onboarding new things: projects, teams, frameworks, products, and ideas. The quicker we can do this, the more effective we are as employees.

Here's what this chapter covers:

- We begin by looking at the *contribution curve*, which is a journey that we all go through when we find ourselves in a new job, team, project, or programming language.

- We introduce an *onboarding function* that comprises three onboarding areas that are important when an employee begins anything new: technical, managerial, and cultural. For each of these, we'll identify *North Stars* that we can align our activities around in a way that equalizes the experience for remote workers.

- We consider how *everything you do to make onboarding better will benefit all your existing staff*. We'll see how applying the onboarding lens to any situation can potentially make it better, especially for remote employees.

Without further ado, let's look at a graph.

The Contribution Curve

When an employee starts a new job, they transition through a *contribution curve*. It looks like the figure on page 132.

At the beginning and end of the line, there are two outputs for the employee:

- *Net negative.* An individual produces a net-negative output for the business as they ramp up. As horrible as it sounds, the organization would produce

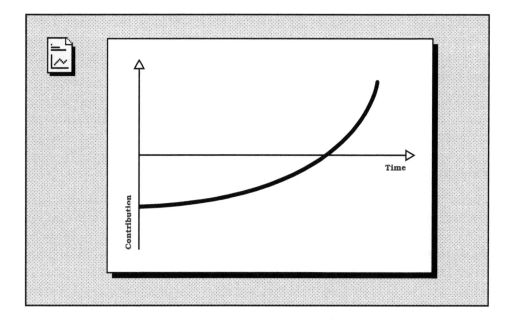

more output if the new person wasn't there because they need help from others.

- *Net positive.* An individual produces a net-positive output for the business. Some people produce more of a net-positive output than others, and you would hope that those people are rewarded fairly for doing so.

This is completely normal. Regardless of how senior or motivated a new member of staff is, starting a new job is initially disorienting and requires a ramping-up period. After all, the new starter has never seen this codebase before, has never worked with their new colleagues before, isn't well-connected inside the company, and hasn't really experienced how to get things done effectively in their new role. They've had no feedback loops to learn from yet.

This is where good management and mentorship come in. Existing employees should be allocating as much time as they can to accelerate an employee through the contribution curve so they can become net positive in their output. The new employee needs to understand the technology being built, the business problems being solved, and the codebases and tools being used to solve them. As they produce code of their own, they may need increased guidance as it's being written, and the code may need more scrutiny as it's being reviewed—hence, a net-negative contribution. It's an additional pull on everyone else's time.

However, gradually, the new employee becomes net positive in their contribution. They require less support when developing new code, and they may be able to begin mentoring others who are less experienced. They understand the business problems and the codebase so they can operate more autonomously.

The Onboarding Equation

Onboarding is the action or process of integrating a new employee into an organization. Successful onboarding is a function that moves an individual through the contribution curve as fast as possible.

This function looks like the following figure.

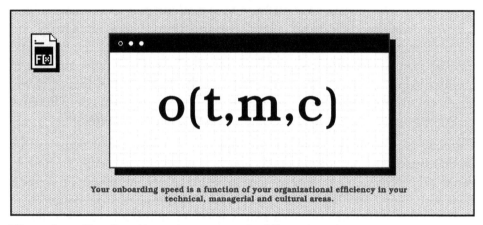

Your onboarding speed is a function of your organizational efficiency in your technical, managerial and cultural areas.

The onboarding function o is composed of three inputs:

- *Technical onboarding (t).* A new employee needs to understand what's being built, what the business problems are that are being solved, and how to begin to be productive using their primary skill set.

- *Managerial onboarding (m).* A new employee needs to grow their relationship with their manager to understand how their work fits into the wider picture of the team, product, and company.

- *Cultural onboarding (c).* A new employee needs to connect to others in the wider company, gaining the feeling that they're among friends and colleagues sharing a united purpose.

The better the job we do in each of these onboarding areas, the faster the new employee becomes a net-positive contributor. In fact, it's about more than just their output. It's about their satisfaction and happiness. A useful model to use to think about this is that of *autonomy, mastery, and purpose [Pin09]*:

- *Autonomy.* We have a desire to be self-directed. With the right management, a new employee can exercise choice in how they approach their work while still contributing to the collective goal. They can tackle problems in their own way while understanding the boundaries that they're working within. They can feel empowered by their freedom.

- *Mastery.* Everyone likes to improve their skills. Not only does it benefit the company they're working for, it benefits them too. With the right mentorship, new employees can not only perform well but they can improve their skills and begin to see tangible progress in this new phase of their career.

- *Purpose.* We all want to contribute to something greater than ourselves. With exposure to the right message and people, new employees can understand how their work fits into the wider purpose of the company. This could range from helping users get their own jobs done quicker, to improving the efficiency of a delivery supply chain, to enabling people to have fun while playing a video game. Understanding the real difference you're making to the lives of others makes work more fulfilling.

Thinking back to our onboarding function, you can see how it maps to this model. Successful *technical* onboarding is the beginning of the journey to achieve mastery. Good *management* ensures that a new employee can develop their autonomy. Feeling *culturally connected* to the company ensures that they can find their purpose. This is why good onboarding is so essential. In technology we're often not only turning up to work to get more dollars, we're turning up due to our work being an important part of our lives. Many of us want to make a positive contribution to a cause greater than ourselves.

In the physical office, this onboarding function can be satisfied to an acceptable level purely through osmosis. New employees observe the behaviors of those around them and gradually find their way. They have daily opportunities to easily meet others, ask questions, and receive guidance and mentorship. However, for remote employees, the opportunities for osmosis are limited. Instead, we need to be deliberate in how we onboard.

We're going to go through each of the inputs to the onboarding function in turn and consider a North Star for each. We will then unpack each North Star to see what kinds of processes, artifacts, and people we need to have in place to ensure that we can satisfy it. We will begin by addressing technical onboarding.

Technical Onboarding

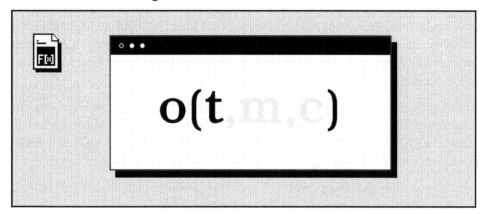

As shown in the previous diagram, let's start with the *t* in the equation. When we talk about technical onboarding, we mean everything to do with becoming a productive engineer. This can cover a number of different areas:

- What the software does and what users do with it
- Codebases and architecture of the system
- How to write code locally and test it
- How to propose changes to the codebase and how to have them reviewed
- How to deploy to the live system
- How to monitor changes via the logs and metrics in place

That's a lot of things to learn. And that's why many formal onboarding programs are ineffective. Capturing all of this information in one place isn't only a significant task if the documentation doesn't already exist, but learning this information by digesting it all in one sitting is somewhat intractible.

Instead, we need to embrace learning by doing and ensure that anything that would be beneficial for the next person to onboard faster is documented. Additionally, we need to understand that unless the company is very small, the problems being solved and the technology and processes to solve them will vary from team to team.

This means that aside from a small portion of high-level information, technical onboarding is something that should be owned separately from within each engineering team. This has the effect of decentralizing the process away from one monolithic technical onboarding program to rule them all, instead of allowing separate teams and divisions to craft their micro-onboarding programs however they see fit.

With that in mind, here's the North Star for technical onboarding: *"How do I push a change to production on my first day?"* This is the beginning of the journey for any new engineer. It allows them to start putting the scaffolding in place to understand the system that they're working within and then incrementally increase their knowledge and confidence in making bigger and more impactful changes with time.

Depending on where you work, this may currently be straightforward or downright impossible. However, it's the North Star that your team should be continually trying to move toward. Even if you never hit it, you'll still make giant leaps in streamlining your processes if you keep it front of mind.

The reason that this is a powerful North Star is because from an onboarding perspective, it assumes that the following are all in place:

- *Mentorship and support.* Making a change on your first day isn't something that you can do alone. Typically, it requires guidance from someone already within the team, either by walking through what needs to be done or by pair programming. Having synchronous support lined up for a new employee's first week, either by their manager or by a nominated mentor, dramatically accelerates productivity.

- *Technical documentation.* How's the part of the system that the team works on structured? Is there an annotated diagram that explains it? What about pointers to the correct codebases with high-quality README files? Are there any specific guides for people contributing for the first time?

- *Development and QA environments.* You can't change production until you can do some work locally. Is it straightforward to check out a codebase and get it building and running locally? Does anything else need to be in place first, such as getting logins created or credentials created for security reasons? How streamlined is this process?

- *Processes for submitting code changes.* Once a change has been implemented locally, what's the path to getting that code reviewed and merged, and is it clear what happens after that?

- *Straightforward deployment.* Once a change is merged, who has the power to push it live? What kinds of processes are in place to roll back changes in case of problems? Is deployment low risk?

- *Observability and monitoring of production system changes.* Once a change goes live, does an engineer have access to the logs, graphs, and dashboards needed to view the metrics that ensure that the change has had the desired effect?

The more that you apply the North Star to these areas as a lens, the more that you're able to make improvements in all of these areas. This doesn't have to wait until you onboard someone for real. Instead, you can bear it in mind with everything you do and ask yourself this question regularly: If a new remote colleague were to join today, how easy would they find this process? You can use the following table to guide your thinking. It's filled out with some hypothetical examples.

Area	Status	Improvements Required	Next Goal	Actions
Mentorship	Good	None. We have good overlap across all time zones.	None	None
Technical documentation	OK	We have no architectural diagrams of our system or the context it sits within.	Publish the diagrams and link to them from our codebase README.	Lara is doing this for next week.
Development and QA environments	Bad	Still experiencing sporadic errors when building and running webapp for the first time. There are always random issues to debug.	Solve this.	Spend time debugging these issues as a team. Consider containerization to normalize dev environment.
Submitting code	OK	We can review and merge changes quickly within our own codebases. However, sometimes we have to change dependent services, and review can take a long time.	Investigate how to improve review speed in other codebases.	Ben to discuss this with Infrastructure team.
Deployment	OK	Similar to the previous. We can deploy all of our own codebase changes, but the Infrastructure team typically has a two-week cycle.	We can limit the types of work given to a new engineer to be entirely under our control for now. But, again, this needs to be discussed.	Ben to raise this.
Monitoring	Good	There's no single place that has all of the links to monitoring dashboards. We are all using our own browser bookmarks.	Produce an index page with all dashboard links.	Lara to do this.

If the answer to the previous question is that they would find it extremely difficult, you need to identify what's lacking. It could be that your processes need refining or that you need to create documentation. Perhaps wider change needs to be lobbied in your department, such as allowing teams to release whenever they like, assuming that it's safe to do so, rather than needing to batch up changes every few weeks.

Even if some of the issues are outside of your control, there are still plenty of places that you can make improvements within your team. You can make sure that your codebases are documented well with architectural diagrams of the systems they sit within. You can improve and document your monitoring dashboards so that they're easier to locate. You could even write a guide for your first day as a dry run of all of the previously stated principles. What would a new engineer experience? Would they know where to look, what to do, and who to ask for help? How would that experience change if they were in a dramatically different time zone, if at all?

Your Turn: Technical North Star

Find some time to discuss the technical onboarding North Star with your team:

- Measure where you are as a team when it comes to being able to deploy on your first day. Focus on the areas described earlier. For each one, highlight what stands in the way. Are those obstacles solvable by your team, or do they need outside help? Use the preceding tabular format to help guide your thinking.

- Categorize the improvements that you can make into short-, medium-, and long-term initiatives. Then assign actions to the short-term ones and make improvements.

- Continue to look at all of the work that you do as a team through the lens of the North Star. If a new remote employee joins tomorrow, could they deploy a change on their first day? If not, why? And is this situation getting better with time?

Managerial Onboarding

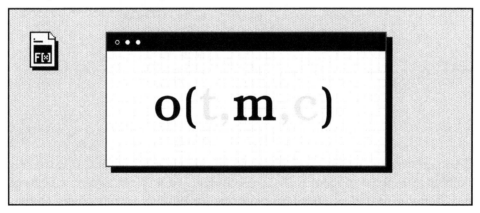

Next up, we tackle the *m* in the equation. When a new member of the staff is getting oriented, their manager plays a crucial role. Good management can provide the structure that helps new employees feel psychologically safe, able to set and achieve their goals, and empowered to make a difference. This is even more true when remote working. It's hard enough being the new person in an office. Being the new person somewhere out there on the Internet is even harder.

Imagine that you've just started in your current role. Who do you turn to to get specific technical help? Where do you go if you're struggling? Where do you learn more about the product that you're building and how it has an impact on the business? Who are the key people in product, design, and engineering worth meeting to learn more? How exactly does the team collaborate in terms of getting work done and shipping code? A good manager is the hub that connects all of these spokes together.

If you're not a manager yourself, don't worry. This is equally as relevant to you. This is because the manager-employee relationship doesn't need to be based on a *push* of information and assistance from the manager to the employee. Instead, it can work equally well as a *pull* in the other direction. This can even make a manager's life easier; their employee is just asking for exactly what they need without them having to guess.

The North Star for managerial onboarding is, *"What am I going to achieve in the next ninety days?"* The reason that this is powerful is because it requires a number of supporting structures to be in place:

- A positive start to the relationship that sets a foundation on openness and an understanding of how each person likes to work

- Regular catch-ups to build rapport and ensure good progress

- Discussions around career progression, covering where the new employee is and where they might like to go

- Creation of a plan for thirty-, sixty-, and ninety-day milestones.

So if you're a manager, consider putting the preceding structures in place whenever you onboard a new employee, especially if they're remote. If you're a new employee, tell your manager you'd like to do these things. It's extremely likely they'll be happy you're taking the initiative. With these in place, the first ninety days of employment can be exciting and rewarding—clear steps on the journey to autonomy, mastery, and purpose. Let's see how to do this.

Book Weekly One-to-Ones

One-to-one meetings (sometimes called one-on-ones) are the backbone of the relationship between an employee and their manager. You'd be surprised by just how many employees don't even have one-to-ones. Some go weeks or months without talking to their manager at all. No more. Instead, we want to make sure that every employee feels that their manager is the colleague they can be the most comfortable talking to. This comes through building rapport by regularly spending time together, week in and week out.

It begins with the booking of a weekly meeting between the new employee and their manager. Remember, if you're the new employee, just *pull* on your manager and take the lead on booking them yourself, but do ask first. An hour is a good length. Have the meeting recur every week at the same time. Don't move it around unless absolutely necessary; it's all about having a safe, predictable, regular touchpoint for discussions. If one of you isn't remote, ensure the meeting happens in a private space such as a meeting room. If you want a candid and transparent relationship, it needs to be built behind closed doors.

You'll also want to create the artifact that drives your time together: a rolling agenda. Have a shared private document that only the two of you can see. This is an excellent way of recording what you discuss in the one-to-ones and what the actions are and who they're assigned to. Over time, good note taking in these meetings builds up an archive of your interactions. The link to the document should be attached to the calendar invite.

Have a Contracting Session

The first one-to-one is a special one because it's all about getting the relationship off on the right foot. It involves performing an exercise called *contracting*. It's simple and straightforward and forms a wrapper in which you can talk about each other's needs in a structured and safe way, promoting a candid and transparent conversation that should continue into the future.

Before the first meeting, both the manager and the new employee should prepare the answers to five questions. Then you spend the time in the session going through them in turn. This allows you to discuss candidly what you hope, want, and need in a structured way that doesn't make either party feel uncomfortable. It also means that the relationship has begun by talking openly, which should set the tone for further interactions.

Here are the questions:

- *Which areas would you like the most support with?* This covers anything and everything. However, perhaps the manager can provide direct technical mentorship because they have the same skill set as the new employee. Perhaps the new engineer has never worked on a product like this one before and needs additional help understanding the market and the users. There may even be interpersonal or language issues to overcome.

- *How would you like to receive feedback and support?* This is about how both people like to operate, highlighting preferences, comforts, and discomforts. For example, would both parties prefer a stream of feedback and updates asynchronously throughout the week, or would they prefer topics get batched together until a synchronous weekly meeting? In a remote world, what's the best way for a new team member to get to know their team and build rapport with them? Can the manager help here?

- *What could be a challenge of us working together?* There are a whole host of concerns that are worth pointing out. Some are practical, such as being in different time zones or not having the same technical skill set. Some can be based on personality traits such as introversion and extroversion. Strategies to confront these challenges can be discussed here.

- *How might we know if the relationship isn't going well?* It's good to be aware of the signs. What does being quiet on chat and email actually mean? Is that deep focus, or is it a sign of overwhelm?

- *How confidential is the content of our meetings?* Sensitive issues are often raised in one-to-ones, so it's worth sense-checking with each other as to whether that information is private by default unless permission is explicitly given to follow it up with others.

Performing the contracting exercise gets the relationship off to a fantastic start and ensures that all employees, regardless of where they're located, are able to feel sufficiently supported in their new role. This can be especially crucial when somebody joins a new company remotely because they may worry about bugging people they've never met before. A quick contracting chat can make it clear that the manager can be messaged or booked for a chat at *any* time.

Explore Career Progression

In addition to a new employee feeling like they understand what they need to do, it also benefits them to orient themselves to where they are and where they might be going in their career.

Having a one-to-one session around the topic of career progression is a great way to do this. Depending on the company, there may or may not be clear career development tracks provided to employees. Typically, progression in technology companies is along one of two tracks:

- *Individual contributor.* These roles have titles such as software engineer, senior engineer, staff engineer, and principal engineer. They involve progression through increasingly impactful technical contributions, both by themselves and via the colleagues they support.

- *Manager.* These roles have titles such as engineering manager, director of engineering, vice president of engineering, and chief technical offier

(CTO). They involve progression via managing ever larger and more effective teams, divisions, and even whole departments.

If you've not encountered these career tracks before, there are many available to view online that have been published by reputable companies.[1] These are often accompanied by a list of competencies that outline what's expected of staff at the different levels. For example, competencies could include industry experience, technical knowledge, mentorship, conflict resolution, and communication.

A new employee should work with their manager to align themselves with where they currently are on a career-progression track and then have a discussion about what they're aiming for in the future. Are they looking to be promoted within the next couple of years? Are they looking to make the switch to management? By discussing this right at the start, the manager can help the new employee look out for opportunities and experiences that can support their growth in the long term. It also allows the manager to connect the employee with others who can help them work toward their career goals. And the beauty of being remote is that anyone is just a chat message or video call away.

Write a Thirty-Sixty-Ninety-Day Plan

An autonomous employee is a happy employee, especially when they're remote. A thirty-sixty-ninety-day plan is a way to capture important milestones during the onboarding process so that both the manager and the new employee know that they're on the right track.

All this involves is creating an artifact with headings for thirty, sixty, and ninety days. Then the new employee works with their manager to set some ambitious but achievable goals for them to work toward. The focus of these goals is to produce a happy onboarded and productive employee. It's not about stretching them to produce more and more code.

It can be beneficial to assign different themes to the first thirty, sixty, and ninety days. For example, the first thirty days could be about getting to know the team and regularly committing some code. The next thirty could be about meeting important people outside the team and understanding the architecture and function of the product and the department. The ninety-day milestones could be about focusing on what the team could do better and helping implement those changes.

---

1.   https://progression.fyi

Fundamentally, how you decide to structure it is up to you. Some examples of milestones that could form part of a thirty-sixty-ninety-day plan are as follows:

- Deploy your first change to production. Work with the team to find a bug or change of suitable size and get it deployed. Ask for help whenever you need it.

- Have a one-to-one catch-up with everyone on the team. Understand their skill sets, what they're working on, and what they feel are the best and worst parts of the team.

- Have a virtual coffee with one of your stakeholders. Why are they so interested in what we're building? Find out how you could serve them better.

- Look at the architecture of the system. What do you think some of the best bits are? What are some of the worst bits and why?

- Discover which teams your team is most dependent on, either in terms of shared codebases or specific knowledge. Why is this, and what could be done about it? Could artifacts be created to alleviate some of these problems?

Having a thirty-sixty-ninety-day plan as a remote employee can provide a great source of comfort, especially if you're in a different time zone. By following that plan each day, you can feel confident that you're doing the right thing and making an impact, regardless of whether your manager and team are there to talk to all of the time.

Your Turn: Re-onboard Yourself

Talk through what you learned in this section with your manager. Then go through the process as if you just joined the company for the first time:

- Ensure that you're having weekly one-to-ones. If you're not, get them booked and start that habit.

- Have a contracting session. You may surprise yourself with what you learn.

- Explore your career progression with your manager. If you don't have your own career track, spend some time looking at publicly available ones together. Where are you now, and where do you want to go?

- Write a thirty-sixty-ninety-day plan and do it. Set yourself some interesting and challenging goals. Do you feel more excited about your work now that it's wrapped in milestones for you to hit?

Cultural Onboarding

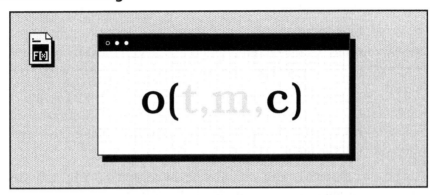

The final part of the equation is cultural onboarding. Having a new employee able to quickly make technical contributions and begin building a strong relationship with their manager is key. However, truly feeling a part of what the company is trying to achieve and strongly connected to the people who work within it makes all of the difference.

But let's face it: work isn't all excitement and victories. Sometimes it's frustrating, boring, annoying, and stressful. Going through these more challenging times is far easier when you know that you're going through them for a reason with other people you care about.

The North Star for cultural onboarding is *"How do I become an integral part of the wider company?"* This explicit focus ensures that a new employee is well on their way to feeling like they're among kindred spirits. We unpack this North Star in two parts, focusing on work and play:

- *Establishing vision, mission, and values.* This is the part that wears the smart business suit. It's about the new employee knowing why they're here and the greater goals they're contributing toward.

- *Plugging into culture.* This is the part that wears the Hawaiian shirt. It's about the new employee forming connections with other people outside of their team.

Establishing Mission, Vision, and Values

If we want new employees to rapidly become autonomous, the quicker they understand *why* and *how* they're doing their work, the better. This enables them to make progress and decisions with the end goal in mind. To do this, it helps to have a mission, a vision, and values:[2]

---

2.   https://open.lib.umn.edu/principlesmanagement/

- *Mission.* This communicates the reason that the organization exists and how it aims to serve its customers, employees, and investors.

- *Vision.* This is a future-oriented declaration of the organization's purpose: What does it want to become?

- *Values.* These are the beliefs of the organization in which employees are emotionally invested.

Sometimes these are best explained by example. Let's look at Nike:[3]

- *Mission.* Our mission is to bring inspiration and innovation to every athlete in the world. If you have a body, you're an athlete. This mission drives us to do everything possible to expand human potential. We do that by creating groundbreaking sport innovations, by making our products more sustainably, by building a creative and diverse global team, and by making a positive impact in communities where we live and work.

- *Vision.* We see a world where everybody is an athlete—united in the joy of movement. Driven by our passion for sport and our instinct for innovation, we aim to bring inspiration to every athlete in the world and to make sport a daily habit.

- *Values.* Do the right thing. Be on the offense always. Serve athletes. Create the future of sport. Win as a team.

That's pretty inspiring, right? It clearly states why the company exists and why it does what it does. It also defines some key values that employees can align themselves toward in their day-to-day work. New Nike employees can read these on their first day and feel an immediate alignment with their colleagues, regardless of how far they are from the headquarters in Beaverton, Oregon. Wouldn't it be amazing if *you* had something similar written for new employees too?

We're aware that you may not be running the company, and we're also aware that your company may not have a clearly defined mission, vision, and values. But you know what? That's actually fine. Does this mean that you're not going to be able to provide this for your new employee? No, you still can. You just address the part of the organization that you can influence, and then you can work with it to define the mission, vision, and values. If that part of the organization happens to be your department, division, or even just your team, that's fantastic. Just pick the level you can work with. Even if your whole company feels a bit rudderless, a new employee onboarded on to a team with

---

3. https://about.nike.com/

a strong mission, vision, and values can make a huge impact on their experience of joining your company.

Your Turn: Define Your Mission, Vision, and Values for Your Team

Let's start small:

- Book a session to discuss mission, vision, and values. What does your company provide already? Are you happy with it, and is it directly applicable to what you do in your team?

- Discuss whether you would benefit from defining a localized mission, vision, and values for your team. What's important to you collectively? What does it really mean to do the work that you do together?

- Run a session to sketch out your mission, vision, and values. When you're done, document them in an artifact and share how this discovery process went with the rest of the department.

Plugging into Culture

Lastly, we look at the fun stuff.

Walking around an office at lunch time often allows new employees to get involved in all sorts of activities, from making connections and having conversations with new people to playing a game of chess or Ping-Pong. Working remotely doesn't offer an employee the chance to accidentally stumble upon these interactions, so new employees need to know where to find them.

Fortunately, you can provide this experience by using all of the tools that you already have access to. They might not be the same as a game of foosball, but they can provide a multitude of opportunities for employees to feel connected to their peers. Here are some ideas for providing opportunities for new employees to plug in to the culture of the company:

- *Create a buddy system.* All you need is a shared document. Have willing volunteers in your company put themselves forward to be *buddies,* which can range from being a friendly face to being a full-blown technical mentor. All they need to do is add to the document their name, role, skill set, contact details, and willingness to help. New employees and their manager can look through the list and choose an appropriate buddy. This works especially well if it encourages different departments to connect, such as sales and engineering.

- *Have virtual coffees.* When a new employee joins, have their manager select three to five people for them to connect with over a virtual coffee break. No agenda is required, just a video call and a nice conversation. It's welcoming and fun, and it may just start some new friendships or generate some innovative ideas.

- *Connect around hobbies and interests.* Ensure that you have a whole host of chat channels and mailing lists set up around hobbies and interests and that they're indexed in an easily findable shared document, just like we covered in Chapter 4, The Spectrum of Synchronousness, on page 53. Make sure that new employees join the channels and get involved in the conversations. The vice president of sales isn't so scary when they're posting pictures of their dog.

- *Slack off!* Make sure you actively encourage new employees to have a bit of fun. Ensure that you too are slacking off from time to time and chatting about hiking, animals, or sewing—whatever interests you the most. New folks orient themselves by observing what goes on around them, so set that example by being part of the culture you want to see.

And Here's the Trick

So there we have it, the three North Stars for onboarding:

- For *technical* onboarding, the goal was, "How do I deploy to production on my first day?"

- For *managerial* onboarding, the goal was, "What am I going to achieve in the next ninety days?"

- For *cultural* onboarding, the goal was, "How do I become an integral part of the wider company?"

If new employees are guided through their initial months at the company by these North Stars, they'll move predictably onward and upward through the contribution curve. Cool, right? Well, yes. However, there's also something sneaky that happens.

It turns out that everything you do to help your team onboard new employees via the North Stars that we outlined doesn't just help new employees. It actually benefits all of your existing staff.

The reason for this is because we all go through the contribution curve again and again, as seen in the chart on page 148. We face it whenever an existing member of the staff changes teams. We face it whenever one project ends and

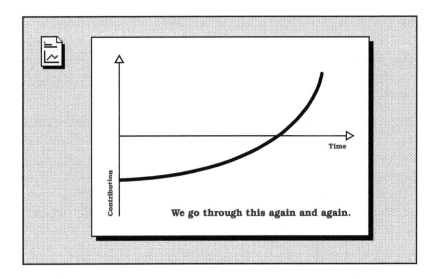

We go through this again and again.

another one begins, or when there's a new company objective to work toward, or a product pivot. Just when you get comfortable, everything changes. It's just as true in work as it is in life.

Applying the lens of onboarding can improve the experience for all staff at your company. The more process, artifacts, and connections that you produce for your North Stars, the more effective that everyone will be in the future, regardless of whether they're new to the company or a seasoned veteran, or whether they're working in an office or remote.

So really, the onboarding equation isn't the onboarding equation at all. It's the equation for having a strong, healthy department. So we've updated the following equation.

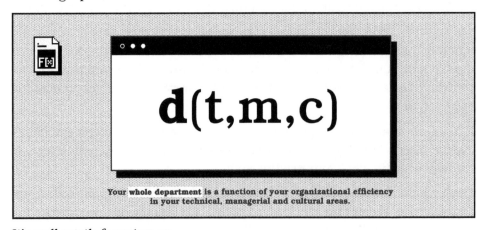

$$d(t,m,c)$$

Your whole department is a function of your organizational efficiency in your technical, managerial and cultural areas.

It's well worth focusing on.

Coming Up: Considering Communication

Phew! You've been sneakily deceived for this entire chapter. But you've come out with the tools for creating an even bigger impact than you may have thought when you first started reading it.

Here's what we covered:

- We looked at the *contribution curve*, which is the process that new employees go through when they join a company. It starts with them being net-negative contributors. Then, with time, they ramp up and become net-positive contributors. This is harder for remote workers because often learning is done through osmosis in offices.

- We considered the *onboarding function*, which outlines the three areas of onboarding that need to be considered for people to progress quickly through the contribution curve. These areas are technical, managerial, and cultural. We considered the North Stars that you should aim for in each of these areas.

- We saw that making progress on improving your onboarding process doesn't just benefit new employees. It benefits everyone. This is because we all go through the contribution curve again and again as we face new challenges, projects, teams, and objectives. The better our onboarding, the faster we all become net-positive contributors as we go through change in the workplace. The processes, artifacts, and connections that are put in place can be reused and improved iteratively and indefinitely and have the effect of increasing equality for remote workers.

In the next chapter, we're going to consider effective communication techniques for the remote world. Many of us are hard-wired to use synchronous communication and are well-versed in the associated etiquette. Should it be different when working remotely?

Let's find out.

CHAPTER 8

Effective Communication Techniques

You click on your chat app. It seems you had a new message during the night. You open it.

```
[01:45] kate: call me please (edited)
```

Oh no. Kate is the CEO. Why would she want you to call her? And what did the message actually say before it was edited? Was it something bad? Has something gone wrong? You rewind through yesterday's events to try to recall something that may have warranted her attention. You only deployed a few small bug fixes. Nothing went awry.

Or did it? You panic. You look through the application logs and the monitoring dashboards. It all looks pretty normal. What else could it be? Wait a second, when was her message sent? 1:45 a.m. What was going on at that time of the night? Could she be in a different country at the moment, perhaps with a potential client, and she needed your input? But—hang on—you've barely even talked to her. This has to be something bad.

You stand up and pace around the room. Have you said anything to anyone recently that may have offended them? You think back through your recent meetings and interactions. No dice. You think of writing a message to your team to see if Kate messaged them as well. But wait, is that a good idea? What if she wanted to speak to you privately about something? Oh no, what if you're being acquired? You don't want to start rumors. Maybe you should speak to your manager. But what would she think if she knew that the CEO was messaging you? Argh!

You sit back at your computer. You read the message again.

```
call me please (edited)
```

OK, let's not get carried away here. This is a simple request. Someone has asked you to call them. Please. You should call them. But how can you call them? You don't even have their number. Who has her number? Did she mean a phone call or a video call? And surely she's in a different time zone at the moment, given the time that the message was sent. You think about booking something in the calendar. No, no. That's too formal. That's not putting the right message across. You know that your CEO likes to be straightforward and get things done.

What would *she* do in this situation? She'd just make the call, right? Right. You should just call her. Then you remember that you still don't have her number. How do you find that out? You can't just go around asking people for the CEO's number. Does she have an assistant? You have no idea. You tap your fingers on the desk.

```
call me
```

What's going on? What should you do? Surely something has to be wrong. There's no reason that she'd message you otherwise.

```
(edited)
```

What did it say before? What didn't she want you to read? It has to be something bad. It can only be bad. It wouldn't be anything other than bad. This is bad. You're bad. Why are you such a terrible person? What do we do when *everything* is bad? Everything is so bad right now. Should you apologize? How can you apologize when you don't even know what you've done wrong? Your hands find the keyboard.

```
[09:03] you: Hey, sorry I missed your message. Is everything OK?
[09:03] you: Happy to call whenever. Shall I book a slot?
```

You're going to get fired aren't you? Yep, this is definitely it. The end. Game over. No, snap out of it. This is probably something really mundane. Or is it?

We've all had situations like this. Simple, benign, but ambiguous messages that are open to interpretation and catastrophizing. Even if you haven't gotten into as much of a spin as in this scenario, it's likely that you've experienced asynchronous communication that has made you confused, annoyed, frustrated, or bewildered or even made you question your very existence.

It's easy to get communication wrong. It happens all of the time. We can say the wrong thing. We can use ambiguous phrases. Our emotions can get in the way of what we're actually trying to say. These misfires and mistakes then go through a correction phase, where the recipient expresses their confusion, which then allows the person that made the mistake to understand and correct it. They may even apologize if they were feeling strong emotions at the time.

When this sequence of events happens synchronously, the length of time taken to resolve the issue is usually short. An auditory or visual cue can be picked up immediately. A question can be asked. A comment can be made. A clarification can be given. When this happens asynchronously, the duration of time to the resolution is much longer. There are fewer cues to pick up on. There's typically only the written word and an interpretation of it.

While many people in the workforce have a good baseline of synchronous verbal communication skills, not everyone has the same baseline of asynchronous written skills and etiquette. As we spend more time on the right side of the diagram seen in Chapter 4, The Spectrum of Synchronousness, on page 53, we need to be aware there is more opportunity for mistakes to be made in how we are communicating but also in how we are being interpreted.

We need to be clear and concise in our communication, and we need to stop using synchronous interactions as a crutch that we revert to in order to say what we actually mean. When we do this, we avoid tackling the problem directly, which is to invest the time and effort into making our asynchronous communication as good as our synchronous communication. Workers who are remote to us, especially those in different time zones, don't have as many windows of opportunity to patch up poor asynchronous communication with a quick synchronous chat. Poor asynchronous communication is detrimental and contributes to them feeling excluded.

But this isn't just about improving our skills for those in different time zones. It's much more than that. With the right investment in communication techniques, we can supercharge our work lives. We can lower frustration in our interactions. We can be better understood. We can increase our influence and impact. We can be more productive. This chapter is all about principles, techniques, and tools that you can use to get better at communicating in a way that keeps remote and distributed workers front of mind.

Here's how we're going to try and slay the dragon of complex communication:

- We'll begin by looking at *why humans communicate*. We'll categorize some different ways in which we interact in our daily lives.

- We'll consider some *principles for good communication* and understand what those mean while you're working remotely.

- We'll cover the *techniques* for both synchronous and asynchronous communication. We'll study common antipatterns and consider new ways of thinking about how we communicate.

- We'll lay out all of the *tools* that we have at our disposal and suggest which ones you should use for different types of situations. Then we'll consider how all the tools carry with them a series of *dichotomies* that need you to use your intuition to navigate.

Why Humans Communicate

Let's dig a little deeper in to why being an effective communicator is so important. Although we often take it for granted, our ability to communicate is a unique and powerful trait of our species. In fact, it may be one of the core reasons that modern humans were able to survive while Neanderthals became extinct.[1]

While some theories suggest that Neanderthals were less able to deal with the chilling temperatures of the last Ice Age, and while others pin their demise on their lesser intelligence, there's evidence that humans' superior trading abilities are what made us the dominant species. This evidence shows that when humans joined Neanderthals in Europe more than 40,000 years ago, they were able to trade with each other to survive. Whereas Neanderthal survival involved primarily hunting for food, human survival included skilled individuals contributing in other ways, such as making clothes or building shelters in return for meat.

In addition to a human individual developing valuable skills, there had to be a way for those skills to be traded. Part of this equation is the token of trade, and evidence has shown seashells were a valuable traded commodity more than 120,000 years ago.[2] It's likely that valuable items were exchanged for other items and services over and over again.

These foundations of economic activity also suggest the origins of our need for language. Whereas animals have a very limited vocabulary that covers, for example, alerting others to danger and asserting dominance, humans would need to also develop the ability to symbolically reason about the world to perform trades. They would have to be able to compose communication that

---

1.   https://www.newscientist.com/article/dn7221-free-trade-may-have-finished-off-neanderthals
2.   https://www.theatlantic.com/business/archive/2015/06/why-humans-speak-language-origins/396635/

covered what they wanted, what they had to offer, and how to settle disputes and persuade others that they were getting a good deal.

No other species has developed such complex communication; it has become innate to us. Human babies acquire language naturally through interaction with the world around them. We don't need to sit them down and teach them all of the grammatical rules first.[3]

Development of our language is a central part of the human experience. Language enables collaboration at scale. It's a fundamental part of evolution and of our society. In fact, it could be the most sophisticated tool we possess. It's our social technology. It's used within our families, friendships, and in our workplaces to describe, organize toward, and achieve complicated goals.

Blending our social technology with other advances in technology has further amplified its effect. With the Internet, we can communicate with anyone, anywhere, at anytime. We can do so in written, auditory, and visual forms. However, as this book frequently mentions, this blend of old and new technology is relatively new in the lifetime of the universe, and we're having to adapt rapidly to what it means to use these supercharged abilities effectively.

When we communicate with each other, especially at work, we do so for a number of reasons. These can include the following:

- *Negotiating exchanges and trades.* Although we're probably not trading seashells anymore, we may be trading stocks, our time, or our focus.

- *Giving and seeking information.* We may be stuck on our work and need the input of others to continue. We may be mentoring a new colleague through the contribution curve. Perhaps we're trying to find the answers to our questions on the Internet.

- *Expressing our feelings.* We may have had a disagreement and are now working on resolving that situation. Perhaps we're excited and want to share that excitement with others.

- *Persuading others to see our viewpoint.* We may be writing a design document that describes our idea for a new addition to the application, with the hope that others will agree on the direction that we're proposing.

Good communication techniques ensure this all happens smoothly. However, in an increasingly remote world, we rely more on new technologies to communicate rather than the methods that we've evolved to use over hundreds of

---

3.   https://www.linguisticsociety.org/resource/faq-how-do-we-learn-language

thousands of years. After all, our ancient human relatives weren't outlining a complex seashell trade in a shared document. We have to adapt to a new world where many of us have access to far fewer nonverbal cues such as eye contact and body language, of which some studies suggest form 70 percent or more of our communication.[4]

Remote working and increased asynchronous communication do increase efficiency and the global impact of our existing social technology, but they do so in a way that dramatically reduces access to many of the cues we follow. To counteract this, we need to make sure that we are communicating with each other more clearly, succinctly, and unambiguously. It reduces the energy wasted on misunderstanding, frustration, and repetition that can be caused by ineffective interactions.

Principles for Better Remote Communication

Before we start looking at specific techniques, we should establish some principles that you can carry through all of your communication, regardless of the platform that you're using to communicate, whether it's synchronous or asynchronous.

A principle by definition is a foundation for a system of belief or behavior, and these principles can be the foundation of how we communicate effectively, regardless of the location of the recipient.

Establish Norms

Because we have many more ways in which we can communicate via digital means, and because we have access to far fewer nonverbal cues in our interactions, we should establish norms with each other to know what to expect from our communication.

Given that you have access to email, video calls, chat, direct messages, and possibly other forms of communication, which should you be using with your team and when? Do particular situations warrant a particular choice of platform? Is it OK to only check your email once per day?

Ideally, at least within your team, the following should be clear:

- *Software to be used to communicate and whether people should be expected to monitor it.* For example, there may be an explicit expectation that people monitor chat; however, the comments that are left on your

---

4.   https://www.lifesize.com/en/blog/speaking-without-words/

diagramming software are probably not expected to be explicitly monitored by everyone on the team.

- *Expected response times per platform.* List all of the platforms that you use and make it clear when people are expected to check them. For example, there may only be an expectation that people read their email once a day, or maybe even less. This ensures that other platforms are used for more urgent communication and helps people refrain from continued checking.

- *Tools to use for particular situations.* For example, more formal communications may be done via email. But day-to-day interactions may be expected to take place on chat. What happens if you need to contact someone urgently? Is it OK to phone them?

- *Level of formality expected.* Chat is usually less formal than email. What are the expectations within your team, and what's observed in the wider company?

Establishing norms may seem like a chore, but there are big benefits. It makes it easier, more predictable, and less stressful to communicate.

Your Turn: Establish Norms in Your Team

Bring up communication norms with your team. Use the preceding list to work out what your norms currently are and whether that lines up with what the ideal situation would be:

- How far do your current norms deviate from your ideal?

- Are the norms within your team different from other teams in the department or other parts of the company? For example, compare chat usage in engineering versus sales.

- Document your communication norms on your team's index page so that others know how you communicate.

- Discuss making any changes that get you closer to your ideal.

Optimize for Understanding

Although it's likely that you work in a complex technical domain, it doesn't mean that all of your communications need to be overly complex and technical. Einstein is attributed with the quote, "If you can't explain it simply, you don't understand it well enough."

Whenever you communicate, optimize for understanding. This means pitching information at a level of detail that aims to allow as many people as possible the opportunity to understand it. Consider the following message from one of the customer support agents that you need to reply to.

```
[14:23] dave: Customers are reporting some issues with the app. Can someone help?
```

Here is the first of two possible replies:

```
[14:24] alex: 504 on gateway, gonna bounce it
```

Here is the second:

```
[14:24] alex: I'm seeing timeouts from the login screen.
[14:25] alex: I've restarted the API gateway. Does that fix the issue for now?
[14:25] alex: I'll look into the root cause further.
[14:25] alex: More detail will be posted shortly.
```

The second reply uses more words, but it's understandable to both technical and nontechnical people. This second message would have informed both the customer support agent and the engineers reading it. The agent would be able to use that message to further update customers, and the engineers would gain more understanding of the issue. The first would not necessarily have made sense to the agent and would require more communication to deliver a message back to customers.

Context is always key in choosing exactly how to communicate. But you should always optimize for understanding:

- *Consider the audience.* Whenever you communicate, regardless of whether it's synchronous or asynchronous, always be mindful of your potential audience. Use the simplest language you can to compose the simplest messages. Remember that your own native tongue may not be the native tongue of your colleagues.

- *Widen potential readership rather than narrow it.* When you have to choose how to get your message across, consider whether you could make it immediately understandable for more people. For example, if somebody from marketing stumbles across your design document, is it possible for them to understand it? You might just help other engineers understand it as well.

- *Use simple, nontechnical language wherever possible.* Making things sound complicated isn't a badge of honor. Do the work yourself by making it easy to understand rather than putting that burden on the people receiving your message.

- *Ask questions to ensure understanding.* If you're unsure whether your audience has grasped what you've said, just ask them. Sometimes people are afraid to look like they're the only one who didn't understand, so invite them in by letting them know that it's OK if they don't.

Practice Brevity

Brevity is the concise and exact use of words in communication. Emergency services often use radio codes to quickly and clearly communicate what's happening across the airwaves. For example, the code 10-23 orders units to stand by. This ensures that in time-sensitive and noisy situations, the message gets through quickly and clearly.

Everyone has limited time and attention. Even though we might not be chasing criminals or fighting fires, we're fighting a battle for our attention among email, chat, calls, family, friends, and even our own minds. As such, we owe it to each other to practice brevity in our communication.

There's a tension between brevity and understandability. If we were communicating about technical matters, perhaps the most concise and technical language would reduce understandability to a wider audience.

Conversely, increasing understandabilty may make communication a lot longer because it requires more explanation. Only you will know the right balance. However, there are some tips that you can use to help you:

- *KISS.* We've probably all heard of this acronym before: *keep it simple, stupid.*[5] Although this is a design principle that was coined when building complex aircraft that still needed to be easily repairable, the same can be said for constructing your sentences. Aim for short, simple, and understandable, regardless of the complexity of the subject.

- *Think, edit, send.* It's easy to type responses in a rush. However, just by slowing down and pausing before you hit the Enter key, you can sometimes restructure your communication to be shorter, simpler, and more impactful.

- *Use the active voice to increase engagement.* The active voice is typically clearer and easier to understand than the passive voice.[6] A sentence in active voice typically follows a formula of actor, verb, target—for example, *The cat sat on the mat.* The passive voice sounds more academic, following

---

5. https://en.wikipedia.org/wiki/KISS_principle
6. https://developers.google.com/tech-writing/one/active-voice

a formula of target, verb, actor. For example, *The mat was sat on by the cat.* Active voice often shortens sentences and makes them feel more alive.

Be Unambiguous

Every time you communicate with somebody, you're asking them to switch their attention to you. The greatest respect that you can bring to this situation is to make it unambiguously clear as to what you're communicating and why. For example, have you logged in to see a chat message like this?

```
[17:01] bob: hey, are you there?
```

Like in our opening story, ambiguous messages cause all sorts of problems. After your attention as been drawn to the message, you begin to waste brain cycles deciphering it. What did they want? Is something wrong? Do I need to reply because I clearly wasn't online at the time? Have I missed out on something?

Ambiguous communication is a pain. It's even more of a pain when the communication is asynchronous. If your communication raises more questions than it solves, it can, in the best case, waste someone's time, but in the worst case, it can send them into a spin. Instead, be unambiguous.

```
[17:01] bob: Hey! No reply needed on this one
[17:01] bob: I just put the pull request up for the bug fix
[17:01] bob: It's there for you to review and/or merge whenever.
```

Much better. The unambiguous message clearly states what it's about, what happened, and what needs to be done. Always think about what you're going to communicate. Are you communicating primarily for the benefit of others, and are you making it unambiguously clear what you're contributing to the discussion?

Make the Next Step Clear

The final principle is making it clear when there are next steps to be followed in any communication. If there are actions, spell them out! If you have time expectations, state them. If you don't need a reply, be explicit and say that. This may initially feel like you're having to state the obvious, but it'll greatly improve the satisfaction you derive from your interactions.

Weave the following techniques into your communication when relevant:

- *State whether a communication is just for informational purposes or whether an action is required.* Are you sending this email just to keep everyone informed? That's great! Say that this is the case. Are you wanting the readers to go and do something else? That's also great. But make it clear. Consider stating this first to ensure that people have digested it before the main content.

- *Suggest explicitly what the actions should be.* If you want people to go to a shared document and make comments, say so. If you want them to check something over, make it clear what you want them to check and why, for example, the integrity of the data, or that there might be some information missing.

- *State the time frame that you expect the actions to be taken in.* Doing so is a considerate act; it helps your recipients slot your requests in to their busy to-do lists.

- *Link to any artifacts that need actions performed in them.* People greatly appreciate quick access to any artifacts that you're referencing, and you'll also want to make sure that people are going to the right place. If you're requesting comments on a document, explicitly link to it at the time of the communication.

- *State whether any follow-up communication is required.* Once people have performed the action that you're suggesting, should they just go and get on with something else, or are you expecting them to drop you a note to let you know that they're done? Ease their minds by outlining your expectations. It makes everything go smoother.

Principles: In Summary

Before we look at specific techniques, let's remind ourselves of the principles for remote communication that we should carry through all of our interactions:

- *Establish norms.* Explicitly discuss how and why you communicate as a team and what that means for the expectations you have for each other.

- *Optimize for understanding.* Use simple language to widen the possible readership as much as possible without losing the core of the message.

- *Practice brevity.* Time is precious, so practice making your communication as short and concise as possible.

- *Be unambiguous.* Ensure your communication covers exactly what you want to say and what's expected of the recipient.

- *Make the next step clear.* If there are actions to take, spell them out and give the recipient access to whatever they need to get them done.

You could print these out and stick them on your wall. Bear them in mind as we now explore specific techniques to use when interacting.

Techniques to Improve Interactions

With the principles in mind to guide you through your communication, let's now look at specific techniques that you can use to navigate through each day. We'll split these techniques into two parts: those that are specific to synchronous interactions and those that relate to asynchronous ones.

Synchronous Interactions

First, we'll look at techniques for synchronous interactions. To begin with, you're getting another diagram with an arrow on it. Lucky you.

Fighting Formality Clashes

It can be difficult to get formality correct in the workplace. We're trying to be friendly, but we're also trying to get things done. We want to have fun, but we also need to be understandable, accurate, and concise. No wonder it's so easy to get it wrong.

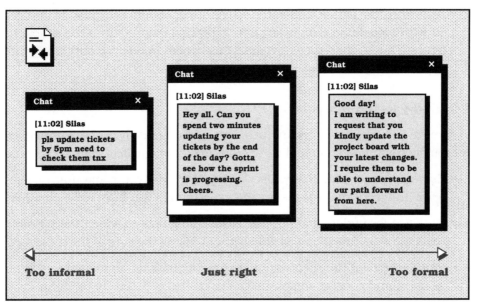

What makes matters difficult, especially when using written forms of communication, is that past experiences and habits can have an effect on our interactions. Take chat as an example, which is mostly synchronous. Many of us had our first experiences with chat in an informal and social context, perhaps with friends or as part of an online gaming community. This means that you may have already developed a tone of voice for chat that isn't quite the same tone you would adopt in email or when speaking to someone in person.

We need to be mindful of potential formality clashes that can take place, where we subconsciously slip into ways of communicating that aren't ideal for workplace interactions. Look at the examples in the previous diagram. The formal example is dry and boring and likely to make people not want to read it. The informal example is less likely to be taken seriously because some basic care wasn't taken in crafting the communication. The example of *just right* is an active, concise, and friendly tone that's easy to read and simple to understand.

Even if you become a master at getting your written tone right, not everyone else will exhibit the same skill. This is where you need to build an interpreting layer somewhere between your eyeballs and your brain that's able to take in and translate any communication you read from others that feels too formal or informal and makes sure that your brain interprets it as if it's *just right*.

Lead by example and translate others where necessary. Over time, others will follow your example, and the quality of interactions will improve.

Stop the World with Care

In Java the process of deallocating memory is automatically handled by the garbage collector. This is a neat feature because it allows programmers to not worry so much about deallocating memory as they do in languages like C. However, one of the downsides of automatic garbage collection is that it doesn't come for free. To find objects on the heap that need cleaning up, the application needs to *stop the world* for a brief period of time so the garbage collector can find the unused objects and delete them.

Depending on the size of your JVM, the number of objects being created, and the computing power available, garbage collection can sometimes take a prohibitively long time. In the worst case, it can make your application repeatedly unresponsive and unable to get done the work that it needs to do.

Conversely, a well-written program and well-tuned JVM with enough computing power will be able to run and garbage collect indefinitely without the user of that program even knowing that it's happening.

There are many parallels between how you decide to balance synchronous and asynchronous communication—especially meetings—and how garbage collection works in the JVM. Imagine an all-hands company meeting with mandatory attendance. This has the effect of stopping the world for the entire company; everyone's focus is on that meeting for its duration and no other work is happening. If the meeting is packed full of information and is a positive experience, then after the stop-the-world event the company runs better. However, if it isn't, productivity has been lost.

The bigger the meeting, the bigger the stop-the-world event. The more frequent the meetings, the more stop-the-world events there are. Consider the following:

- *Pay close attention to how often you decide to call meetings* versus using asynchronous means of communication. Meetings are fantastic for debate and discussion, complex subjects, and tricky interpersonal matters. However, a weekly project update could easily be written instead. Choose wisely and only stop the world when needed.

- *Only invite those who need to be there.* Make use of calendar features such as marking attendees as optional to reduce unwanted interruptions to others.

- *Record the meeting and take minutes* to distribute afterward so others can catch up at their own pace if they wish.

> ### Your Turn: Are You Continually Stuck in Stop-the-World Events?
>
> Have a look at your calendar over the previous few weeks and upcoming days.
>
> - What observations would you currently make about the stop-the-world impact of meetings within your team and more widely within your company?
>
> - Are there meetings within your team that have a high stop-the-world impact that you could convert into ones with smaller attendance? Could they even be converted into asynchronous exchanges instead?
>
> - How do your colleagues feel about the amount of meetings they have to go to compared to the time that they have to get their work done?

Enable Flow

Another consequence of too many meetings is that it interrupts *flow*. This is especially important for individual contributors. Coined in 1975 by Mihály Csíkszentmihályi, flow is a mental state in which a person is fully and enjoyably immersed in the activity that they're performing.

You may have experienced this highly productive state, also known as *being in the zone,* when programming, drawing, writing, knitting, fixing your bicycle, or doing numerous other activities that require skill and concentration.

Programmers often rely on the flow state to be at their most productive. This allows them to fully immerse themselves within the task that they're doing. This is especially important when they're debugging an intricate problem.

The mortal enemy of flow is meetings. There are two reasons that this is the case. The first is straightforward: having to drop everything to go to a meeting means that you lose the flow state. The second is more subtle. Often, to lose yourself in an activity and achieve the flow state, you need to forget about everything else that's going on: the time of day, what's coming next, and what you want to eat for lunch. When there's a meeting coming up in forty-five minutes, it can be difficult to get into the flow state in the first place because you know that you're soon going to be interrupted.

Discuss with your team how best to enable the longest possible periods of flow each day. Is it possible for your team to block together meetings so that they happen either at the beginning or the end of the day? Is it possible to shift them all to one day of the week, leaving the other days with as much opportunity for finding flow as possible?

Maker's Schedule, Manager's Schedule

Y Combinator cofounder Paul Graham wrote an article, found in his book *Essays by Paul Graham [Gra09]*, outlining the key differences between the daily schedules of makers (e.g., programmers) and managers.

 Managers typically schedule their days around hourly blocks in their calendar, whereas makers are most productive when they can schedule their time in blocks of half a day. This is because the work of makers is deep and takes time to achieve productivity.

Try your best to protect the time of those on a maker's schedule. Have meetings at times that allow people to be focused and productive during the rest of the day.

Widen Inclusion

The final technique for synchronous communication is to widen potential inclusion as much as possible. By its nature, synchronous communication requires all parties to be available and present at the same time. This becomes harder when a workforce is globally distributed because people can easily become left out if they're in a different time zone, have busy calendars, or work flexibly so they can do the school run.

Sometimes it's hard to avoid synchronous communication. There can be crises where the production system has gone down, and those who are online need to drop everything and have a video call to discuss the strategy for getting it back in action. Perhaps a design document attracted so many comments and conflicting opinions that it's getting a bit messy and needs a discussion to iron it out. Perhaps it's just impossible to get the whole team together synchronously because of vacations and public holidays.

In these situations you shouldn't shy away from synchronous communication. It should still be embraced to get people aligned and heard and unblock progress. But when it's impossible to have everyone present at the same time, *do remember that they're still there.* It's your job to widen inclusion as much as possible. Think of it as leaving a breadcrumb trail, much in the same way that Hansel and Gretel did. Your breadcrumb trail consists of messages and artifacts that allow those who aren't able to be present to be able to find their way home at another time. Here are some ways that you can do this:

- *Summarize synchronous meetings in text.* If a subset of the team gets together to discuss something and make a decision, have one of the participants write up a summary of what was discussed in a place where everyone can see it, such as the team chat.

- *Produce artifacts in the meeting and distribute them afterward.* Perhaps you could use collaborative drawing software to produce a diagram. Maybe you could produce some meeting minutes. If the discussion is particularly interesting, a recording of it could be circulated.

- *Offer a follow-up meeting for those who weren't there.* Give them the option to get together with everyone at a later time to give their input.

- *Go up a level when necessary.* If the content is relevant beyond your team, let more people know where that breadcrumb trail lives. Share your discussions and content more widely using chat channels or email. Think of stakeholders who would be interested in what you discussed, either from a technical perspective (e.g., your peers in the department) or from a user perspective (e.g., people in the commercial side of the business). Radiate that knowledge.

Accessibility

With videoconferencing being used more than ever, it's essential that the platform is accessible to individuals with disabilities. Accessibility needs must be considered for staff who require it. If an individual is deaf or hard of hearing or blind or has intellectual, developmental, or mobility disabilities, videoconferencing can present challenges for ensuring that the conversation is accessible to all participants.

This may mean that the company should carefully consider the platform that it uses to perform video calls.[7] There are a number of features and functionalities that should be present to serve current members of staff who have disabilities but also to support future staff with disabilities.

Examples of the kinds of functionality to consider are as follows:

- Support for live transcription and automatic closed captioning
- Support for screen readers
- Keyboard shortcuts to use the software without a mouse
- Ability for sign langugage interpreters to be present and visible throughout
- Features for visual modifications such as screen magnifiers and high-contrast and colorblind modes.

These areas are often overlooked and are challenging to roll out support for quickly, especially if it means moving to another videoconferencing platform. So do your research up front and ensure that there are accessibility options that you can use now and in the future.

Asynchronous Interactions

The techniques that we covered as part of synchronous interactions were predominantly based on getting the formality right, introducing additional artifact creation, improving the scheduling of meetings, and ensuring that nobody misses out on what's being discussed. The actual interactions themselves happen in pretty much the same way as they would in the physical office. As long as people are polite, clear, respectful, and professional, we're well on our way.

But as we mentioned in the opening of this chapter, people—on average—are far less experienced in asynchronous interactions. So the techniques that we're going to look at have less to do with exact processes and more to do with getting your mindset right and ensuring you take your time to express yourself properly.

Slow Down and Practice

Just because you can write it quickly doesn't necessarily mean that it's going to be any good. (Believe me; just ask my editor.) The beauty of asynchronous

---

7. https://www.americanbar.org/groups/diversity/disabilityrights/resources/covid-resources/virtual-meetings-checklist/

communication is that time is on your side. It doesn't matter if you're able to reply to the chat message in ten seconds or ninety seconds. Likewise, it doesn't matter much if you reply to that email immediately or give yourself five minutes to think of the best possible reply. You should use this to your advantage.

The only way that you can get better at understandable, concise, and unambiguous communication is to practice. Usually practicing things is challenging because you have to make space outside of work and life to focus and do your drills. However, practicing your asynchronous communication is something that you can mindfully and purposefully do every single day at work. It might even make the drudgery of clearing through your email inbox a little bit more enjoyable because you're working on mastering your craft rather than getting a chore done.

Make a habit of slowing down to practice. Even if you doubled the time that you took to reply to asynchronous messages, it's likely you'd still get all of your work done. Use each message as an opportunity to improve your sentence structure. To read back what you've written and improve your choice of words by using a thesaurus. To insert more line breaks. To rejig the order. Or to use bullet points to make your message clearer. These are all small details, but they make all of the difference in the impact of what you're saying.

Most importantly, they put you back in the driver's seat. Here you are, every day, with tens, maybe hundreds, of opportunities to practice your craft of communication. Don't miss that opportunity. This purposeful practice, compounded over days, weeks, months, and years, will make you a highly skilled written communicator.

Measure Twice, Cut Once

An old proverb suggests that you should measure twice and cut once. This originates from traditional crafts such as carpentry, where double-checking your measurements can save you from making an expensive mistake. For example, there are no other negative side effects from ensuring that the measurement is correct before sawing through a piece of wood, other than the additional time that it takes. However, there are some drastic side effects of cutting too soon, especially if the wood is expensive or has had a number of processes already applied to it. It gets wasted.

You can apply the same proverb to asynchronous communication. As we mentioned previously, little will change if you decide to take one minute or five minutes to reply to a message. By slowing down and taking that additional time, you can measure twice and cut once. There's no worse feeling than rushing out a reply, realizing that you've misread what was said in the first place, and then frantically rushing to redact and edit your message while the conversation goes off in the wrong direction.

When you write something, ensure that you read it back before you slam your finger on the Enter key. Then read it again. Does it convey what you intended to convey? Are there any typos or ambiguous, woolly phrases that need to be removed? Would it be better if you wait for the conversation to unfold further before chipping in?

Measure twice, cut once. You won't regret it.

Your Turn: Pause Before Sending

Practice measuring twice and cutting once throughout this week:

- Resist the urge to send a message as soon as you've written it. Instead, read it back to yourself and consider whether you could make it any better.

- Are there any messages that you wrote that you then completely rewrote after reading them back? Why did that happen?

- Did you decide not to send a message at all after reading it over? Why did that happen?

Remove Your Ego

One of the reasons that you may decide to hold a message back is because it puts too much focus on your ego. This can manifest in a number of ways. Hasty responses may be driven by the need to satiate one's ego. Perhaps there's a need to be first or a need to be right. Perhaps a viewpoint strongly opposes your own and it raises the pulse and gets the fingers flying on the keyboard.

However, you're working for the good of your team and the company first, not yourself. Communication is always better when you're able to remove your ego from it. Now, the first time you write a reply, it may be nigh impossible to remove your ego from it. That's why you measure twice and cut once. Read your response and ask yourself the following questions:

- *Is everything that I'm saying coming from an unbiased point of view?* Are you implicitly pushing your own agenda, or are you genuinely being impartial?

- *Am I considering the other sides of the argument?* When others read what you're writing, will they feel that you have considered how they feel and what they think?

- *Am I using any language that makes me appear superior, aggressive, or boastful?* Remember that you should be contributing to discussions so you can make collective progress, increase knowledge, and facilitate understanding. This can be done without needing to inflate your ego.

You're all working toward the same thing. There's no need for your ego to get in the way. So edit it out.

Mind Your Emotions

A closely related concept is controlling your emotions in conversation. As we just touched upon, not keeping your ego in check can generate unwanted emotion in your communication. However, there are plenty of other reasons that you may not say exactly what you want to say. You may be feeling stressed because your day has been busy and overwhelming. Perhaps you are frustrated because your progress keeps getting blocked by dependencies you have no control over. Perhaps you're afraid that you're going to miss your deadline and everything is spiraling out of control.

All of these emotions are totally natural, but they can dilute or distort your message. Employ the technique of measuring twice and cutting once to center yourself before you commit and hit Send. There are a number of techniques that you can employ here, but the most important one is being able to observe yourself and your emotional state in order to understand how you're feeling at any given time. Throughout the day, make time to pause what you're doing and make a mental note of how you're feeling. Are you feeling optimistic or pessimistic? Productive or frustrated? Progressing simply through the day or among stress and friction? As you do this more often, you'll build up a picture of the emotional states that your communication may be frequently coming from. Sometimes you can surprise yourself; you may be less happy and carefree than you think.

Once you've understood the different emotions that you frequently feel, you should be able to spot them in your communications before you send them out. If you do, ensure that you create a larger time gap in which you can measure before you cut. If need be, delay your response until you have centered yourself. Go and do something else for a while, such as fixing a snack or making coffee. Perhaps you could go for a quick walk if things are getting too stressful. It's hard to communicate well when you're in a maelstrom of emotion, so try and do something to defuse it.

If you aren't able to defuse it, just be open about how you feel. Prefixing some communication with your current emotional state can help to frame your responses. For example, you may state that you're having an incredibly stressful day at the beginning of a written communication. Or perhaps you could state that you're aware that you have a particular viewpoint because of the emotions that you're currently feeling and then follow with that viewpoint. This helps the recipients to frame the communication based on the emotional state from which it's being generated rather than have them misinterpret you.

Prune Your Inputs

Our final technique for you to use is less about continually attacking all of the communication that's assaulting you; instead, it's about knowing how to channel it, avoid it when possible, and organize it so that you're the one who is in control. Think like a strategist rather than a soldier on the offense with guns blazing. What you need to do is prune your inputs. Remote work naturally relies on digital communication, so there's little you can do to escape it. But you can take steps to give it order and predictability.

Doing so is important because without some careful attention, you can feel like your back is against the wall while you're continually being bombarded with email, direct messages, chat-channel updates, GitHub notifications, and alerts from the production system. Multiple applications and multiple ways of being contacted mean multiple stresses.

You need to survey all of your communication channels and bucket them into three categories:

- *Those that are critical and need you to stay on top of them.* This could be alerts when the production system is down or direct messages from your teammates.

- *Those that can be batched together for reply when it's convenient for you.* Perhaps this covers general email and activity in some of the other chat channels that you're in.

- *Those that can be ignored unless you're curious.* Perhaps these are passive notifications on your ticket tracker that you're subscribed to or other less-important and less-active chat channels.

Once you've bucketed your inputs into these three categories, see whether you can implement a strategy for dealing with them. For critical messages, decide whether you want to get push notifications to your desktop or your phone, or whether you could route them into your email inbox with a tag to filter them with. That way, only the most important things interrupt you.

For inputs that you can batch, pick a couple of times per day that you read and process them. Keep your eyes away from them for the rest of the time, and resist the urge to look. Maybe once in the morning, once after lunch, and once after the day is over will suffice. When it isn't that time of the day, keep the tabs closed. Better still, see if it's possible to route all of your inputs in this category to your email inbox with a tag so you can batch-process them in one go for maximum efficiency.

For inputs that you can ignore, utilize functions such as muting chat channels, tagging email based on filters, and automatically archiving messages that aren't that important to you. At the beginning, you may feel like you're missing out, but after awhile you'll forget that these messages exist. Well done! You've just boosted the signal-to-noise ratio significantly.

Your Turn: Pruning Time

Take an audit of your own inputs and categorize them into the three buckets mentioned previously:

- How would you describe your current signal-to-noise ratio? Are you keeping up with conversations and notifications that could otherwise be ignored?

- Is it possible to funnel your communications into one place, such as your email inbox, so you're able to keep fewer separate pieces of software open at any given time?

- Implement the previous strategies and try it out for a week. Has it had any impact on your focus? Are you experiencing a fear of missing out? How can you address this?

The Right Tools and When to Use Them

It's all well and good having a host of techniques to improve your communications, but you get a huge head start if you're choosing the right tools in the first place. The exact tools you'll use will depend on you, your team, and even your company culture. However, the advice in this section is broadly applicable. If you start with the goal in mind, you can better choose the way in which you're going to communicate. That's half the battle. Let's take a look at the different communication tools and the scenarios in which they work well, and the situations in which they don't.

Medium	Good for ...	Bad for ...
Phone call	An interruptible urgent matter, since a video call is typically used for regular scheduled meetings.	Anything else. Calling someone's phone directly can feel intrusive.
SMS	An urgent alert, such as the system going down.	Anything else.
Chat	Informal conversations and light interactions that require near-synchronous responses, both for work and social purposes.	Finding important information later due to limitations in retention and searchability. Not as suitable for formal communications due to lack of archivability. Also can suffer from poor signal-to-noise ratio.
Video call	Rapid discussion, feeling connected to fellow humans, and discussing nuanced issues such as interpersonal matters.	Finding time for everyone to be available and needing to *stop the world*. More introverted personalities may have a harder time communicating in meetings than in asynchronous mediums. Complex matters can be hard to discuss without preparation.
Email	Formal and archival communication, broadcast updates, and nonurgent matters that don't need immediate replies.	Matters requiring quick replies and ensuring that everyone has read your message. Big email threads become unwieldy and actions can be unclear.
Recorded video	Material that will be rewatched repeatedly, such as for onboarding and training. Preventing large synchronous meetings from happening.	Searchability and discoverability of content. Can sometimes take a lot of time and effort to create and distribute.
Written document	Developing complex ideas and getting others involved through shared editing and commenting (e.g., design documents and idea papers).	Time-poor recipients who may not engage. Repelling people more than attracting them if documents are poorly written.
Wiki/README	Discoverability and searchability. Treelike structure is well-suited to browsing. Evergreen content.	Easily going stale and becoming misleading. Continually changing content can become a pain to maintain because collaborative editing functionality is weaker than shared documents.

Dealing with Dichotomies

As a final note in this chapter, it's worth mentioning that any communication, in whichever format, is always subject to dichotomies. This is just part of being human. There's never a perfect answer for how to be, act, and respond. You have to be aware of the trade-offs and then do your best. What do we mean by this? Have a look at the following dichotomies:

- *Fun versus noise.* Having some fun while you're communicating is brilliant, but it has the side effect of generating more noise in written communications that can make it harder for people to easily understand what has been said.

- *Flexible working versus communication out of hours.* Staff working flexible hours in different time zones can be enabled by asynchronous forms of communication, but it has the side effect of producing things to read at all hours of the day, making people potentially feel guilty for not logging in and keeping up.

- *Friendliness versus lack of assertiveness.* Being friendly and jovial is great, but sometimes it can dilute your messages if you just want to get things done.

- *Being resolute versus being overbearing.* Conversely, being assertive and resolute may make people think that you're overbearing and uninterested in communicating with them as humans. You can come across like a robotic taskmaster.

- *Process and organization versus rigidity in approach.* Those who like to carefully organize their work and wrap everything in processes may have the unwanted side effect of boring others to tears who just want to get on with things.

- *Humility and humbleness versus passiveness.* Being overly humble by accepting and deferring to others in conversation as a means of being polite can have the side effect of making you seem like a passive participant. You may get looked over for your input into decisions in the future.

- *Detail-orientation versus dryness.* Infusing all of your communication with detail may be a sign to some that you're diligent, but to some it may make you come across as overly dry and dull and distract from your message.

So there really is no right way of doing things that will please everyone. You have to ride the line among the dichotomies whenever you communicate and be mindful of the different ways in which you can be interpreted. It seems that in communication, as is the case in life, you just have to try your best. You can't please everyone.

Turning Inward

And there we are, the end of another chapter. What did we cover?

- We looked back through history to explore *why humans communicate* and then categorized some of the ways in which we interact with each other and why.

- We defined some *principles for good communication* and saw why they were important when working as part of a globally distributed workforce.

- We gave *techniques* for communicating effectively. These covered both synchronous and asynchronous communication methods.

- We looked at all of the *tools* that we use to communicate and what they are good for and bad for.

- We concluded by touching on the *dichotomies* you face when using any form of communication.

In the next chapter, we're going to turn inward and look at ourselves. Don't worry, this isn't going to be spiritual or challenging. Instead, we're going to focus on simple but frequently overlooked daily habits for managing your time, your to-do list, and your flow, which can be more interruptible than ever in a remote environment. Let's get to it.

CHAPTER 9

Managing Yourself

You knew that today wasn't going to be your finest when you woke up in a mental fuzz. As you sat up in bed, you felt yourself begin to panic about the load testing not being complete ahead of the release tomorrow, only to realize that the release wasn't actually until next week. Phew. Just what day was it again? The rainy weather made the past two weeks seem like a gray, wet blur.

You spent the morning trying your best to concentrate on your programming, but it just wasn't happening. Every time you started to write a new load test configuration to run against the new search index, you found your mind wandering. You stared deeply into the YAML syntax. While you fixated on the colon character at the end of each line, your brain fired thoughts at you. A colon is such a strange character isn't it? And what's it got to do with your stomach? Oh, wait. Come on! Snap out of this. Focus. This isn't going to get these scenarios written.

After several hours of feeling like you were getting nowhere, the guilt set in. You imagined the rest of your team busily tapping away at their keyboards and being productive. You're probably the only person on your team who hasn't raised a pull request today, aren't you? OK, OK. You need to focus and get this done. Just concentrate.

But wait, has anyone needed you for anything? You open your browser and check the team chat channel. Hmm. No conversation of note here. Wow, everyone must be incredibly busy. You bet they've gotten tons of code written. You open GitHub and check the pull requests to see just how far behind you are today. Hmm. Interestingly, there's nothing here. Are you just being paranoid? Why are you spending more time on thinking about what other people think of your output than on your output itself?

OK, back to your work. What were you doing again? Yes, the load test scenario configurations. YAML. Yams. You're hungry. But you've got work to do. But you can't concentrate. You feel an overwhelming urge to get out of your chair and go and chat to your colleagues in the kitchen. But the only thing that's in your kitchen now is the dishes, and they're not the best at conversation. You notice that you're staring at the colon character again.

Wasn't there something else you needed to do today? Perhaps it would be better to do something different for a while. You scroll back through yesterday's chat to remind yourself what you needed to do, but you can't seem to see it. Where was it again? Was it the back-end channel? Or maybe the infrastructure channel? You flick around. You sigh. It's just not happening today. Tired, wired, distracted, disorganized. There has to be a better way.

When it comes to performance, talent is only a small piece of the puzzle. World-class Olympians did more than just realize that one day they were pretty good at running. Yes, it's likely that athletes have a bedrock of innate talent that they're able to build their skills upon; after all, no matter how hard I try, I'm really not tall enough to be a basketball player. However, that innate talent alone needs to be fostered, grown, challenged, and improved for many years for it to blossom into the athlete who wins a gold medal on the global stage.

Often talented younger athletes are spotted by coaches and then enter into sports clubs and training programs that allow their talent to flourish. This allows the young athletes to work on improving themselves in some different areas:

- *Developing their talent into skills* that are essential to their sport. Athletes repeatedly practice so they can build the portfolio of skills they'll need to perform. If you've dunked 5,000 times, it'll be easier to do it at the critical moment of a game than if you've only done it a handful of occasions before.

- *Coaching the right training and habits* to allow them to continue to improve. Professional athletes need the right conditions, physical training, nutrition, and rest to allow their bodies to be in peak condition.

- *Working on their mindset* so they are able to be level-headed and strong during performances. This can involve understanding the dynamic of working within a team, recuperating from losses, making good decisions during clutch plays, and dealing with natural human emotions such as self-doubt.

There's a lot of different work that needs to go into making an athlete the complete package. The same is true about our working lives. A programmer can have world-class talent and problem-solving skills, but without the right conditions, mindset, and habits, their performance in their job isn't going to live up to their potential.

Working in an office can help you perform in ways you may not have previously noticed. The commute from home to your workplace can help your mind adjust to performance mode. Sitting around your colleagues who are all working diligently can make you want to sit down and do the same. Your company may provide a good work space with ample screen real estate, an expensive ergonomic chair, and good lighting. It's game day every time you turn up.

Working remotely, especially from home, may make you slip away from your peak performance. There may be more distractions. There are no other colleagues to mirror. Mentally, it can be difficult to shift between home mode and work mode continually throughout the day, especially if you're observing that pile of dirty laundry every time you go to the kitchen. You may struggle to get started at the beginning of the day because you've not physically gone anywhere. Instead, you need to build the strength of your mindset and habits to give you the advantage that you need.

In this chapter, we focus on managing yourself so that, like an athlete, you can better create the conditions that you need to perform at your best. We can't help you with your talent, although we're sure you have plenty of that already. Instead, here's what we're going to cover:

- We'll create an *organizational bedrock* for you to build your day around. We'll look at how to *manage to-do lists, build habit loops, and plan out daily, weekly, and monthly goals with milestones* that you can feel good about hitting.

- We'll consider *the effects of being unobserved*, ranging from the ease of slacking off and the guilt that can drive you to work even harder and subject yourself to more stress than you need.

- We'll look at *emotional peaks and troughs* that we all go through, sometimes on a daily basis. We'll talk about how you can manage yourself by thinking about how smart investors use the stock market.

So let's begin by getting organized.

An Organizational Bedrock

A large part of being productive is *feeling* productive. It's a virtuous cycle that keeps on giving. When working remotely, it's imperative that you set a foundation that allows you to feel like you're making progress and checking off achievements, even if you have days that are stressful, busy, frustrating, or contain limited interactions with other people. To do this you need to set an organizational bedrock for yourself. It involves a small selection of simple habits that you can implement, and you can even do it with just a pen and paper.

The following ideas are just suggestions; fundamentally, you can organize yourself how you want. But what's most important is that you do organize yourself. This way, you can check off your progress through each day against the plans that you set for yourself rather than the plans that somebody else may have for you. It puts the control back in your own hands, and this is a powerful position to be in.

Your Organizational Tools

When it comes to organizing yourself when working remotely, you really only need three tools:

- Your calendar, for organizing your *time*
- Your to-do list, for organizing your *tasks*
- Your email inbox, for organizing your *incoming messages*

With these tools you can create a simple system that ensures that you're structuring your day, prioritizing what needs to be done, and keeping everything in one place that's simple to sift through.

The habit loops that form this system are easy to implement. Once they truly become habits, you won't even think about what you're doing to stay organized. It'll just become natural. The best part is that you'll find that your brain just *feels better,* primarily for two reasons.

The first is that you can trust your system to capture what you need to do. This ensures that you don't need to keep wasting brain cycles on remembering what you're doing and what you need to do next. The second is that once you trust your system, you can find comfort in knowing that it has your back at any given time of day. If you get interrupted, it's no bother; your system tells you what to do next.

Your Calendar

First off, let's cover your calendar. Learn to love it. Make it the de facto record of how you spend your time, and live your day by your calendar.

The golden rule is that you should only use your calendar for organizing your time. Your calendar isn't your to-do list (your to-do list is your to-do list). Only put the following things in your calendar:

- *Meetings with other people.* This way others will know that you're preoccupied at a given time.

- *Events that indicate that you're unavailable.* Ensure that you mark what your working hours are so that people in different time zones don't accidentally annoy by booking you in a 7 a.m. meeting. Make sure that you also book time for lunch, physical activities, doctor's appointments, and so on.

- *Blocks to prevent others from interrupting you.* Block out deep work time for yourself between commitments so you know when you can close other distractions and focus on the tasks that you need to complete.

If you can, make your calendar public to others in your organization so they can see what you're doing. That way your coworkers (assuming they're nice) won't book over your scheduled blocks for deep work without asking you first. A remote colleague with a well-organized calendar is a wonderful thing. You can quickly determine if they're busy, where the free slots are if you need to book a meeting, and at a glance what kind of time zone overlap you have with them, which may suggest when you're likely to get a response.

Your calendar is an excellent tool—not just for yourself but for people collaborating with you.

Your To-Do List

Now, we said that your calendar isn't your to-do list, because your to-do list is your to-do list. Your calendar is for organizing your time. Your tasks belong in your to-do list.

Your to-do list should be the only place where tasks live. Tasks shouldn't be unread or starred email, or pinned chat messages, or all-day events in your calendar. This is a recipe for quickly forgetting what you should be doing. Instead, form a discipline around continually adding to and working from your to-do list.

> ## Your Turn: Organize Your Calendar
>
> If you don't already have good a calendar habit, now's the time to get started. Be disciplined, manage it daily, and manage your own time with it:
>
> - If it isn't already, make your calendar public to others at the organization to indicate when you're available. Some calendar software has specific functionality that flags when a meeting is being booked outside of your working hours.
>
> - At the end of the day, organize your calendar for the next day. Ensure that all of your meetings are recorded in it, and create blocks for deep work, lunch, and anything else that you need to add to your schedule.
>
> - Run tomorrow solely from your calendar. See how you feel waking up on a day that you've already organized.
>
> - Repeat this process for a week and see how you feel reviewing your time at the end of the week. Do you feel more or less satisfied about how you spent your time? Would you change anything?

There are many different to-do list applications, and you can use whatever you please. The benefit of using a software to-do list is that it can sync to multiple devices, and it's right there on your computer where you're working. It's also right there in your pocket on your phone, so you can capture a task when it pops into your head away from your computer.

The golden rule here is that if it's not on your to-do list, you're not doing it. This may seem strict, but it forces a habit: you need to actively keep your to-do list up to date and prioritized. There are some big benefits to this. Driving your day from a single to-do list is straightforward. At the end of the day, week, or month, you can easily look back at all of the things that you've done and feel productive. Additionally, knowing that everything you need to do is on your to-do list means that you don't have to continually worry that you've forgotten something and then go searching around trying to find it.

Your to-do list is your single source of truth. If a task is generated, you put it on your to-do list. If someone sends you an email asking you to do something, it goes on your to-do list. If something comes up in chat that you need to action, it goes on your to-do list. If you're in a meeting and you say you're going to do something, as you've probably already guessed, it goes on your to-do list. Practice this repeatedly and it quickly becomes habit. And you'll equally quickly feel the relief of knowing that everything that you need to do is recorded in one place rather than in thirty browser tabs that you need to come back to later.

Some to-do list software can even help you automate your days by creating recurring to-dos. Perhaps you check through pull requests once per day or send a weekly summary digest to your team. By setting these up as recurring tasks, you need never forget to do them again. Bliss.

Your Turn: Organize Your To-Do List

Let's get your to-do list into shape:

- Choose how you're going to keep your to-do list. Pen and paper can work fine, but there are many benefits to using an application.

- Think of all of the tasks that you perform daily, weekly, and even monthly. Record them for the coming week. Use recurring to-do items if your software supports it. Remind yourself of absolutely anything that you want.

- Make your to-do list the first thing that you look at in the morning and the last thing that you look at before you sign off for the day. Record every task that you need to do throughout the working day and reprioritize as necessary.

- Drive the coming days from your to-do list alone. How does it feel checking off all of those tasks? How much of your time are you thinking about what to do compared to actually doing what you need to do? Has it changed for the better?

Your Email Inbox

With your time and tasks taken care of, the remaining piece of the puzzle is having a single place that your messages will come to. Depending on where you work, the platforms you use for chat, direct messages, and videoconferencing may differ. But there's one thing that you're guaranteed to have no matter your employer: an email inbox.

Most—if not all—other software that you use for communicating will offer the ability to generate email notifications. You can use this to your advantage by following the golden rule that your email inbox is your primary source of incoming messages. Consider all other software as secondary sources and set up notifications so that an email is generated whenever there's something that you need to pay attention to. This means that you only need to be on top of your email and everything else will follow.

If you're driving your schedule from your calendar and your tasks from your to-do list, you can similarly drive your communication from your email inbox. Rather than needing to keep ten platforms continually open, you just periodically refer to one. And the best part is that you can close it while you're doing deep work and come back to it later. Those messages won't go anywhere.

Speaking of not going anywhere, email by design is searchable and archival. How often have you left a chat message unread to come back to it later only to accidentally mark it as read during a moment of busyness? That reply you should have written disappears into the abyss, and the person who asked you a question now thinks that you're ignoring them.

Email, on the other hand, is much better, and it has some key features that you can use to ensure that your inbox is kept tidy and Zen-like. Following an inbox-zero approach works well:

- *Once you've read an email, archive it.* If don't need to do anything, archive it. If you have to do something, put that task on your to-do list and archive the email. This means that your inbox is kept neatly pruned, but the email hasn't gone anywhere. If you search for something, you'll still find it in the archive.

- *Never delete email (unless it's spam).* Because email is a transactional record of communication, just archive everything so you can find it later if you need to. You can just search.

- *Unsubscribe from lists you don't read.* If there's clutter in your inbox, be proactive and unsubscribe. It just gets in the way.

- *Set up rules for important messages.* If you get a lot of email, consider using rules to star, flag, or sift incoming messages, sending them to folders that help you stay on top of it.

By performing several batch-processing passes through your email every day, you can quickly get to a state where you have the pleasure of archiving it until there's nothing left on the screen. Empty inbox, empty mind, pure bliss. There's a reason that email has been around a long time. If managed correctly, it's hard to beat. It works on multiple devices, is stored server-side, stores drafts, and can be accessed without an Internet connection.

A note, however: don't be an inbox watcher. When you're done with your email session, close your inbox and come back to it later. The main benefit of having all of your communication come through your email inbox is that it allows you to close it and forget about it while you get on with your work. Don't get addicted to responding to new messages. Instead, become addicted to your organizational system and the peace that it brings you.

Chat

Depending on where you work, chat may be the preferred form of written communication. How you interact with it depends on your team and those

Your Turn: Organize Your Email

OK, last one. It's time to get your email inbox into shape:

- Think about how you use email at the moment. Is your inbox a neatly pruned garden, or is it a jungle? Why is this? What's your current way of staying on top of all of the different communications that you receive?

- Spend some time implementing the email approach previously outlined. If you're not an avid archiver already, see how it feels when you archive every email in your inbox. Ahh. Try it out for a week.

who you talk to. As mentioned in the previous section, you can set up filters that send direct messages and conversations in important channels to your email inbox so that you don't miss them.

However, it's not possible to route everything through your inbox. Also, depending on how much chat is used, if you don't check it occasionally, you may miss out on opportunities to contribute and help others and to get involved in making decisions.

There's clearly a tension here because you don't want to ignore chat all day, nor do you want to be glued to it and unable to get any other work done. So instead, work out the right cadence to check on chat between tasks that take up larger blocks of time. Some chat applications have the ability to quickly view all unread messages in your channels and direct messages in one pane and then mark them all as read when you're done.

In the same way that you need to work out the filters and habits that make your email inbox manageable, it's likely you'll need to do this for your chat application.

Milestones and Reflections

Being in an office exposes you to all sorts of beginnings and endings. Walking through the space, you might see a team sketching out the design of a new feature on a whiteboard. You might see a sprint retrospective taking place through a glass partition, with the team reflecting on the good and bad points from their last iteration. In the breakout area, new staff may be getting shown around the space.

These are all constant reminders that companies are continually entering new phases, making changes based on past learnings, and moving forward with new knowledge. You see and feel progress all around you. When working remotely, the visibility that you have into these small yet significant events is reduced. Furthermore, if your team is engaged in a particular large or slow-moving project, you may find that each subsequent day can become a blur with few distinguishing features from the previous ones. With time, you can feel like you're making little progress in your work at the company and also within your own growth and development.

In the same way that you're able to take your daily organization into your own hands through your calendar, to-do list, and email, you can take setting milestones and reflecting on your progress into your control. Now, you may already have milestones to achieve and subsequent points of reflection as part of your team. However, given the increase in isolation that we experience when working remotely, having more structure in which to progress and achieve—even if those achievements are small—can greatly affect your mood.

In fact, research has shown that regular reflection can improve your performance.[1] In this research, call-center staff who spent fifteen minutes at the end of the day reflecting on what they had experienced and learned went on to perform 23 percent better after ten days than those who did not reflect. A similar U.K. study prompted commuters to use their travel time to reflect and found that those who did reported that they felt happier and less burned out.

Make a habit of setting milestones for yourself. But don't worry about setting the bar extremely high to begin with. The important part is that you're able to achieve them and then celebrate when you do. You can start by defining daily and weekly milestones. You can do so like this:

- *At the beginning of the week, think about the most important things that you would like to achieve.* For example, this could be completing all the tickets that you have assigned to you in your sprint, completing that design document for a new feature, getting out each day for a walk, or ensuring you finish on time every day and get away from the computer. Write these down somewhere you can see them.

- *At the beginning of each day, repeat the same process but on a smaller scale.* For example, it could be getting that bug fix deployed, getting that job description posted on the website, or just getting through that big block of meetings.

Then each day, measure your progress against your daily and weekly milestones. Check them off with happiness and celebration. At the end of each day, spend five to ten minutes reflecting on your milestones and whether you achieved them or not. Ask yourself the following questions:

---

1. https://hbr.org/2017/03/why-you-should-make-time-for-self-reflection-even-if-you-hate-doing-it

- Did I manage to achieve my milestones for today?
- If not, why?
- What else happened today that was notable? Was it good or bad?
- What is one thing that I learned today that I can carry into tomorrow?

After all, we often overestimate what we're going to achieve in a day but underestimate what we can achieve in a week. A neat way of forming this habit is to start a private journal, which can be as simple as a text document in which you record your thoughts each day.

Before you log off for the weekend, spend a little longer thinking about the whole week. You can refer to your journal if you've made one. Make a conscious effort to acknowledge everything that you've done. If your to-do list software lets you view completed tasks, you may be pleasantly surprised when you look back over them.

If you'd like to take this habit further, you can encourage an accountability partner, or even your whole team, to do this process more visibly. This could take the form of writing your daily or weekly reflections in bullet points that you share with each other in your team chat channel. This will inform everyone how everyone else is doing and what they've been working on.

Give it a go. There's ample opportunity to feel proud of yourself, even for achieving the smallest things. Why not take advantage of that?

On Being Unobserved

For those of you who've worked in busy and noisy open-plan offices, distractions may have driven you to despair. You may have been deep in thought about the problem that you were working on only to have a colleague interrupt you to ask you a question. Perhaps you've experienced what it's like to be on the cusp of finally figuring out where that problem is happening via the debugger only for noisy colleagues to start talking and laughing in a huddle by your desk. Maybe you had a day where wearing headphones only seemed to be making everything more distracting when combined with all of the movement around you.

On those days, you may have wished that you could take a trip back in time to when offices had cubicles so you could at least have some privacy. In your wildest dreams, you may have wished to have your own private office. You'd be able to close the door and exist in a world of silence where you could contemplate your stack traces in Zen-like peace.

Certainly, this is one of the motivations that draws people toward working from home. Even if your home setup isn't as plush as those who are in the office, it's often possible to have much more control over the environment and the number of distractions when at home, especially if you're someone who's fortunate enough to have a private space or separate office to work in. Thus, the private work environment that was once reserved for high-flying executives is now available to many more people through remote working. So surely you're now feeling you have everything you ever wanted, right? You're putting in just enough work on your own schedule and then skipping out for a game of tennis at 4:30 p.m., aren't you? No?

Not so much. In 2021, studies showed that employees who were working from home were facing a bigger workload than before and working longer hours.[2] The studies showed that after one year into the COVID-19 pandemic

- Workers had increased the amount of time that they were working on the computer by more than two hours a day, with U.K. workers increasing their workweek by 25 percent. Many employees in the Netherlands reported that they weren't logging off until 8 p.m.

- Workers were taking shorter lunch breaks and working through sickness. And the split between working and leisure time was becoming increasingly blurred.

- Workers felt that their companies weren't addressing burnout well enough, with communication and work expectations often drifting outside of work hours.

This is clearly a long way from the breezy dream of working from home, or even the long-standing view that some industry leaders held about it: that those who work from home slack off and don't put in the work. If anything, the global, mass work-from-home experiment of 2020–2021 showed quite the opposite. Workers who were at home were subject to a barrage of situations and emotions that encouraged them to work harder:

- Tough economic times meant that workers were increasingly worried about whether their company was going to continue to thrive and whether they would be able to keep their jobs. Thus, they put in more hours.

- A shift to digital-only communication meant that the visible ebbs and flows of the office (e.g., people arriving, impromptu chats, lunch breaks, and people departing at the end of the day) that influenced the working

---

2. https://www.theguardian.com/business/2021/feb/04/home-workers-putting-in-more-hours-since-covid-research

patterns of others were not there. Those who were always contactable and responsive could implicitly, and accidentally, signal to others that this is the new normal.

- Whereas the office often provided clear signals and physical spaces to make slacking off collaboratively OK—such as the presence of a foosball table—the home had no equivalents. People took fewer breaks.

- Being at home, which has often carried stigma in the industry, can bring with it feelings of guilt and anxiety around what others may or may not be thinking of you. If you're quiet today due to deep work, will others feel that you'd gone AWOL?

This snowball of anxiety, guilt, stress, and overwork is a common pattern for people who are new to working remotely. Not all of this can be avoided. For example, if a company makes unreasonable demands on its staff, then they are unreasonable, full stop. However, some of the feelings and behaviors are heavily influenced by the self and often feed into a vicious cycle, forcing workers to spend less time concentrating on their actual work—which is exactly what they should be doing to be impactful—and instead spend more time spinning while checking email, messages, and notifications repeatedly, giving the impression that they're always on and always there. This is often described as the fear of missing out, or FOMO for short.

Let's touch upon four techniques that you can use to manage these feelings:

- *Overcoming FOMO* by implementing, and trusting, your self-organization techniques

- *Letting go* of your inner demons

- *Strengthening the muscle of stepping away*

- *Creating just enough visibility* through signals and regular updates

We'll visit these in turn.

Overcoming FOMO

The good news is that you learned the necessary self-organization techniques earlier in this chapter that allow you to be productive. You've touched upon how to manage your time, your tasks, and your incoming messages. You even learned about making a habit of using milestones and reflections to bring structure to your day. However, even if you've begun to use these, and even if you're darn good at doing so, it's likely that you'll find yourself thinking of deviating. Just what is everyone else doing right now? Should you go and check just in case you're missing anything? FOMO is real.

The deeper that you get into a problem and the more involved you get in your code, the more likely that your brain will send you an unwanted push notification. It may ask you the following questions: What if there is an important email sitting in your inbox right now? What if it's from your manager? And what's happening in your team chat channel that you might've missed? Should you go and check? You might not even catch yourself doing this. And before you know it, you've opened up your messages purely by muscle memory and, there you are, distracted from what you were doing, getting lost in a thread that really isn't all that important.

The great irony of this behavior is that the open-plan-office engineer, who may have dreamed for decades of having an environment with reduced interruptions, has now become their own worst enemy, continually interrupting themselves! This isn't entirely the fault of the individual, however. Short, dopamine-driven feedback loops have been a part of our smartphones and our social media platforms for years, and there have been studies that link checking for updates with the same neural circuitry used by slot machines and even cocaine.[3] We've all experienced anxiety when misplacing our phone. Why? FOMO and the inability to scratch the itch of checking for new updates.

Unfortunately, the tools we're using for our work exhibit similar behaviors. The email inbox tells you that you have ten new messages waiting. The chat client lights up with red dots at all of the information that you haven't read yet. It screams "Read me!" regardless of whether the information is important or not.

What you need to do is be mindful of your impact. What is it that you do each day that increases your impact? This is what you should be primarily seeking with how you focus your time and energy. Is it writing code? Is it producing a design document? Is it blocking out an hour to deeply think about a problem on paper? Is it reviewing pull requests for your team so they can deploy their features to production? These are your core activities, and you need to continually remind yourself that when you're doing these, you're making your most impactful contribution.

Your email, chats, bouncing notifications, and messages will always be there, and sometimes they're important. They're the connective tissue between you and your colleagues. However, they're not what moves the needle for you or

---

3. https://sitn.hms.harvard.edu/flash/2018/dopamine-smartphones-battle-time/

your team. Be mindful of FOMO. See it arise in your mind. But then breathe in deeply, remind yourself of what you're doing, and go back to your task calmly. You can check those messages when you're done.

> ### Your Turn: Impactful Activities
>
> Think over a given week and list all of the activities that you do. This can range from reading and answering chat messages to programming and doing code reviews:
>
> - Rank each of these activities by the impact that you feel they have on your team.
>
> - Think about the least impactful activities. Why do you end up doing them? Are they required for your job, or are they driven by other factors like FOMO?
>
> - How could you increase your time doing the most impactful activities? What changes would you have to make to your day? Are these changes within your control?

Letting Go of Your Inner Demons

FOMO can drive you into relentless, unproductive cycles of checking messages. However, there's another, often more difficult, force at play. Being remote means being away from an office full of people who may subconsciously feel at ease because they're mirroring the behaviors of the group. Even if they're having a bit of an off-day, they can feel comforted by simply being at work. But when you're on your own remotely and left to your own thoughts, your inner demons can come out to haunt you. A simple off-day can escalate.

Suddenly, you begin staring at the wall and asking yourself questions. Am I struggling here? Am I performing badly? Are my colleagues wondering why there hasn't been much activity from me on GitHub this week? Do they think that I'm taking too long on this particular ticket? Is it because they know that I'm a liability? Is the reason that my manager moved our one-to-one meeting this week because she's writing up a formal warning for my bad performance? Am I in the wrong job? Am I a fraud?

It's amazing what the mind can do when it's left to wander. And it's also amazing that it never tends to generate particularly useful thoughts when left to its own devices. You need to learn to let go of your inner demons. They don't want to help you while you sit there stuck on a bug. They certainly don't want to help you when you take time out of your programming to prepare your lunch. They aren't on your side when you're yet again interrupted by your daughter, or when the dog starts being a complete nuisance. They'll just make you feel like you aren't doing enough. The irony is that if you don't get these thoughts in check, the increased isolation of working remotely can bring you down, down, down. And then you really aren't able to do your job.

Thoughts are just that: thoughts. They aren't the reality that you're living in. If you find yourself getting sucked into negative thinking, remember that it's just thinking. Nothing more. Take a step back. Try a simple breathing exercise that has been proven to trigger a relaxation response.[4,5] Observe your breath passing your nostrils as it comes in, filling your lungs. Observe it exiting your body on the out breath. See whether you can observe that thought from afar for what it really is: a thought. Move on.

Impostor Syndrome

Often, high-achieving individuals may experience an internal contradiction about their ability, resulting in a feeling like they're a fraud or a failure. This phenomenon is known as *impostor syndrome.* Individuals feel like they're faking it and that they'll soon get found out.

If you feel this way, don't worry. It's normal. Know that it's because you want to do a good job to benefit of others. You were given this role in the first place because you were qualified for it. Remember that. You will feel more confident with time.

Another technique for fighting your inner demons is to partner up with someone who can tell you the opposite of what your demons are telling you. This involves getting yourself an accountability partner. Here's what you can do:

- *Pick someone you work with whom you respect.* They could be your manager, your peer, or someone you're mentoring. It doesn't matter what role they have. But ensure that they're someone you feel produces good work and holds themselves to a high standard.

- *Ask whether they'd like to be your accountability partner.* Tell them that you're looking for someone to regularly share your progress and your successes with and that you'd like to offer them the same service in return.

- *Choose a format and regularity.* Perhaps you'd both prefer to write to each other in an ad hoc manner on chat, or maybe a biweekly video call could work best for you.

- *Get going, and be bold and positive.* Start sharing! It might feel awkward at first, but make sure that you both offer motivation, questions, and

---

4.   https://www.thecut.com/article/4-7-8-breathing.html
5.   https://www.ncbi.nlm.nih.gov/pmc/articles/PMC5455070/

genuine interest when you exchange information. Soon, you'll always look forward to checking in. It can give your spirits a real boost.

You've got to fight back at those inner demons by leaning on yourself and others. The demons only want to make your life harder, when in reality, you've got everything much more under control than you might think. Press on.

Strengthening the Muscle of Stepping Away

So far, we've painted a scary picture. Your inner demons may prod and tease you to make you feel like you're not performing, and your FOMO may keep stealing your focus away from your work. This vicious cycle can become paralyzing.

Not only can this deprive you of your mental space, it can deprive you of your mornings, evenings, and weekends. While you're making a sandwich, you're not actually focusing on making a sandwich. Instead, you're mentally replying to an email that's waiting for you, or perhaps wondering whether decisions are being made without you. Your weekend walk with your family is continually interrupted by looking at your email on your phone. Even though you're technically not being paid for working these hours, you're still working. And your hourly rate is ever decreasing as a result.

Being able to step away requires willpower. It requires training. It's like lifting weights, or running, or cycling. To become really good at it, you need to practice. But stepping away consistently is scary. If you're offline, there may be conversations going on without you. What if people think you're lazy for signing off at 5:30 p.m. on the dot? You become gripped by FOMO, and the inner demons tell you that you're a failure for not working harder, harder, harder. But it has to stop. To do good work, and to be a balanced person, you need to have your evenings and weekends free to do everything else in your life that's important, from being with your partner and family to exercising, watching movies, reading books, and playing video games. The yin needs the yang.

But you can't escape the fear, the fear that putting solid boundaries in-between your work time and your personal time will somehow make you a worse employee and a worse human being. It's not true. The fear is all you. Former U.S. Navy SEAL Jocko Willink, now a podcast host and author, was once asked how to face your fears and step into bravery.[6] His answer was that you do just that. You take the step. No matter how big your fears, no matter how gripped you are, you just have to take that step. You step. You go. And the more that you do it, the better that you become at it.

---

6.   https://www.youtube.com/watch?v=CgKAFyZNApM

Are you putting off that lunch-time walk because Steve might reply to your email? Step. Go. Are you worried about signing off in case your boss replies? Step. Go. Are you reaching for your phone when you're spending time with your daughter? Step. Go. Strengthen the muscle of stepping away. Nobody looks back at their life to remember the times they checked that chat message. People look back and remember the times they spent with their loved ones, on their passions and hobbies, and being present in moments that defined what it is to be alive. When it's time to stop, put down the phone, close the tabs, put the laptop in the drawer. It's time for your life now. Step. Go.

Creating Just Enough Visibility

There are simple ways you can increase your visibility, even if you aren't online at a given time. This can also make it easier for you to step away. Earlier in this chapter, we mentioned that a great way to better understand and take pride in your progress is to set your own milestones. You can measure your progress against these and regularly journal about how you're getting on, through the good, the bad, the successes, and the failures.

Some people find it hard to keep a journal. They wonder why they would put so much effort into something that only they can see. So here's the trick: Why not journal publicly? Perhaps you could regularly journal your progress to your team. Perhaps you could even start a culture of everyone regularly journaling their progress. This can be as straightforward as throwing three to five bullet points into the team chat channel at the end of each day, detailing what your goals were, what you achieved, and where you're picking things up tomorrow.

This accomplishes a number of things in a remote setting:

- It implicitly *signifies that you're signing off* and that you're on top of what you're working on.

- It *informs others of your progress* and allows them to comment or ask questions if they wish.

- It *increases the accountability* that you're putting on yourself by candidly sharing your progress with others.

- It possibly *makes others look up to you* both in terms of the great progress that you're making and in being so transparent and honest.

You'll notice a cathartic feeling as you drop your end-of-day or end-of-week update to your colleagues. As you look back over what you've done to prepare it, you'll feel a sense of accomplishment. As you share it, you'll feel that marker being plunged into the end of the workday that lets you break away. It's like the school bell. You're free. And while you're free, anyone can see exactly what you've been up to, so you can confidently step into your evening or weekend without fear. They can leave comments, and you can get back to them tomorrow because both you and they know that you're signed off.

Riding Peaks and Troughs

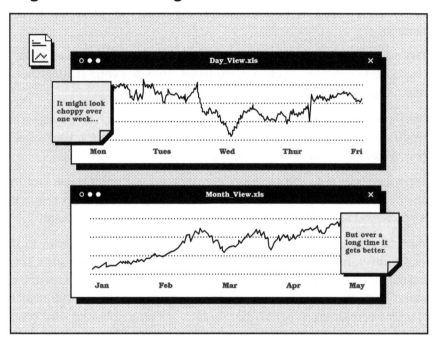

When you think about the stock market, what comes into your mind? Is it traders wearing blue jackets screaming at each other across the floor of the New York Stock Exchange? Is it black-and-white images of the Great Depression? Is it the irrational exuberance of the dot-com bubble?

Many of our thoughts about the stock market gravitate toward times of great highs and great lows, of speculation and headlines. Not all of us immediately think about the steady, day-to-day, gradual building of capital that makes the economic world tick. Generally, over a long enough time span, the market always increases in value, as shown in the previous diagram. And a certain famous scientist once said that mankind's greatest invention was compound interest.

However, many people see the stock market as a risk. Those who have never invested may think that the stock market is a game to be played by picking stocks, except with real money and with dire consequences if you lose.

A book on this subject, *Smarter Investing [Hal13]*, lays out all of the traps that usually bewilder novice investors. In it, the author states that when it comes to investing your money, you should favor the following:

- *Investing over gambling.* In short, don't put your life savings into that hot company that your friend told you about.

- *Evidence over marketing.* A lot of stock tips are just marketing in disguise, so you should look at what works already to decide what to do with your money.

- *Logic over emotion.* You should keep away from situations that allow your emotions to rule you, such as completely changing your strategy because of a temporary fall in the market.

- *Low costs over long shots.* Try not to incur costs, such as paying fees for trading or becoming enamored by an expensive investor who says they can quadruple your money in a year.

- *Discipline over delusions of grandeur.* Instead of thinking you can invest small amounts of money from time to time and expect the market to quadruple it yearly, you should be realistic and do the same thing every month.

An index fund is a low-cost vehicle that you can invest your money in that's by default diversified in many different markets, equities, and bonds. It takes the hassle out of choosing a portfolio. You just pop your money into one place the same way, over and over again. This is a long way from the traders in blue jackets screaming at each other. In fact, it's almost boring. But it works.

But what has all this got to do with remote working? Well, instead of thinking about the peaks and troughs of the stock market, think about the peaks and troughs of your energy, mood, and motivation. When it comes to working remotely—and working in general too—you want to be the smart investor when managing your effort, sticking to a strategy, and building for the long term.

Let's revisit the advice for smarter investing in the context of how you should be working:

- *Investing over gambling.* Unless you get very lucky, you're going to be working for many days in your life. You need to do so at a steady, pre-dictable pace that respects that you're running a marathon, not a sprint. Each day, do your work well but ensure that you make time to eat prop-erly, take breaks, and exercise. Work your allotted hours and then step away from the computer and do something else. Going too hard for too long will burn you out. Conversely, giving in to the attraction of slacking off while being unobserved won't only make your performance suffer, it'll make you feel unhappy and unproductive.

- *Evidence over marketing.* You already know that to get the work done well, you've got to focus on the essentials. Manage your time, your tasks, and your communication. Get the most impactful work done. No matter how many articles you read that promise to reveal five secrets that you can use to increase your productivity, and regardless of whatever the early-morning habits of top CEOs are, the evidence is already there when it comes to managing yourself. Just do the basics that you've already read about. The rest will follow.

- *Logic over emotion.* Try your best to put the same amount of effort in every day, regardless of whether you feel like it's wartime or peacetime at work. Yes, there'll sometimes be periods of crunch before deadlines. Yes, there'll be weeks where it feels like there's far less important work that needs to be done. However, don't let your emotions dramatically ramp up or ramp down your effort. Slow and steady wins the race.

- *Low costs over long shots.* You should keep our fees down in investing, and you should keep your fees down in your remote working. But what are the fees? The fees are the taxes that you put on yourself for context switching and reacting to FOMO and your inner demons. Structure your day so that you get as many periods of single-minded focus as possible, especially if you spend a majority of your day writing code. You can't do everything at once; and you can't communicate with everyone at once. Prioritize and focus to keep your fees down.

- *Discipline over delusions of grandeur.* Clayton M. Christensen, a late Harvard Business School professor, once wrote that it's easier to hold your principles 100 percent of the time than it is to hold them 98 percent of the time. The idea is that once you let your standards and your discipline slip, regardless of how talented and amazing you believe you are, they will continue to slip, slip, and slip. So if you're having a bit of an off-day, don't slack off. Try your best to do your work anyway so that you feel proud that you've put in an honest effort. It's actually easier to maintain this in the long run, and it strengthens the muscle of discipline. The most gifted geniuses can't complete their PhD programs if they aren't writing their theses gradually and incrementally, day by day. They can't do it all in one go when a moment of inspiration strikes.

You need to be a smart investor when it comes to managing yourself when remote working. Your mood, energy, and motivation will always fluctuate with time. However, if you zoom out enough, it all averages out. You just need to play the long game by doing the basics. You manage your time, your calendar, and your messages. You look after yourself. You do the same, predictable hours every day to the best of your ability at the time. Over longer periods, this compounds your effectiveness, your happiness, and your professional growth.

There's no need for heroics, or for overdoing it when you feel hyperproductive, or for getting yourself in a state if you can't produce today as well as you could yesterday. You just work on the discipline of doing your best each day, while learning about yourself and how you work best, and adjusting accordingly. That's how you win in the long term.

From Yourself to Teams

The end of another chapter is upon us. Here's what we covered during our journey through the habits and discipline of pacing yourself through the marathon of work:

- We looked at the *organizational bedrock* that you can build your day around. This covered how to manage your time, your tasks, and your incoming messages and how to use milestones and reflection to ensure that you get to feel progression and celebration even on the hardest days.

- We looked inward at the *effects of being unobserved* while working remotely. We saw how a mindful approach means that you can beat FOMO, shake off the inner demons, and strengthen the muscle of stepping away from your work while creating visibility into what you're doing for others to engage with.

- We concluded by looking at how, like the stock market, you'll always be riding *peaks and troughs* when it comes to your motivation and mood. We saw how you need to consider the bigger picture and act like a smart investor by staying focused, contributing your best each day, and coming back the next day and doing the same. Keep the tortoise in mind, not the hare.

Even if you're not a permanent remote worker, the insight in this chapter will help you understand some of the hidden issues that your remote colleagues may be dealing with on a day-to-day basis. Next time you speak to them, why not ask them how they tackle some of the problems that we've been describing? You may get some valuable insights into their work; and you're now primed to help them out with sage advice.

In the next chapter, we're going to transition into looking at what effective remote teams do. When you're ready, we'll see you there.

Teams usually take on the personality of the coach.

Khris Middleton

CHAPTER 10

Managing Teams

It's Tuesday morning and you're catching up with Alice, who manages the search infrastructure team. You're having a virtual coffee. Y'know, over a video call. You're interested in how she's finding her job now that she's remote.

"How's it all going anyway? I always remember that your team seemed so close when they were sitting together in the office."

Alice thinks. "Well, it's good and bad."

"What's good about it?"

"Well, I seem to get way more time to focus on my individual work than I used to in the office. I was always getting interrupted all the time and sometimes it would take me a whole day to get twenty lines of code written."

"OK, well that's good. But what about your team?"

"Well, I hate to admit it, but I don't really know."

"You don't know?"

"I just don't really hear from them. As time has gone on, I hear from them even less. They're just not a very talkative bunch."

"That makes sense. But are they getting their work done OK?"

"I think so. Nothing's on fire yet."

You smell that something is a little off.

"How are they all getting on, you know, personally? Emotionally? What sort of things do they talk to you about in their one-to-one meetings?"

"Ah, we don't do those. We never used to do them in the office. We'd just chat every day. I'm here if they need me. I just guess they're busy."

Later, you send a direct message to Kevin who is on Alice's team. You're after some advice on how to best update the data schema of the search index. You figure you might as well see how he's doing at the same time.

```
[10:59] you: how are you doing anyway? we haven't spoken in a while
[11:00] kev: i'm ok. some days are better than others
[11:00] you: what's up?
[11:00] kev: please keep it confidential
[11:01] you: sure, of course!
[11:01] kev: alice just isn't there at all for us these days
[11:01] kev: I have no idea what she's up to and we never talk
```

You had a feeling that this might be the case. It seems that even the best managers in person may not realize how to make that shift when working remotely.

Have you ever worked in an office with a leader who seemed to be larger than life? Perhaps you couldn't help but notice whenever they were in the room: their presence would make their staff gravitate toward them. Maybe you noticed that they were a compelling speaker, both in presentations in front of large groups and in private meetings. When they were around, their team's area of the office was a hive of energy and activity.

That is, apart from the days when that particular leader wasn't in the office. On days when they were in other offices or working from home, they seemed to either vanish or be a shadow of their physical self. Maybe they just hadn't gotten the hang of asynchronous communication. Perhaps the effectiveness of their writing style would always let them down. Possibly the gravitas that they radiated when they were physically present wasn't paralleled when they weren't.

Now, this can be a real challenge for managers who have either gone remote themselves or now have remote teams. When their management style is to typically overindex on the nature of the physical office, they may find themselves with fewer tools in their toolbox to be as effective when they aren't there. For example, they're no longer able to have immediate impromptu check-ins with staff, nor can they observe what their team is up to firsthand. And they can't stay connected to their network and gather information by mixing with others at the coffee machine.

So let's fix that. This chapter is full of tools and techniques to enable effective management remotely. But before we get going, there are a couple of important points to cover:

- First, if you're not a manager, don't think that you should skip this chapter because it's not relevant to you. It absolutely is. All of the content is applicable for nonmanagers as well. Changes within teams can happen by changing your behavior and having others see the benefit. A team can be influenced to work differently by osmosis.

- Second, if your manager could benefit from getting better at managing others remotely, why not use the knowledge that you gain in this chapter to have conversations with them about it?

Here's what we're going to cover:

- We'll look at *an equation that describes the output of a manager,* and we'll see how remote working can cause their output to either diminish or increase depending on whether they're able to adapt their management style to suit this new world.

- We'll cover the many *reasons that a manager's output can decrease* when a team is remote. This will include topics such as relying too much on face-to-face interactions, having limited access to information, and experiencing social isolation. We'll consider some remedies for these factors.

- We'll study the additional *techniques to supercharge a manager's output in the remote world.* And, like we said, not only are these techniques that'll be useful for managers, they'll be pertinent discussion points for both you and your team.

OK, so let's start by revisiting an oldie but a goodie. Let's go back to the '80s.

The Output Equation Revisited

In 1983, Andy Grove, the cofounder and CEO of Intel, published a book called *High Output Management [Gro95].* In a period of time where many books on how to be a manager and a leader were more aligned with wearing sharp suits and working your way up the corporate ladder, Grove's practical and scientific approach to how he runs a company like Intel was a breath of fresh air in the industry. His background as an engineer shines through in his writing, making the science of management understandable to those of us who have never worn a suit to work in our lives.

One of the concepts visited early in the book, which frames much of the rest of the content, is an equation that acts as a rule of thumb for the output of a manager. He states that a manager's output can be measured by the following formula:

The output of their team + The output of others they influence

This seems simple, but it's powerful: managers can use it to make decisions about how to spend their time. By framing their output in this way, they may realize that

- Ultimately, they are accountable for the output of their team. If their team is underperforming, fundamentally, they need to work out how to improve that performance.

- Their team's output is more important than their own output. This means that they should be spending their time coaching and mentoring their team to improve their collective skills and also should be delegating tasks rather than doing them themselves.

- Additionally, the right side of the equation shows that it isn't just about getting projects done on time. Good managers also spend their time on key activities such as information gathering, decision making, nudging the decisions of others, and being a role model for the behavior that they want to see. Highly influential managers can impact a much larger area than just their team. This is also explored in detail in *Become an Effective Software Engineering Manager [Sta20]*.

Thinking back to our hypothetical leader who excels when they're physically present in an office but ultimately suffers when they're away from it, let's consider why that might be happening with this equation in mind:

- When it comes to the *output of their team*, the effective physically present manager is able to rapidly observe, chat, and intervene where they see fit. If people are getting blocked or stuck, they can quickly spot it and seek out solutions.

- To be an *influence upon others*, they have their network all around them. They can walk through the office and engage in conversations with others and offer their opinion or discuss the diagram that's drawn on another team's whiteboard.

Earlier in the book, we mentioned how the design of the physical office allows so many of these behaviors to happen implicitly. Shifting to remote work means that effective managers need to understand the implicit interactions they were having in physical offices and then embark on a journey of translating these into explicit digital interactions. The good news is that there's also the possibility that when they do this effectively, managers can increase their output beyond the maximum that they were previously able to achieve.

We can take the earlier equation and introduce a scale factor to represent remote working.

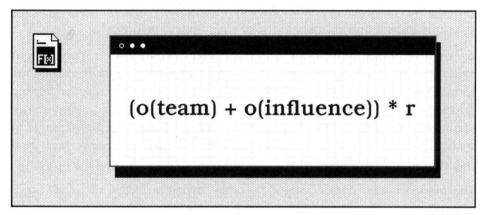

$$(o(\text{team}) + o(\text{influence})) * r$$

Here's how to read the previous equation:

- The first part is just the management equation that we introduced earlier. It's the sum of the output (o) of their team and the output of those they influence.

- The second part is a representation of their ability to adapt their skills and output to remote working (r). It can scale the previous part of the equation up or down. If they have no idea how to manage their team remotely and stay connected to others, we could imagine the scale factor being something like 0.1, thus diminishing their output. However, if the opposite is true, and they're using all of the techniques we're learning in this book to their full effect, we could imagine them having an even wider influence, thus scaling their output as a manager to 2, 3, 10, or beyond.

For the rest of this chapter, we'll first look at how the remote environment can decrease the unprepared manager's r number. Then we'll focus on ways that it can be increased.

Shrinking the Scale Factor

So let's begin by considering the manager who is unprepared for making the required changes for transitioning to the remote world and seeing how this manifests in their output shrinking as a result.

The Disappearing Manager

A highly extroverted manager like the one we previously described may all but disappear when they're without the physical office and close proximity to their team and colleagues. Like an actor without a stage, they may find themselves relegated to the wings. For them, this is highly demotivating. The energy that they used to absorb from spontaneous interactions with their colleagues is no longer available. They may feel powerless and unable to create the same impact and change that they were able to before.

Even worse, if they're unaware that they need to change their management style, they may feel like remote work is an untenable solution in the long term. This conclusion is especially worrying for those in senior leadership positions who have the power to influence or even dictate company policy about remote working. The truth is that you can be a successful manager in both a globally distributed and physically colocated company. Both just require some tweaks and adaptations to the style used to lead a team.

The manager who doesn't adapt becomes invisible. Years of practicing a leadership style based on physical presence can be detrimental to the skills needed to manage remotely, such as clear and concise asynchronous communication through writing. A dependence on impromptu interactions that require no planning can mean a lack of comprehension in how to book regular, structured, knowledge-sharing sessions with key people in wider business. Suddenly, the tools that they had access to implicitly don't work anymore.

Worse still is the effect that this has on their team. A manager who is unprepared and unable to reform their style to suit a remote environment begins to fade away into the ether. This effect is especially pronounced when the team has adapted well, as is often the case with diligent engineers who are already well suited to distributed collaboration due to the tools that they use. Our increasingly invisible leader can appear like they aren't doing a good job, even though they may be trying their best with their old tools. Their team can begin to not get what they need, and they can begin to lose trust in their manager even if they're trying their best.

The disappearing manager has a diminishing impact on their team and the organization that they influence. The r number is working against them.

Rethinking Access to Information

In an office a manager can become a hub of information, helping route others to the right people. So there needs to be some changes made to the search index schema? OK, well, that's one for Alison, and she sits upstairs by the back wall. A question about payroll? Third floor, and Kevin's your guy. What about getting an overview of the production database? Rebecca's great at walking others through how it works, and she's over there by the whiteboard. When people are physically colocated, the answers are often found within the walls of the building. You just have to know where to go and who to talk to.

For those who have experienced companies growing and expanding to multiple locations across different time zones or for those who have worked at large companies, we may have seen how there are limitations to this approach. If employees are online at different times due to being located all around the world, relying on synchronous interactions with a manager of a team to get information simply does not scale. It establishes a manager as a single point of failure for connecting with and informing others.

The same is true for other types of information. Employees onboarding in the company across the world cannot rely on a manager to continually point them in the right direction. Additionally, other teams that may wish to find out more about how to contribute their own code to the codebase that another team owns cannot rely on the synchronous guidance of the manager.

Even if a manager who prides themselves on being the custodian of a team's information feels like they're being useful because of the feedback that they get from the people who they're helping, it's likely that there are other people thinking quite different thoughts. Out of sight, out of mind.

Others across the world in another office or working from home may be wondering who owns a particular codebase and how they can get in contact with them. They may be getting frustrated at the lack of documentation and the absence of any indication as to the names or contact details of the team. Others may be trying to find the team's chat channel to make them aware of a bug that they found because they don't know what the team's project is in the ticket tracker software. A new starter in a different time zone may be stuck waiting for the manager to respond to a new question because previously all other questions were routed through them. Being a synchronous hub of information simply does not scale in the remote world. It just drags a manager's r number down.

All Work and No Play Makes Jack a Dull Boy

In an office environment, the manager may engage in a multitude of interactions. They may lead a discussion about how to approach a new feature. They may catch up with others in both group and one-to-one settings. They may spend some time chatting to others they happen to walk by.

Even if all of these interactions are about work and work-related topics, the fact that they happen in person implicitly injects some social satisfaction into them. Conversations may include joint observations about something funny that happened that day or perhaps a conversation about the weather. The social nature of human beings often adds kindness and humor to make interactions feel more fully rounded and wholesome. They just feel good. This all tends to happen fairly naturally, and it's easy to take it for granted.

When working with a remote team, pleasantries can become more difficult. Not everyone is in the same place, so making observations about the immediate surroundings is limited. There's no office gossip because nobody is in an office. You can't even have a laugh at the squeaky chair in meeting room 3. So those elements of interactions fade away, especially when there's more written, asynchronous communication. What this means for managers is that, with time, interactions within the team become predominantly functional, lacking all of the extra feel-good facets that make them more fulfilling.

This can lead to a feeling of social isolation. Without enough connection and happiness weaved into the day, people can begin to feel like they're just doing any other job. Sometimes they can even forget they work with other people. There are a whole bunch of tickets, and they just need them done. And there's another message from the boss, and they just want to know what the status of something is. Great joy. Whatever happened to joking around and drawing stupid things on the whiteboard? This feeling can hit staff hard who are used to having their colleagues as major contributors to their social lives.

With time, fundamentally, this erodes culture, which is likely to be one of the reasons that you may have joined a company in the first place. This can then lead to a decrease in feeling included and part of a highly functioning, psychologically safe team. It makes the team's output suffer, which in turn makes the manager's own output decrease due to a shrinking r number.

Managers must remember that even though many more of the interfaces that they have with their team are digital, there are still human beings at the other end of the email and the direct messages. These are the same humans who used to like chatting about what they ate for lunch that day and what the new coffee place on the corner is like. A little "How are you doing today?" and "How was your morning?" goes a long way. When leaders make time for fun, it gives permission for others too. It's surprising how it can even make them a more effective manager.

Inflexible Means Ineffective

Being in an office means that many other things get taken care of elsewhere. Deliveries go to the reception desk. Snacks and drinks might be provided. Childcare may be arranged while the parent is away from home. Depending on the company that you work for, there may even be free meals and a laundry service. Perks, perks, perks. Offices are often organized to remove any unrelated distractions so that staff can focus on getting their work done. As many parents may know, when children are old enough to go to school, it's an immense pleasure to get that time back in the day to focus.

Some managers develop a leadership style that capitalizes on the office environment where everyone is together, at the same time, with little additional distraction. However, this doesn't always translate to the world of remote work. Remote workers don't necessarily have the same provisions in their homes as in offices. The snacks don't turn up in the kitchen by themselves. One compelling reason for remote work is being available for family, but this means many distractions during the day. Another reason that some prefer remote work is it allows them to work more flexible hours during the times of the day they feel they're most productive. But this means that a manager forcing a highly synchronous way of working does more harm than good.

Managers need to adapt their style to support flexibility. If they don't, working remotely can be even more of a pain than a noisy office. Workers end up frantically checking messages while they're making lunch for their children. Or they suffer the burden of having to think about work and life all the time rather than having them automatically compartmentalized by being in different physical locations.

Some managers are able to make this shift naturally, especially if they, too, find themselves with young children, dependents, or a variety of other things that they're responsible for. However, other managers who have never been in this position, either through their life choices, their role in their household, or even just their mindset toward work, may not naturally keep others in mind who are subject to these conditions. A continual push toward being online all of the time through core office hours, an expectation that everyone has a quiet and distraction-free place to work, and a disregard for the flexibility required to live a busy, modern life only serves to increase friction and frustration and reduce trust between them and their staff. Remote staff need to be able to work at times that suit their productivity best. Flexibility should be granted to create high-performing teams. If it isn't, people may vote with their feet.

The Panopticon

The behaviors of a team working together in an office are highly observable. In fact, a manager may see this as an integral part of their team's culture: that they arrive and leave from the office at a similar time each day and are seen to be working hard around each other.

There's a potentially more sinister side to this observability of the team from the manager's point of view. Consider this. A concept called the *panopticon* is a type of building and a system of control that was designed in the eighteenth century.[1] The idea is that a ring-shaped building design for prisons would allow a small number of prison guards to observe all the prisoners from a central location without the prisoners knowing whether they're being observed. This means the prisoners are motivated to behave as if they're being watched at all times, which in turn means that less bad behavior is expected.

Although open-plan office environments are thankfully a long way from prisons, the lack of screen privacy and the ability to be observed at all times could be seen as a way of enforcing behavior. If you're not at your desk, it's clear that's the case. The same is true if you're browsing the news instead of working. Everyone can see.

When managing teams remotely, the visibility of the team is dramatically reduced. The manager can't see them. The manager may not even necessarily know that they're working because they can't look at where they're sitting and see that there's code on their screens. This can cause some managers to begin to micromanage. They may start enforcing team video calls or synchronous message exchanges at various points throughout the day to satiate their own desire to observe their team rather than to help them work. This slowly descends into meddling.

Managers who are unable to trust that silence from their teams means that they're diligently working and also balancing their home lives start to decrease the output of their team by interrupting them and making them feel like they're being watched. This is ironic, isn't it, because that's exactly what they feared in the first place.

Supercharging the Scale Factor

We've just spent a lot of time seeing all of the ways in which managers can make themselves less effective by not adapting to remote work. What a downer! Now, let's bring back the positivity and see a number of ways in

---

1. https://en.wikipedia.org/wiki/Panopticon

which a manager can supercharge their scale factor and increase their effectiveness in a remote setting.

Write Once, Run Anywhere

Engineers of a certain vintage will remember the 1995 slogan created by Sun Microsystems to highlight the cross-platform nature of Java: Write once, run anywhere.[2] Any device could run the Java Virtual Machine, which would in turn allow any Java program to run on any device. So Java programmers would only need to write one version of their program, and the execution of it on a mainframe, PC, or phone would be taken care of.

Managers who embrace remote work will understand that they, too, can adapt how they work and communicate clearly, efficiently, and, most importantly, in a way that they don't have to repeat themselves again and again.

Whether a manager is running one team or multiple teams, part of the job is gathering and distributing information. They have unique access to what's going on in the rest of the department and company, and it's their duty to ensure that others are informed. Organized managers may feel like they should batch up news and updates into weekly one-to-one meetings to share with their staff or let people know on an ad hoc basis. However, there may be ways for them to better increase their output.

After all, if you're programming and writing the same code over and over, you would probably refactor it so that the code is only written once and reused in multiple places. Managers who are able to supercharge their output in a remote setting are the ones who are able to embody the write once, run anywhere approach.

For example, they might do the following:

- *Provide written summaries to their staff* of all the key developments and updates that they need to know.

- *Organize regular information-sharing sessions* across the team and the department. Has the team just built something that others could leverage? They could help create a recorded video series that anyone could watch at any time.

- *Keep a document or wiki of nice-to-knows about their team's progress* that staff can browse at their leisure. This way, rather than having their inboxes overwhelmed, people can browse at the frequency that suits them.

---

2. https://en.wikipedia.org/wiki/Write_once,_run_anywhere

Even if it takes a manager thirty minutes to prepare a broadcast communication, it likely requires way less time and energy than communicating it to others individually. What's more is that managers can be sure that everyone receives exactly the same information.

Extract, abstract, and broadcast. Write once, read everywhere, with high consistency.

Overcommunication Encouraged

There's a common adage on how to structure your presentations: Tell them what you're going to tell them, tell them, then tell them what you've told them. Regardless of how good you are as a presenter, no matter how clear and beautiful your slides are, delivering a message that sticks requires repetition.

How many times have you been surprised that many people didn't read that important email? Or that your carefully crafted summary in chat that explained exactly where everything was on your project was overlooked only for you to face multiple questions about the project status the next day. Come on, people!

No matter how diligent the people you work with are, communication is always going to be missed by some of them some of the time. If you spent ages writing an intricately detailed update, some eyes may glaze over it because it's too long. Maybe when they looked at it, their mind was preoccupied with fixing a bug. Perhaps they flagged it to be read later, but their discipline of returning to flagged messages isn't too great. Perhaps some of your recipients were on vacation and just never got on top of older communication when they got back.

In short, the odds are never stacked in your favor. And for managers who need to regularly communicate and achieve consensus as part of their jobs, ensuring that all recipients have had a chance to digest it is key. That's why overcommunication is a manager's best friend. How much communication is too much? Probably much more than you actually think.

This is even more true in a remote setting because there are fewer opportunities for osmosis to spread a message via informal conversation or overhearing what others are talking about. Overcommunication is the solution for managers to ensure that they've given others the most opportunity to receive and digest messages.

Think about it in terms of marketing. Managers need to become the marketers of their messages. In the same way that a new drink gets repeatedly advertised on the television, in print media, and online, managers need to advertise their messages multiple times and in multiple formats.

Managers need to continually overcommunicate. They could write a document containing a project summary and then remind people to read it during their stand-up meeting and also follow up later with a link in chat. They could also include a link to the document in a weekly summary that they send out to the team. Even though managers may feel like this behavior is annoying to others, it very rarely is. If someone hasn't read it, they'll be thankful for the reminder. If they have, they'll just ignore the message.

Regular overcommunication can become the heartbeat of a team in a remote world. It keeps everyone focused on the tasks at hand, makes everyone feel connected to a shared narrative, and gives plenty of opportunity for questions and celebration. Managers: remember, if people haven't read your message, don't get annoyed. Just try again from a different angle. Be a marketer for what you want to convey. And if you think that you've communicated it enough, you probably haven't. Keep going.

Mastering New Tools

One of the challenges all managers face is the nature of their job moving them further away from contributing lines of code. They need to make that shift to be effective. It's the output of their team that matters. However, preventing technical stagnation through lack of practice is something many managers have to contend with. They may ensure that they're reading about the latest open source frameworks and perhaps have hobby projects on the go.

In the physical office, the tools of the manager haven't needed to evolve. Conversations, whiteboards, and meetings have been around for a very long time indeed.

But in the remote world, the tools of the manager are changing rapidly. When everyone isn't present in the same room, being able to better use technology to improve communication and collaboration becomes an area in which managers can supercharge their output. Being leaders, they can also set a higher standard for interactions. Instead of taking photographs of a diagram drawn on paper, they can learn to use collaborative drawing tools to create artifacts that the whole team can interact with. They can get better at recording and editing videos to broadcast their message to a wider audience. They can facilitate better group meetings by using built-in breakout group functions in videoconferencing software. And the list goes on.

Managers who do take advantage of all that technology has to offer have the chance to increase their output. Not only are they able to facilitate better communication within their team and also increase the impact of their messages, they're able to set new standards for how everyone can work together that others will follow. And, hey, it's also a lot of fun!

So, managers, you now have a new toolset of your own to master. It's not just the engineers who need to be learning and using the latest and greatest technology to do their jobs. You need to be doing the same as well. Otherwise, you'll get left behind.

Output over Observed Activity

If managers are responsible for the output of their teams, what does that really mean? It means that the time of day that employees are working doesn't matter so much, assuming that the work can be done individually or asynchronously. It means that if the day's work is finished an hour early, the day can end there rather than having idle employees waiting for 5 p.m. Output matters, not the hours at the desk or the number of meetings.

This phenomenon has often been called *competitive sitting,* where someone sitting next to their team or manager experiences anxiety about going home because it may give the impression they aren't working hard. Taken to the extreme, you could imagine a whole office waiting for the CEO to go home before making their move.

The problem with this is that it's purely theater. The presence of an employee has no connection with their output. A PepsiCo workplace initiative called Leaders Leaving Loudly encouraged leadership to reduce *presenteeism* by encouraging people to go home and announcing when they're doing so.[3] When PepsiCo's CEO leaves at 4 p.m. to pick up his children from school, he tells everyone, because if it's OK for him, it's OK for everyone else too.

Even though remote working prevents the physical competitive-sitting problem, there's the risk of the digital equivalent occurring. However, managers that make it clear that their teams are being judged on their output and impact also create space for flexibility. This means that employees can work at hours of the day that they feel most productive. It also means that they can set expectations that people may be slow to respond to messages. They can encourage others to log off when they've done their work for the day. When

---

3. https://www.news.com.au/finance/work/leaders/why-pepsico-ceo-asks-his-team-to-leave-loudly/news-story/5467b3ffff387c3a5dd79ac3a245c868

a team finishes their sprint commitments for the week, their manager can encourage them to wrap up and get outside in the sunshine.

More autonomy and flexibility create better teams and more effective managers.

Leading with Empathy

The route for managers to fully embrace flexibility in their team is by practicing empathy. Leaders who were resistant to remote work would sometimes state that working from home was in some way lazy or a route to slacking off and avoiding interactions. But one of the reasons that people choose to work remotely is that it can allow them to better balance the other areas of their lives in a way that they couldn't when they were commuting to an office.

For example, a remote worker may be in a situation where they're dealing with the integration of all other aspects of their lives into their workday, spanning from the needs of their partners, homes, families, dependents, pets, and sometimes all of them at once. This is, overall, positive but hard. Unlike the predictable daily ebb and flow of an office, none of these life commitments like sticking to a fixed schedule. Children get sick and need to be picked up from school; the dog might need another walk; and the Internet connection will always stop working at the most critical part of that presentation. This is just life. It happens.

Given that remote working means that workers have to be their own office manager, taking care of their surroundings and their environment, managers need to have empathy for this situation. Yes, working from home is a wonderful perk. But it doesn't come for free. Defining flexible working hours, shifting the culture of a team toward asynchronous communication, and being mindful that there are many unseen tasks to take care of go a long way toward building teams where people feel safe, understood, and protected from the anxiety of doing a bad job when everything blows up on them.

In addition, managers need to be mindful of the other hidden costs of remote working and managing a busy household, or even the perils of living alone or in a noisy house-share. Overwork, burnout, the inability to switch off at the end of the day, the fight against FOMO, it's all real. Great managers understand the burdens of life and the strain that can be put on the mental health of their staff that takes place invisibly, out of frame on the video call and out of mind on the chat channel.

Leading with empathy builds trust, increases psychological safety, and makes for a happier, more supported, and more productive team in the long term.

Out of sight, but present in mind. Everyone is trying their best, but not everything is in their control.

Exposing the Connective Tissue

Don't worry, this section doesn't have anything to do with surgery. By the nature of their role, managers have many links to the rest of the department and wider company. This can come through their peer group, their own managers, and their influence and involvement in initiatives outside of the team. One way to think about it is a bit like the human body: each of the main functions, systems, or internal organs could be represented by each team and their manager. However, each team is busy performing their own special function in isolation for most of the time. They don't necessarily know what else is going on elsewhere.

However, the knowledge that managers have forms the *connective tissue* among all of the different functions. For example, if it looks like there may be external dependencies coming up with the team's work, they'll know the right people to talk to in order to work out a path forward. But managers sometimes keep a lot of this information in their heads. It becomes a *pull* relationship between the manager and their team. If someone needs some information, they can get it, but they typically have to ask.

Managers can supercharge their output by externalizing all of the connective tissue that they have in their head. They can turn the interface that the team has with this information into a *push* relationship instead. They can do this in a number of different ways:

- *They can keep an updated index page* that outlines all of the key people in the organization and what they can offer help with.

- *They can frequently broadcast updates* to their team when they find out important information about what's occurring elsewhere in the organization. A weekly summary in chat would be a fine example of doing this.

- *They can have frequent Ask Me Anything sessions* where the team is encouraged to discuss anything that's on their minds about the team, product, and company. If the manager doesn't know the answer, they can find out and report back.

Over time, the team will become less reliant on the manager to find out information for them. They can seek it out themselves. Engineers will understand the connective tissue and talk directly to other engineers, which encourages better collaboration and communication across the department. Managers will feel less like they need to funnel information and can instead focus on making their team even more impactful. This lets their r factor go up, up, and up.

Time to Take It up a Level

We hope that even if you aren't a manager, there are plenty of ideas here that you can share with your boss and encourage discussions within your team. Here's what we covered in this chapter:

- We learned about an *equation* coined by Andy Grove that describes the output of a manager. Given that managing remote teams involves managers adapting and refining their style to suit remote working, we extended the equation to add a *scale factor* based on their ability to do this.

- We explored the many ways in which a manager's output could *diminish* when their team is remote. Examples we explored include too much reliance on synchronous interactions, the difficulty of surfacing information, and a lack of visibility and interactivity.

- We considered how managers could increase their scale factor by making a number of adaptations in how they manage their teams. For example, we considered overcommunication, empathy, flexibility, and measuring output over activity.

In the next chapter, we move into the third part of the book, which is about creating a world-class remote culture. We'll begin by going back to New York City in another time of great change in the technology industry: the dawn of the new millennium.

Part III

Creating a World-Class Remote Culture

Now it's time for us to widen our gaze to consider the bigger picture.

We're going to explore what it means to work for a forward-thinking remote company, and we're going to look at designing a handbook for your department that can serve as your repository of important information. Then we'll explore what it means for companies to be fully remote.

Next we'll consider how remote work can affect your mental health so you can look out for yourself and others. Then we'll explore the challenges of diversity and inclusion in our industry and how remote working may help or hinder efforts to improve it.

Lastly, we'll look to the future and see how remote working could pave the way to equality.

CHAPTER 11

The Remote Working Test

It's the weekend, and you're catching up with your longtime friend and two-time colleague Alex. You've both made the trip downtown to spend some time together hanging out. You're walking through the park after grabbing a coffee. Alex has recently been going through some big changes. She's moved several hours outside of the city into a beautiful house and is now working for a new company remotely.

"So how's that big house treating you?" you ask.

"Ah, the house is great. I'm so glad we live somewhere where we can have a garden. And we all have so much space! Especially the kids. Y'know, I'm already tired of mowing the lawn each weekend, but, yeah. I can't complain. It's lovely."

You smile. "I've gotta admit, I've been jealous. You've done what we've been thinking about doing for years now, but we never summoned up the courage."

Alex takes a sip of coffee. "You should go for it. It's not all panned out brilliantly, though."

"What do you mean?"

"Working remotely hasn't quite worked out how I expected, if I'm honest."

"Oh, no! But I remember you showed me the job you applied for. The company looked great, the product and the culture looked awesome. What gives?"

"Yeah, that job posting made everything sound perfect. The reality is it's not that perfect. I feel really disconnected as a remote worker. Despite it saying they were remote-friendly, most of my colleagues are all in the office. They talk among themselves in person, and I feel like I'm always playing catch-up. Conversations and decisions just happen without me. Email and chat some days is totally dead, but so much is happening I have no idea about."

"I'm so sorry. That sucks," you reply. "But what was all of that stuff they said about giving you the perfect environment to work in?"

"I know, right? I assumed there would be some support in getting my home office sorted, like a desk and a chair, or maybe a monitor. We're tight on cash after moving. But they've offered nothing. It seems you only get that perfect environment if you go into the office. They have food, drinks, games, amazing workstations, and I've got my thrifted $20 desk. It squeaks when I type."

You sigh. "I honestly thought that they'd provide all of that for you based on their website."

"Me too. I've been considering commuting into the office a couple of days a week so I don't feel so left out, but I'd have to sort out childcare and stomach the three-hour round trip on the train. I'm not sure if I can face it. But I'm worried I won't pass my probation because I don't feel like I'm actually doing any useful work."

You wipe off a drip from the side of your coffee cup. "Bah, that sucks. How could you have known?"

We've all been there. Teetering on the fence. You know how it goes. You might be comfortable in your current job, but there are more bad days than there are good days. Maybe you're unsure whether you changed or the role changed, or whether you're just getting tired of working on the same old problems year after year. You find yourself looking at job advertisements just a little more than you usually would. You may have even replied to that message from that recruiter on LinkedIn.

However, even though you're tempted, we all know that changing jobs is incredibly stressful. Sure, your current job might be a little frustrating from time to time, but at least you're safe there and you know your colleagues well. They trust you, and you trust them. And sure, you could probably get paid more or have a more flexible working environment at that cool company you read a news article about, but what's the likelihood of even getting an interview there? You haven't updated your resume in years. And even if you did get an interview, what's the likelihood that it's going to consist of running a gauntlet of impossible and unrealistic programming problems that will make you feel completely stupid, even though you'd never be exposed to those kinds of problems at work? Might as well just stay put.

The fear of taking risks sometimes makes us stay in suboptimal employment situations for too long. After all, when you find yourself browsing through job postings, don't they all begin to sound the same? You trawl through pages of listings from companies that all say that they're solving important problems, have inclusive cultures, pay competitively, and use cutting-edge technology. Is it really true that everywhere else, aside from your current job, is wonderful, or are they all just hiding their warts?

Fundamentally, a job advertisement is exactly that, an advertisement. It's there to attract candidates to the interview pipeline. This means that it might not always reveal all of the gnarly parts of working for a particular company, such as a looming technical debt problem or bad, angry management. Part of the challenge of going through interviews as a candidate is to try to uncover as many of these bad smells as possible as you go so you can ensure that you're making the best decision you can if you decide to accept the offer. After all, if your current role is OK but perhaps a bit boring, it's still a better option than working somewhere that's going to work you to the bone.

For larger companies, it's sometimes possible to do a little research before deciding to apply. Websites such as Glassdoor enable workers to leave anonymized reviews about where they work, which can expose both the good and the bad aspects of working for a particular company. However, for start-ups and other small companies, it can be difficult to gain any insight into what it's like to work there. It's a gamble.

Remote workers can find themselves with an additional challenge: What is it really like to work for a particular company while being remote? As you've seen in this book so far, a world-class, remote-working culture is the result of continual decisions, practices, and habits that may not be visible to the outside world. This makes it challenging for a remote candidate to understand whether they're going to have a good experience. So could this be easier? Could there be a way for companies to publish a scorecard that encapsulates whether they're a good organization to work for remotely? You know what? We think so. It also turns out that this isn't an entirely new problem. It's a new take on something that has existed for some time in a slightly different domain.

Here's what we cover in this chapter:

- We look at the Joel Test, which is a twelve-point scorecard to see whether a software team is good to work for. We'll see where it came from, how it's used, and what you can learn from it.

- We come up with our own Remote Working Test, which is our own twelve-point scorecard to see whether a company is good to work for remotely. We'll dig in to each of the points and explore what they mean, and then you'll see how your own workplace currently scores against it.

- We examine how to be an agent of change. You'll see what can be tackled autonomously and locally within your own team and which changes need support from managers or the executive team.

So let's get started. We're heading to Manhattan at the turn of the millennium. Here we go.

The Joel Test

It's the year 2000. For the previous five years, significant growth in the use of the Internet has fueled investment and speculation in Internet-based companies.

This period, called the dot-com bubble,[1] saw the Nasdaq Composite index rise around 400 percent as investors clamored to invest in any dot-com company, often at any valuation, overlooking traditional metrics of company health such as profitability, or even revenue. As Alan Greenspan, chairman of the Federal Reserve, described it, it was a time of "irrational exuberance."

Venture capital was easy to raise and it flowed freely into plentiful, hyped dot-coms. Investment banks added to the speculation by encouraging investment in technology so that they could profit from hundreds of initial public offerings (IPOs) that were happening that year.

But as the months unfolded, there were concerns that the market was at a tipping point. Investors began to back away from tech companies that were spending too much capital on marketing and too little on securing revenue. Some even hedged against their success. By November, most Internet stocks had fallen in value by 75 percent, wiping out $1.755 trillion in market capitalization. Pets.com went out of business just nine months after a successful IPO. Layoffs and closures heavily affected the technology industry as capital dried up. Many developers found themselves out of a job.

Around the time of the dot-com bubble bursting, Joel Spolsky and Michael Pryor founded Fog Creek Software, backed by their own savings.[2] Despite beginning as a consulting company, work was becoming harder to secure. The market conditions meant that many companies were cutting ties with

---

1. https://en.wikipedia.org/wiki/Dot-com_bubble
2. http://www.foundersatwork.com/joel-spolsky.html

third parties to stop hemorrhaging costs. As such, Fog Creek pivoted into a product company making its own software and gained notoriety through the Joel on Software blog.

One seminal post introduced the Joel Test, which was a response to overly complicated ways of measuring the productivity of software teams. Instead, the Joel Test was written as—in the words of the author—a "highly irresponsible, sloppy test" to rate the quality of teams that only took a few minutes to answer. The idea was that if a team can answer each question with a yes, they're likely a productive team. Questions answered with a no suggest improvements should be made.

The Joel Test questions are as follows:

1. Do you use source control?
2. Can you make a build in one step?
3. Do you make daily builds?
4. Do you have a bug database?
5. Do you fix bugs before writing new code?
6. Do you have an up-to-date schedule?
7. Do you have a spec?
8. Do programmers have quiet working conditions?
9. Do you use the best tools money can buy?
10. Do you have testers?
11. Do new candidates write code during their interview?
12. Do you do hallway usability testing?[3]

Each question is answered with a quick yes or no, and each question is also sufficiently generic. For example, it doesn't matter exactly which source control you're using; it just matters that you're using it. Although the test may have aged since it was first published, there's consensus that it still remains relevant today.[4]

In 2008, Spolsky cofounded Stack Overflow, a question-and-answer community for developers to find help from others with their programming questions. As the website gained popularity, it launched a successful jobs board. A unique feature was that it allowed the companies that were listing their job openings to score themselves on the Joel Test as part of the listing. This was a neat way of helping candidates understand if they would likely be joining a high-quality software team.

---

3. https://en.wikipedia.org/wiki/Usability_testing#Hallway_testing
4. https://rknuus.github.io/blog/2020/02/22/yet-another-joel-test

So given that it's also hard to understand from a job listing whether a company has a high-quality remote culture, wouldn't it be neat if there was a similar twelve-point test for their approach to supporting remote work?

You're right. It would be great, and we think so too. So let's come up with our own test.

Your Turn: The Joel Test

Before we jump into defining our own Remote Working Test, take some time to think about the Joel Test and how it applies to your own company. A score of twelve is perfect. Anything less indicates that there are some potential issues to think about:

- Go through the Joel Test and rate your own organization against the twelve questions.

- Which areas do you think that your company needs to improve upon and why?

- Are these areas where you need to lobby for change, or could you make those changes locally within your own team?

- Are there any parts of the Joel Test that you feel are out of date? What would be a more modern substitution for those questions?

Twelve Questions about Remote Working

With the Joel Test in mind, let's create our own version. It will consist of twelve questions that can be answered quickly with a yes or no and will form a scorecard for the quality of the remote-working experience at a given company. And although we'll win no prizes for originality, let's call it the Remote Working Test.

There are many ways that we can use this Remote Working Test:

- We can *score our own companies* against it to see which areas we do well in and which we need to improve upon and why.

- We can *attach our results from the test to our job advertisements* to publicly show our commitment to providing a great remote-working experience, thus increasing transparency at our companies.

- We can *ask pointed questions* when we are interviewing for new remote jobs to find out what the culture is really like.

Taking into account everything that we've learned in the book so far, we can put together the twelve questions that form the test:

1. Do you treat everyone as remote?
2. Do you provide a remote work-space setup?
3. Do you spend money equally on in-office and remote staff?
4. Do you optimize for asynchronous communication?
5. Do you create artifacts from synchronous interactions?
6. Do you measure staff by their impact?
7. Do you allow staff to choose flexible hours?
8. Are the members of the executive team remote workers?
9. Do you use the best collaborative tools that money can buy?
10. Do you hire staff anywhere in the world?
11. Do you support families as well as employees?
12. Do you give back to an employee's local community?

So, without further ado, let's explore each of these questions in more detail.

Do You Treat Everyone as Remote?

The first question is something we covered in detail in Chapter 3, Treat Everyone as Remote, on page 33. Does the company treat everybody as a remote worker regardless of whether they're working in an office, in a meeting room, in a shared work space, or at home? Does this pervade through the culture? Given that this is a mindset that will form a consistent thread through countless habits in the organization, it's important that this question is the first one.

The worst situation for a new remote worker is that they feel like a second-class citizen from the day that they join the company. Without this mindset, remote workers can feel like they're out of sight and out of mind, with discussions and decisions within their team taking place without them being present and with limited access to others in the company. Even synchronous communication can be a pain. Remote workers can have poor experiences in meetings where others are all physically present in a meeting room, with remote participants struggling to properly see or hear their colleagues on a webcam that's positioned faraway across the meeting room.

As we previously learned, treating everyone as remote can't just be an intention. It needs to be backed up with action. One would hope that if a company answered this question with a yes, the interview process would quickly begin to reveal that this is the case. Each interviewer would have a separate connection, webcam, and microphone in the video call. Screen-sharing and collaborative software would be the norm for communication rather than pointing webcams at a whiteboard. People could ask questions about how meetings and socials are organized in a way that everyone is welcome regardless of their location.

Whether everyone is treated as remote is a simple but powerful question. It sets the scene for the remote culture of the company from the start.

Do You Provide a Remote Work-Space Setup?

When employees start a new job in a physical office, they aren't expected to purchase their desk, chair, and computer equipment. That expectation should be the same for those who are working remotely.

We understand that ergonomics are important to ensure that we're looking after our bodies while we're spending a significant portion of our days sitting at desks and using computers. This means using the right equipment. However, the downside is that good-quality office equipment is expensive if you're the one who needs to purchase it rather than your employer. Good chairs can be hundreds, if not thousands, of dollars.

Companies that are invested in their remote workers should offer to purchase home-office equipment for them. It should get shipped to their door. Typically, this will include a computer, a desk, a chair, a monitor, and any peripherals that are required for them to get their work done. This also includes any equipment for individuals with disabilities or special requirements.

Not only does this question highlight whether a company understands the importance of ergonomics and their intent to give remote workers the same treatment as those who are located in offices, it shows that they trust them. For a reasonably sized company, the sum of money invested in buying this equipment for an employee is just a rounding error on the company budget. Being generous with a home setup—perhaps by going in at the higher end when it comes to equipment choice—makes employees feel great when all of the packages get delivered and they get a setup that's way beyond anything that they would likely buy for themselves. Why not even make it a policy that the staff can keep all of the equipment other than the computer if they leave the company? It's generous and a great perk, and it saves the logistics of returning and redistributing large items.

Do You Spend Money Equally on In-Office and Remote Staff?

Employees who work in offices may not think that much money is being spent on them, but often when it all gets added up, it's a reasonable amount. Free tea and coffee, snacks, occasional team lunches, drinks, and so on can sometimes total many hundreds of dollars per year per employee. That's not to mention that employees won't be paying the rent, electricity, or Internet bills for the office for the time that they're working in it.

Remote workers often have to foot these costs for themselves. They might notice that their grocery bills are higher than usual because they're now buying all of the items that they used to get provided to them for free. They may also be missing out on team lunches and drinks that are expensed by the department. Their electricity bills may be higher, and they may need to upgrade their broadband to the fastest package.

So the question is, Does a company realize this and then spend equally on staff who are remote? Perhaps when a team goes out for lunch at the end of the quarter, the remote staff gets the opportunity to expense takeout for themselves. Perhaps workers could be offered a monthly stipend for the same kinds of supplies that the office would provide for free, such as tea, coffee, and snacks. Maybe there could even be an Internet allowance to help staff get the best possible broadband connection. There's a lot of scope here for companies to tangibly help out their remote workers in small but impactful ways that don't put a huge dent in the budget. It's both symbolic and genuinely useful, especially for younger or less-experienced staff who are earning less money than their senior colleagues.

Do You Optimize for Asynchronous Communication?

We covered the topic of asynchronous communication in detail in Chapter 4, The Spectrum of Synchronousness, on page 53, and we noted how important it is for companies to use it to support remote workers. This question gives companies the chance to reflect on how they communicate in general.

Is it the case that information only exists in the heads of staff and then is transferred between them in synchronous communication, or is it well written and documented and easy to find? If a team member has a tricky time zone difference and only overlaps with their colleagues for a few hours each day, is the presence of good documentation able to keep them unblocked and productive? Or are they stuck as soon as everyone else goes offline?

Are companywide broadcasts recorded or written so that everyone has equal access to the content? Is all critical information recorded somewhere centrally, such as in a searchable, well-organized digital employee handbook? We'll look into producing one of these in more detail in Chapter 12, Creating a Handbook, on page 237.

As we learned previously, optimizing for asynchronous communication not only requires a change of mindset and habits, it requires real action to continually create the required artifacts that allow people to discover information, find answers to their questions, and to understand how to do their work.

Candidates who are interviewing should ask about whether important communication is written and archived, whether the codebases and contribution guidelines are well documented, and what proportion of time their prospective team spends in synchronous meetings every week.

Do You Create Artifacts from Synchronous Interactions?

There's always going to be some amount of communication that needs to happen synchronously. Urgent, complex, confusing, or nuanced matters are sometimes better resolved by just getting together and talking about them. Additionally, there's always some number of team meetings, whether it be scrum ceremonies, planning, design sprints, and so on.

The important aspect is that teams create sufficient artifacts from their synchronous interactions so that anyone can catch up at their own speed at a later date. Artifacts can range from video recordings of the meetings themselves to written summaries or design documents that outline the approaches that were discussed.

A continual flow of artifacts from synchronous interactions build up the archive of information and documentation that also serves as the answer to the previous question. It's a virtuous cycle. Isn't that neat?

Do You Measure Staff by Their Impact?

As we learned in Chapter 10, Managing Teams, on page 199, it's important that the performance of staff is measured by their impact in their roles rather than the number of hours that they spend working. This paves the way for flexible working hours. We saw how in the physical office, the worst of this behavior can manifest in staff waiting for their bosses to leave, and they in turn are waiting for their own bosses to leave. In the remote world, this can manifest in staff who feel unable to step away from their computers because they're afraid if they're not able to immediately answer messages, they'll be seen as slacking off. FOMO is real.

Companies that measure their staff by their impact have better ways of understanding performance than with time-tracking software that's installed in their computers. Instead, they have a culture that consists of clear goals for their teams to work on, allowing them to achieve autonomy, mastery, and purpose. They also value staff who are good team players and mentors—those who not only produce work themselves but also amplify the work of others around them.

The key point is that none of this has anything to do with clocking exactly eight hours of work every day. It has to do with clear progress, efficient use of time, good prioritization, and a focus on the quality of the hours rather than the quantity. Measuring staff by impact lets them choose exactly how to spend time, which means that fitting in a busy home life is more possible, working across different time zones is easier, and having a work-life balance that's beneficial to their mental health is attainable.

Do You Allow Staff to Choose Flexible Hours?

Working remotely, often from home, means that there are plenty of other interruptions during the day. School runs, childcare, and looking after dependents can mean that juggling both work and life requires flexibility in the hours of the day in which staff choose to be sitting at the computer.

This can also come down to personal preference. Some workers know that they're extremely productive in the morning and given the choice would start early and finish early. Some are night owls who get into their stride in the afternoon and evening. If a company is able to let workers choose the hours of the day that suit them best for doing their work, it gives them more flexibility in their home lives and allow them to capitalize on when they feel productive. It also is a clear demonstration of the amount of trust that they have in their staff to know how and when to work best.

Supporting flexible work for staff in the same time zone is a localized version of the same issues that are faced when workers are globally distributed in different geographies. It requires good documentation, asynchronous communication, and the ability for teams to organize core hours in which they know people are contactable in order to get synchronous collaborative work done.

Flexible hours, including part-time hours, when implemented correctly can be a boon to new parents. This concept can be extended to include compressed hours, which is where they work the agreed hours over fewer but longer days. Or job sharing is where a job designed for one person is shared by more than one part-time worker. Assuming that a company is measuring its workers by their impact, all of these arrangements should be possible.

Are the Members of the Executive Team Remote Workers?

Culture is set from the top down. If the members of the executive team at the company—that is, the CEO and their direct reports such as the CTO—are remote workers, or at least spend a meaningful portion of their time remote, it's likely that they'll experience first-hand the challenges that all remote workers will face in the company.

They, too, will feel the challenge of having to coordinate significant initiatives and projects over different time zones and geographies. They'll have to address the company via video or by writing. They won't be able to just get everyone in a room when there's something urgent to discuss. They'll have to use the same tools as everyone else and face the pain if they don't. This creates cultural change.

As the company leaders and budget holders, if they're the ones who see the pressing need for software that allows remote collaboration, they'll purchase it for everyone, because they can. If they see that their recorded video messages have poor audio and video quality because of the built-in hardware in their laptops, they'll likely make it easy for everyone in the company to expense a good-quality webcam and microphone. If it's hard to find the information that they need, it's likely they'll spearhead initiatives to centralize documentation and make it easily discoverable.

The best way to gain sympathy and understanding for others is to see the world from their point of view. In the technology industry, we have been taking this approach in UX design and research for many years by improving the technology that we deliver to our users based on what we learn while observing them using it. If the leaders of a company are able to understand first-hand what it's like to be a remote worker, it's likely that the experience will improve for every member of the staff as well.

Do You Use the Best Collaborative Tools That Money Can Buy?

This point is almost identical to the one in the Joel Test. There's a whole host of fantastic collaborative software out there, but often it isn't free. This is especially true when those software licenses are for businesses rather than individuals.

At the time of writing, the best-in-class software for IDEs, collaborative drawing, document editing, spreadsheets, and videoconferencing all cost money. Many use subscription-based models that charge per number of users. This can get expensive quickly. However, if a company holds to this principle and realizes that this is one of those areas that you don't skimp on, it can ensure that all staff have access to the best collaborative tools that money can buy. This makes certain that it has a workforce that has the best chance of being happy, efficient, and productive. It's a competitive advantage.

Any underspending in this area, unless the company is in a financial crisis, shows a lack of understanding of how countless, tiny frictions can build slowly but surely, until staff become so frustrated that they'd rather just give up and work elsewhere. When being forced to use a second-rate tool, a member of the staff may wonder why their daily pain is worth the company saving $10 a month on its license. Imagine how that feels if the company is also announcing that it's opening a new flagship office where each of the designer chairs in the lobby costs several thousand dollars. It's all about relative priorities.

Do You Hire Staff Anywhere in the World?

This is a bit of a trick because the answer will often have more embedded nuance than a simple yes or no. However, it gives companies the ability to highlight a few key things:

- Whether they *hold any biases for hiring in any particular location*

- Whether they're willing to *consider hiring a member of staff who isn't in one of their current locations*

- Whether they're able to *further expand on how they'll achieve hiring in other locations* and what policies or processes decide this

Why is this so nuanced? First, this question can highlight the extent of a company's appetite for supporting remote work. Does remote work to a company mean a hybrid setup where staff can work from home but are expected to be within a reasonable distance of the office in case they need to come in? Or does it mean that they can be anywhere, in any time zone, working mostly asynchronously? There's a big difference in setup and culture between the two scenarios, from how IT support works to how communication takes place.

Second, if an exceptionally talented member of the staff wanted to work for the company from a country that they're currently not located in, what would they do? Typically, companies employ staff by having them work for a given legal entity in the country that they're in. For example, staff based in the United States would be employed via the company's U.S. legal entity, and Spanish staff would be employed via the legal entity that's set up in Spain. This means that staff can be easily added to payroll in existing locations, but staff in new locations may need to be hired initially as contractors while the company goes through the process of setting up a legal entity in their country. Depending on the country, setting up legal entities can be arduous, requiring plenty of form filling, legal advice, and wet-ink signatures.

As you can see, all of this requires significant investment from human resources, and the desire to do this will form a core part of the remote culture of the company. The alternative answer to this question is no, and that's also fine. But it gets expectations straight about what remote work really means if an applicant is applying and also provides a North Star for companies to move toward if they so wish.

Do You Support Families as Well as Employees?

When people work in an office, they're among a tribe of other workers who share that space with them. An office manager may keep the space running efficiently and the tea and coffee flowing, and the maintenance staff keep the hallways, bathrooms, and lobby clean, safe, and tidy.

And few remote workers are entirely unsupported. They're often at home with a partner, children or other dependents, and pets. This is the primary support network that surrounds our remote colleagues. Therefore, a company that's mindful of the hidden support network should elevate it by offering additional support for those in the network as well. This can be in the form of more traditional benefits, such as offering a generous life-insurance policy or whole-family healthcare, vision, and dental plans.

However, it can also extend to other benefits such as widening the scope of work-from-home stipends for household expenses or childcare. Perhaps companies could allow employees to expense health and well-being activities that their families can also use to their advantage. This could include gym memberships, yoga classes, or a set of dumbbells or running shoes.

The key factor here is that the company realizes that few people truly work alone. There is often an invisible supporting cast that could also do with some additional reinforcement from time to time.

Do You Give Back to an Employee's Local Community?

Companies may give to charity, perhaps by donating a portion of their profits every year. Also, they may donate their time, such as staff volunteering at a local nonprofit like a food bank or soup kitchen. In the nonremote world, these activities would typically happen near the office location.

Remote working isn't a reason to stop doing these things. In fact, there's a great opportunity for a company to really give back to the communities in which their remote workers live. For example, all employees could identify charities in their local area that they know make a real difference in their community. The company's charitable donations could then be divided among the charities that have been chosen. Companies could also give regular, paid volunteer leave for their staff to donate their time as well as their money.

Allowing staff to choose local charities is important because every local community is different and facing different challenges. Employees who live by the coast in the United Kingdom may want to donate their money or time to the Royal National Lifeboat Institution because it's sustained by donations and unpaid volunteers. Conversely, another employee who lives in a city may choose a local children's hospital based on their own experience of visiting it with their sick child. Just imagine how many small communities worldwide could benefit.

Your Turn: Score Yourself

Now that we've outlined the twelve questions that form the Remote Working Test, it's time to score your own company against each of them:

- Go through and answer yes or no to each of the questions in regard to what you observe at your own company.

- Ask a colleague to do the same. Do their answers line up with yours?

- For each answer no, think about what would need to change within the company for it to be a yes. We'll consider how you can begin to lobby for change in the next section.

Making Changes in Your Company

Now that we've defined the Remote Working Test and you've considered how your own workplace scores against it, the natural next step is to think about whether there's an opportunity to bring about change. While some of the actions needed to meet some of the criteria do require a shift in culture and decisions to be made at the higher echelons of a company, the good news is that there's a lot that can change from the bottom up.

Let's see how each of the questions in the test can be categorized by what sort of buy-in and approval is required to enact change. We use three different categories for the types of action required:

- *Grassroots.* These are changes that often require no formal approval and can immediately be implemented by individuals, such as yourself. Just go for it!

- *Local managers.* Some changes require formal approval, either because they require budget or because they may result in a change in process compared to other teams.

- *Companywide change.* These changes require decisions made by the company leadership, either because they involve spending larger amounts of money, require legal considerations, or have a deep link to how the company is being run, such as where employees should be located.

So with that in mind, here are the questions broken down by the type of action required and relative difficulty.

Question	Action	Difficulty	Comments
Do you treat everyone as remote?	Grassroots	Easy	This requires a mindset shift in individuals and teams.
Do you optimize for asynchronous interactions?	Grassroots	Medium	This may require individuals and teams to rethink how they collaborate.
Do you create artifacts from synchronous interactions?	Grassroots	Medium	This may require new habits to be enforced through repetition.
Is the executive team remote?	Grassroots	Hard	Difficulty depends on the individuals, their openness, and whether they're contactable and approachable.
Do you measure staff by their impact?	Local managers	Depends	If managers have autonomy in how they do performance reviews, this is easy. Otherwise, it could require greater cultural change.
Do you provide a remote work-space setup?	Local managers	Medium	If managers have discretionary budgets, they can contribute toward home setups themselves. However, this can cause political issues with other teams.
Do you allow staff to choose flexible hours?	Local managers	Medium	Assuming there's no strict companywide policy or tracking of hours, this can be a simple change.
Do you use the best tools that money can buy?	Local managers	Medium	This depends on how software procurement and budgets are handled. It's easier to enact in smaller companies.
Do you spend equally on in-office and remote staff?	Companywide change	Easy	Assuming there's buy-in from the executives, this is a straightforward change. This may require scaling back on spending on office perks to find budget.
Do you hire staff anywhere in the world?	Companywide change	Hard	This requires a knowledgeable, forward-thinking, and well-resourced human resources department. It also requires executives to oversee creation of legal entities in new countries. It can be phased in by hiring in all existing locations rather than a select few.
Do you support families as well as employees?	Companywide change	Medium	This may require significant additional budget to extend healthcare and insurance to whole families.
Do you give back to employees' local communities?	Companywide change	Medium	This is easier if charitable giving is already a part of company culture.

So the positive news is that it's possible that two-thirds of the questions that form the Remote Working Test can start with action that takes place in your team. This is because they either only require grassroots action that you can enact yourself, or they simply require the buy-in of the rest of the team and need some form of local managerial approval. Everything that you need to start making these changes has been covered in the book so far. You already know what to do, so you can start making a tangible improvement to the work lives of current and future remote workers right now. How awesome is that?

For those that require companywide change, you may have different levels of success, depending on the openness, transparency, and progressiveness of your company leaders. Beginning to make some of these changes happen could be as easy as sending one of the executives an email, if you work for a transparent, small company with a relatively flat hierarchy. Change may be much harder for those who work for companies that are either conservative or large in size. But perhaps there are middle managers such as directors and vice presidents you know who could move some of these wider initiatives forward and help you work on lobbying the higher-ups. All change is possible with the right amount of time, energy, and connectivity to key people. You just have to keep working on it and building consensus and momentum with your colleagues.

On the other hand, if after consideration your company looks like it's unlikely to ever change at all, maybe it's time to look for a different company to work for. And the neat thing is, you now know all of the right questions to ask when you're interviewing to ensure that it's exactly the right place for you. Good luck.

Something to Guide Us

There you have it. The Remote Working Test is there to guide you in your journey of helping companies transform their approach to remote working, making it better, fairer, and more effective. We hope that it assists you in creating change for yourself, your team, and your company. We also hope that it guides you as an assessment tool if you're deciding to look for a new role. And who knows, maybe one day it'll become a standard part of remote-job listings.

Here's what we covered in this chapter:

- We explored the Joel Test, twelve questions that can roughly and quickly assess the quality of a software team.

- We defined the Remote Working Test, which is our own twelve-point scorecard to assess the quality of a company's remote-working culture.

- We categorized each question in the test by considering whether change could be enacted via grassroots action or whether it requires wider company consensus.

On the subject of guidance: the next chapter is going to be all about creating an artifact to help you find your way around your company, regardless of your role, experience, or location. Come along with us to find out how a handbook could be the one piece of documentation that can unite all employees.

It's dangerous to go alone! Take this.

    → *Unnamed Hermit from The Legend of Zelda*

CHAPTER 12

Creating a Handbook

It's coming up to 6 p.m., and after a slow start to the morning, you're having an incredibly productive afternoon. There have been minimal interruptions, and you've been enjoying that wondrous state of flow for several hours. It feels like you've managed to construct the entire codebase in your head, and you're mentally jumping around the structure of it, adding tests and code, building out the cathedral walls as you go.

Your partner is finishing work and texts you to say they're going to be checking in on their parents this evening before they come home. They also say they'll grab takeout for dinner. This is great news. After replying, you put your phone to one side and rejoice. You have another hour and a half of pure uninterrupted coding bliss. You crank up the music and put your fingers back on the keyboard. It's time to build and test the fix you've been working on.

You run the build script, and the program compiles and the binaries are created. The tests pass, and it's looking good locally. You run the program, and it does exactly what it should be doing. Awesome. You open a pull request and wait for the build to complete on the server, except it doesn't complete. After several minutes, it bombs out with an error.

```
Permission denied: user lacks group access.
```

OK, that's strange. But then again, you haven't submitted any code in this repository before. Hmm. This is frustrating because you need this fix deployed so that your team can build on top of it. After all, you've already lost several days to fixing this bug so you could get on with what your sprint commitments were in the first place. You pause and think about how you can get unblocked. Right, so this codebase is probably owned by one of the other teams, and they probably have a permission group set up about who can submit pull requests. Seems reasonable. It's time to find out who to ask about this problem.

You start in the usual places. You check to see what it says in the README file. It actually says very little. Huh. OK, next you check the usernames of the repository owners. That doesn't shed any light on the situation either. dscode and froggo aren't exactly names that you can look up in the company email address book, are they? Erm, what could be the name of the team that maintains it? This is the analysis pipeline, so is there an analysis team? You open your chat client and scroll through the channels, searching for *analysis,* but find nothing. You don't know what else to do at this point, so you decide to post in the engineering department channel.

```
[18:15] you: does anyone know who owns the analysis repository?
[18:15] you: i'm having some build issues
```

You sit there for ten minutes. Silence. Most of the East Coast has already stopped working for the day, and Europe is asleep. You find yourself getting frustrated. Why is it so hard to find such basic information? You open your email, searching for the name of the repository. Nothing. You search through the chat history for the same word and also for some names of some of the classes. No dice. And you still have no idea who froggo actually is.

As a last gasp effort, you scroll through the entire list of employees to see if any of them have the same profile picture as the mysterious froggo. Nada.

You check the clock, and you've wasted thirty minutes on this wild frog chase. You close the pull request and resubmit it to see if the age-old guidance of turning it off and on again might solve the problem. You watch the build progressing.

```
Permission denied: user lacks group access.
```

You sigh. You shut your laptop. So much for that flow you had.

Imagine for a second that you're on vacation and you've touched down at the airport in a new city. And yes, your sunglasses look cool. Getting off the airplane, you follow the signs to customs and then onward to the baggage claim. You grab your suitcase and head for the taxi stand, and you're in luck. There's no queue. You jump in the back of the cab and look at your itinerary. You look at the highlighted map that's contained within it.

"Hotel 1882?"

The taxi driver nods and you're on your way. About ten minutes later, you're walking up to the hotel lobby. The desk is straight ahead. You get your room key and check the map on the wall. Fourth floor. You catch the elevator and turn left, and there you are. One swipe of the room key and you're in.

There's a pamphlet standing upright next to the television. You flick through to find the part that's written in English. Breakfast starts at 7 a.m. on the first floor. There's a twenty-four-hour gym on the floor above. The room lights are controlled from the panel next to the bed, and the minibar is excruciatingly expensive. Seems like a normal hotel experience.

When things work how you expect, or when there's a clear guide to follow, even tricky situations can be made to seem straightforward. Good documentation can cut through complexity. On this short, imaginary vacation, you navigated through a city that you'd never visited before by following signs and waypoints and by consulting a number of different maps and models. It's actually quite impressive. You routed through the airport, navigated a hotel, and then quickly worked out how everything functioned in your room, and you'd never been to any of these places before. You were able to do so because you followed particular norms, but most importantly because there were a number of useful guides that were there to help you.

Maps and guides can come in all forms, and they can even be conceptually nested inside of each other, such as a guide to your room inside a hotel inside a city inside a country. They can turn a complex space into a simpler, more abstract one, such as a map of an airport or a subway system. Guides can transform the bewilderment of a first-time visitor into the excitement of a confident new explorer.

So this chapter is all about guides. It's about the best guide that any employee could have for their company. We're going to look at handbooks: the definitive reference manuals for new and existing employees alike.

Here's what we're going to cover:

- We're going to *dive into the concept of the handbook* by examining a real-world example: GitLab's handbook, a central repository for how those who work there run their company. We'll see why it exists, what it contains, and why it's available publicly to the entire world. Yes, that includes us.

- Then it's time to *create our own handbook*. We'll start small by designing a handbook for your team. We'll think about what information should be in it for both team members and other people who interact with your team.

- We *consider what life would be like if the whole company had a handbook*. We'll think about what it would mean for discoverability, transparency, and democratization of data and how that relates to soft power.

Let's get going.

The GitLab Handbook

Before we begin thinking about how to put together a handbook for ourselves, let's get some inspiration from a company that has made its own handbook the central pillar of how it operates. Not only is it written and updated extensively by everyone who works there—including the founder and executive team—at the time of writing, it's a staggering 13,804 pages of text, increasing every year. And it's all available on the Internet. Yep, pretty much all of the company's workings are completely transparent. How's that for a radical idea?

Let's get some background on the company first. GitLab provides a DevOps platform that enables product, development, security, and operations teams to work together concurrently.[1] It's delivered via a software-as-a-service model. You subscribe and access the product via your web browser. Aside from the quality of the product itself, one of the reasons that the company became widely known is that it was an early mover in its approach to supporting a distributed workforce. The company is fully remote.[2] It has no headquarters or offices and no predetermined work hours. Employees work predominantly asynchronously and only meet once per year at an informal event that enables them to get to know each other better face to face.

The strategy that forms the core of how this fully remote company keeps its workers informed and connected with each other is the use of its handbook.[3] It exhaustively documents everything from the formal organization structure and the current company vision, mission, goals, and culture to the minute details of how to raise a ticket to the finance department. It's all there, and everyone, regardless of where they work in the company, is expected to keep it up to date as a core responsibility of their job.

Changes to the handbook are suggested and merged via the software that the company produces. In fact, one of the first onboarding exercises for new members of the staff is to add themselves to the staff page, which involves forking it, editing it, and raising a merge request for the maintainer of that page to approve. It's a great example of eating your own dog food.

The handbook was initially created during the early stages of the company. The first ten employees wanted to make information sharing easier so that important information could be immediately discoverable for new employees

---

1. https://about.gitlab.com/
2. https://about.gitlab.com/company/culture/all-remote/guide/
3. https://about.gitlab.com/handbook/

when they joined the company. This exercise in efficiency soon became core to their culture.

GitLab lists the advantages of its public-facing handbook as follows:

- Reading is much faster than listening.

- Reading is asynchronous, so you don't have to interrupt someone or wait for them to become available.

- Talent acquisition is easier if people can see what the company stands for and how it operates.

- Retention is better if people know what they're getting into before they join.

- Onboarding is easier if you can find all relevant information spelled out.

- Teamwork is easier if you can read how other parts of the company work.

- Discussing changes is easier if you can read what the current process is.

- Communicating change is easier if you can just point to the diff.

- Everyone can contribute to it by proposing a change via a merge request.

While it's possible that some might think that a handbook could be overly rigid or prescriptive in how people get their work done, GitLab argues that writing down its processes and information has the effect of empowering everyone to propose changes and to continually improve how the company works. At the time of writing, the handbook receives tens of modifications every single day.

Your Turn: Browse the GitLab Handbook

Before we begin working out how to define your own handbook, go and visit the GitLab handbook and spend some time browsing around:

- What do you notice about the way that the handbook is structured? What does this layout mirror in terms of how the company is organized?

- See if you can find out what the top priorities are for the company this quarter.

- See if you can find out the technology stack that the company is using to develop its software.

- Who is the maintainer of the handbook? Who contributes to it the most? How many of the staff members contribute in total?

- What are your thoughts on it being public? Would you feel more or less likely to apply for a job at a company that operates in this way?

Creating a Handbook for Your Team

As we see with GitLab, there are a multitude of benefits to investing the effort into creating and maintaining a handbook, most notably that it democratizes information for remote workers. Important information is available for anyone at any time, regardless of whether you have direct access to your colleagues or not. Also, cultural benefits can be gained from interfacing with the wider world because hosting a handbook publicly increases the visibility of a company, which in turn assists in attracting new remote talent.

Therefore, it seems like a good idea for your company to have a handbook. However, unless you're the CEO, or unless you're in a similar situation to GitLab when it started—that is, when it was a small startup—you may have difficulties.

This is because creating a handbook for your whole company is no small feat. Changing the culture to make your handbook a central pillar of how your company does things might be a task that's too big for you to undertake alone. Yet there's still reason to be hopeful.

Earlier you saw how a map of a city could be used to find areas that would in turn have their own separate maps to guide you further. Within those local areas there may be buildings like a hotel, which also has its own localized guide.

You have an area of your company that you work in, such as your team, that you already know a lot about and you have a reasonable amount of influence in. You can begin mapping the metaphorical hotel, even if the wider city hasn't been mapped out yet.

What you can do is focus on creating a handbook for your team in collaboration with your teammates. The handbook concept can dramatically improve access to information for remote workers, assist in onboarding new staff regardless of where they are in the world, and increase the visibility and discoverability of everything your team is doing. You can do this without needing permission and with little to no dependencies on anyone else in the company.

What's more is that if you create something genuinely useful, there's a high likelihood that once you've broken ground, others will follow. When people see excellence, they're often inspired to try and do the same themselves. You might begin to find that the city starts mapping itself around you.

Certainly, as we saw previously, the GitLab handbook is gigantic and is the result of a decade of work. However, even a few pages of a handbook could help remote workers find their way around while their colleagues in other time zones are asleep. Your team having a single page with important information is a significant help for others you work with. And from there, each team in the department having its own page doesn't seem so far away. You can start small and work up to something much bigger.

Before we get into writing the handbook, you'll need to host it somewhere. Let's consider which software to use.

Choosing Software

There's an anecdote that when software engineers get the urge to write a blog post because they have some insight to share with the world, they'll do the following.

Initially, they'll spend a whole week researching the blogging framework, setting up the code repository, and picking a domain name. Then they'll build and tweak the site, get the automated deploy process working, and publish a placeholder "Hello, world!" post. Then, by the time they've done all that, they've lost the enthusiasm to write the article they had the idea about in the first place.

If this sounds like you, don't worry; we've all been there. Sometimes focusing too much on engineering the setup can dampen the enthusiasm for getting the job done. You need to be mindful of this with your handbook so that it's primarily an exercise in creating a useful reference for remote workers rather than an exercise in building the perfect documentation system. Let's break this down into doable steps, starting with choosing the software that you're going to use.

There are a number of factors you'll have to consider. Let's go through them:

- *Cost.* If you pick a free tool, or decide to use documentation functionality that's already available through existing software that your company uses, you can get going right away. If, on the other hand, you're enamored by a paid tool that seems perfect for what you want, there's the hurdle of securing budget and getting sign-off to buy it.

- *Features.* The simplest documentation can be plain text. Fully featured documentation software can have a customizable look and feel, a library of integrations into your workflows for embedding up-to-date information, and whole app stores full of plugins.

- *Learning curve.* Plain text and markdown are fairly straightforward. But some documentation systems can be as complex as spreadsheets, with so many features that they can boggle new users who haven't had training.

This is especially important: whole-company usability needs to be considered because there will be people who are time poor, nontechnical, or both.

- *Access.* How do users log in to the documentation system? How are permissions handled for different types of users? Will everyone in the company easily have the permissions that they need to contribute, regardless of where they're located?

- *Change management.* How are new changes proposed and added, and how does the system handle multiple users editing the same pages at the same time? Is there a way of reviewing changes before they're merged in?

- *Scalability.* How would the documentation system fare if people were updating it every hour from remote locations across the whole company?

- *Portability.* If you had to move from one documentation system to another, how easy would it be to export the data and move it elsewhere?

- *Security.* Is it hosted internally or externally? What are your company policies around this?

Clearly, there's a lot to consider. But don't let choices get in the way of getting started. We would recommend getting going by choosing the option that'll be the lowest friction for your team, ideally by bootstrapping off of the functionality of systems that you already use every day.

What do we mean by that? Well, one possible option, if you're already using GitHub to host your source code, is to use a repository of plain-text markdown files for your team handbook. Why? Well, let's think about it with reference to the previous criteria.

First, it's unlikely to incur any extra cost because you're already using GitHub. Secondly, in terms of features, markdown has a decent array of markup options, from basic text to tables, code blocks, and task lists. GitHub also renders these nicely in the browser, and they can be edited in WYSIWYG mode. Markdown and GitHub also have little to no learning curve for an engineering team. They're likely already being used extensively. Access is easy to arrange. It's done in the same way as your code repositories. Change management is built in. You can use the standard pull request workflow. In terms of scalability, it could, in theory, support the whole company, but there would be learning-curve issues. However, markdown is highly portable, so if the handbook idea did take off companywide, it would be easy to move it onto another system.

There may be other starter systems that will work well for you, based on the tools that your team has access to and is comfortable using. However, do be mindful of the anecdote about engineers setting up their personal blogs. Focus on getting something up and running with minimal effort by bootstrapping off of whatever you have available. While it may be fun building a wiki that's hosted on a web server that you're experimenting with running on Kubernetes, all of this is distraction from the task at hand and is creating future maintenance debt that you're not going to enjoy being responsible for.

Keep it simple.

Your Turn: Pick Your Handbook Software

It's time to choose. What software are you going to host your team handbook with?

- What software is your company already using that you could bootstrap from? Remember to look for software that has documentation capabilities as a side effect, such as GitHub.

- Is there dedicated free and open source software that you could use? How hard would it be to host it yourself? Would it encourage or deter others, especially nonengineers?

- See what your team thinks of your choice of software. If they have other suggestions, how do they align with the previous criteria?

Structuring Your Team Handbook

OK, so you've chosen how you're going to host your team handbook. Now it's time to start creating it. You should approach it the same way that you approach writing software:

- *Focus on the highest value* you can deliver in the shortest space of time.

- *Organize for readability and searchability.* Short sentences, bullet points, and links are better than pages of text.

- *Try to keep the scope under control.* Only try to record the most useful information, and don't be afraid of linking elsewhere for the details.

- *Find some stakeholders* from inside and outside of your team who can give their opinions on what you're creating as you go along. Ideally, your stakeholders should be members of your team who are remote, or others in your department who are remote. Have any of them discovered it's hard to find information recently? If so, they might be a perfect fit for helping you proof what you create.

Adopt the mindset of minimum viable product: everything you write needs to be maintained, so be sparing in what you create until you can prove that it's worth including. A great mass of outdated information or the once hopeful skeletons of sections that were never filled in are broken windows that'll make your handbook look like it's out of date before you even get it going.

To keep it simple for your first iteration, we recommend aiming to keep your team's handbook only two layers deep in total:

- *Index page* that contains high-level, concise information and links to the other pages
- *Whole pages* linked from the index page for topics big enough to fill them

Any information that goes deeper than that—for now, at least—is probably too fine-grained in detail and could be served by links to elsewhere, such as to further documentation in your codebase, specific tickets in your ticket-tracking software, or video recordings.

So what sort of content should you be putting on your index page? Here are some ideas in the table on page 247.

This list is merely a primer to get you started. What you put in your team handbook is entirely up to you. You'll know what's best when it comes to the tone and formality of the content. If you're working for a bank, plastering your handbook full of cat GIFs may not be in line with the company culture; but it might well be if you're a startup. Try to create your content in the middle of the Venn diagram that blends both the individualism of your team and the wider company culture.

Team Handbook QA

Since we're borrowing some concepts from writing software to guide us in putting together our team handbook, such as keeping the scope narrow and creating the highest value elements first, we should also do some QA on it. After all, your team members won't be the only people who'll be using it. The readership will be much bigger than that.

As quick as it is to QA it among your team, there's only so much benefit to marking your own homework. Find other people in the department—ideally remote workers—who can take part in this process. You only get a pair of fresh eyes once, so ensure that you seek them out.

Topic	Content Ideas
Team name	A simple one to begin with: What's your team's name, and what does it mean?
Staff	List each staff member on your team. They could potentially link to email addresses, GitHub profiles, and chat handles so that people outside the team are able to easily contact them. Perhaps your colleagues may also like to create individual staff pages where they can go into more detail about themselves.
Contact details	What are the main contact points for your team? This can include mailing lists, chat rooms, routes for escalating bugs and production issues, and so on. Put yourself in the shoes of someone who doesn't know your team. How would they be looking to contact you and why?
Mission and vision	What's the reason that your team exists? Are there feature areas of the product that you own and develop, or are you responsible for maintaining and scaling storage infrastructure or providing tools for other teams? What do you want to achieve in the future?
Goals	At a high level, what are your goals for this year and beyond? Are those goals focused around your users, the stability of infrastructure, or the success of other engineers?
How you work	What are some of the notable features of how you work together as a team? Do you have core hours? Do you encourage pair and mob programming? Are there local rules or guidelines that you follow?
Latest progress	Here's a great place to summarize some of the notable things that you've shipped recently. Additionally, you could link to your ticket-tracker system so that people can find out what you're up to in your current sprint, or you could link to the latest builds of software that you've released. Either way, what would you love to proudly show to other teams when they stop by your handbook?
Responsibilities	What exactly does your team look after? You could describe and link to particular codebases or architecture diagrams here. What route should those outside the team take if they have a question about something that you're responsible for?
Codebases	List the links to the codebases that you develop, maintain, and contribute to with descriptions of what they do.
Meetings	What are your regular team meetings, when do they take place, and where can people find the agendas, meeting notes, and archive of recordings?
Documents	List any important documents, such as designs, architecture overviews, supporting material for your current projects, or anything else that you'd like to draw people's attention to.
Useful links	If there's anything else that isn't covered, list it here.

Your Turn: Create Your Team Handbook

Now it's time for you to get writing. If you haven't settled on the software that you're going to be using yet, don't worry. You can start in a shared document and port it across later. What matters is that you focus on creating the content:

- Using the previous suggested topic areas, draft your team's handbook. Ensure that you get remote members of your team involved, or if you don't have any, lean on others in your department who are remote.

- Show what you've created to other members of your team and see whether what you've written can be improved or expanded upon. If you have no remote workers on your team, ask one of your stakeholders who is.

- Are there additional topics that would be worthwhile for you to include, either for members of the team or for people who are outside of it?

- Which of the high-level topics are worth having their own dedicated page?

- Run what you've written by colleagues on other teams and, if you can, colleagues who are in other departments. Ensure that a number of them are remote to you in some way. What do they think about what you've written? How can you improve it?

- How can you write your handbook so that it doesn't overly rely on referring to specific individuals? For example, Alice may be the person to talk to about something now, but Alice's role may change in the future or she may leave the company. How can you futureproof what you write, perhaps by referring to people's roles or teams instead?

Here are some ways in which you can test your team handbook:

- *Proofread.* Handbooks and documentation that are full of typos and grammatical errors can be frustrating to readers. Distribute different parts of your handbook to your team so that they can take a fine-toothed comb to what has been written. Given that the simpler documentation systems may not have a built-in spellchecker, it's worth copying and pasting what you've written into other software to pick up any mistakes and copying it back when they've been fixed.

- *Insert links.* Often there are plenty of additional artifacts that are related to what's covered in the handbook. They're well worth linking to. Make additional passes over what you've written, actively seeking out supporting documentation and artifacts in other software systems that you use regularly such as your ticket tracker. Link them from your handbook so others can find them. If you find out-of-date artifacts when you're doing this, either bring them up to date or delete them.

- *Give out challenges.* Test the navigability of your handbook by setting challenges for people who aren't on your team. For each challenge, they should start from your team handbook's home page. For example, you could see whether they can find out what the highest priority item in your backlog is, or what you shipped last quarter, or how to build and deploy one of your services. If they get stuck, improve the handbook so they can continue.

- *Do an onboarding test.* You can expand on the previous technique and have somebody pretend they have just joined the team and their first task is a bug fix. See whether it's possible for that person to orient themselves, find the bug ticket, check out the codebase locally, and deploy their fix into production, all with little to no help.

Since your handbook is living documentation, the quality and the consistency of the writing can succumb to entropy with time. An approach that you could take is to perform some of the previous activities at regular intervals, similar to a spring clean. For example, your team could be responsible for checking and updating the handbook at the end of each sprint, or you could all put aside an afternoon once a month to ensure that it's in good shape.

Getting Others Involved: Marketing and Evangelizing

A contributing factor of any product doing well is good marketing. When you keep seeing that particular soft drink advertised on roadside billboards and at sports events, you're probably more likely to give it a try when you're standing in front of the cooler at the grocery store.

If you've created your own team handbook, you're probably thinking that the department would be a better place if more teams had one as well. After all, it would be beneficial for you to be able to find out important and interesting information about other teams. It would also help them organize themselves better and make life easier for remote workers across the department.

However, even the best products in the world need some marketing. This begins by showing everyone else what you've done. Here are some ways in which you could begin to increase the visibility of your handbook initiative so that others can be convinced to begin their own:

- *Show it off.* First things first: get the message out there. You can take a multichannel approach to this, similar to how companies advertise their products on different mediums. You could share the link with your department. You could write a blog post about your team handbook and how you put it together. You could record a short video walking everyone through what you've done and why it's an important piece of documentation for everyone to have.

- *Give how-to sessions.* Offer to give tutorial sessions on creating a handbook to other teams. You could do these interactively, or you could record them. Just follow the template from this chapter.

- *Create a handbook channel.* To start building momentum, you could create a handbook chat channel in which you begin by sharing links when updates have been made to your team's handbook. Inviting others who are interested in the idea can encourage discussion. You can also share any how-to material that you've created as per the previous points. With luck, a handful of teams will begin to join you in creating and sharing their own progress, which creates a buzz of activity that people want to get involved in.

- *Pitch your department leader.* Once there's some momentum, if they haven't already noticed, show your department leader what you're all creating as part of the handbook movement. See whether they would be interested in further evangelizing the idea to the department, or even making it a required responsibility of team leaders. Maybe they could help create the department index page, with high-level important information and links to the handbooks that have already been written.

Your Turn: Creating Habits and Spreading the Message

Let's put what we've just covered into practice:

- Make your team handbook an integral part of everything that you do. This may require a disproportionate amount of effort from you in the beginning. Ensure that it's kept up to date, link to it everywhere from your team chat channel topic to your codebases, and find opportunities to say, "Hey, we should probably put that in the handbook!"

- Choose a way to spread the message to the rest of the department using the previous suggestions.

- See if you can book some time with your department leader to take them through the idea. If their calendar makes this impossible, why not record a video and send it to them?

A Handbook for the Company

So perhaps at this point you've made good progress within your team, and you've got the beginnings of your handbook in regular use, albeit with a little prodding required from time to time. Perhaps there are a couple of other teams that are putting together their own handbooks, and you're seeing the first few links appear among the information written in them. That's great. But what does it take for this to become something that the whole company buys in to? That's a lot harder than just writing some documentation for your team. It needs to become a cultural movement. This takes time and leadership.

Let's take GitLab as an example. Yes, it's true that the handbook became a core part of their company culture because they created it and used it right from the start. But when viewed from another angle, it was the fact that the founder and early-stage employees—the ones who defined the company culture going forward—believed it to be an integral part of the way that their company operates.

However, probability would suggest that most readers of this book are not early-stage employees. It may also be likely that your decision-making power in your company is limited, and perhaps your influence is scoped to within your team. But that's OK because you can use this as an opportunity to try to make change happen in a different way.

In politics the term *soft power* refers to the ability to attract and co-opt rather than coerce. It's about influencing others through the appeal and attraction of what you're doing. The opposite of soft power, somewhat unsurprisingly, is *hard power.* That's using money or executive order to get things done. The currency of soft power, especially in international politics, is demonstrated through culture, values, and innovation. For example, in 2020 South Korea was ranked second in the *Monocle* magazine soft-power survey.[4] Although a small country, its global influence is significant through its music, television shows, and films and via products created by its companies such as Samsung, LG, and Hyundai.

Getting buy-in at a company level for a handbook can be done with soft power. It needs to first emerge as something that's inherently practical and useful, and that's where your efforts in helping it gain traction in your department have an effect. But to make it spread into other departments and to catch the attention of leadership, it needs to elevate into a soft-power movement. This requires some additional cultural framing of the initiative rather than it just being an exercise in documentation.

Here are some talking points that you can use for why handbooks are crucially important for your company:

---

4.   https://www.korea.net/NewsFocus/Society/view?articleId=192236

- *Efficiency.* As organizations grow, communication becomes a major over-head, with some common questions and conversations repeating themselves when information isn't discoverable. This is especially true when many of the workers in a company are remote from one another in some way. If you found that you were writing the same lines of code over and over, you'd refactor so that the repeated code is in a separate function and only called once. So why not do the same with information? Just think about how many conversations a handbook could save.

- *Discoverability.* Smart and curious remote individuals are greatly empowered by being able to find out what's going on elsewhere in the business. It helps them to learn, to do their jobs more effectively, and to make connections with others. For example, if remote workers could easily find out via the handbook what's going on in sales and marketing, they could better understand the pain points on the periphery of the company and react accordingly, all without needing to book cold meetings with people they haven't yet built rapport with.

- *Transparency.* Putting more information into the open where others can discover it forms a foundation of trust between employees, teams, and departments. It increases morale, engagement, and retention.

- *Data democracy.* Creating new features and products is enriched by the presence of more information, which can be used to make data-driven decisions about what to do next. If sales can easily find out what's coming down the pipeline in engineering, they can better engage new prospects. If feedback from new prospects is easily discoverable, it can inform engineering decisions. It's a virtuous cycle.

- *Practical benefits for remote workers.* If a company is globally distributed, having information available to everyone without needing to depend on synchronous interactions will reduce the amount of blockers for those who have the least availability overlaps with the rest of the business. It can be the difference between a productive day and a wasted day.

- *Onboarding.* New staff benefit greatly from a thorough handbook for the same reason that remote workers do. Having a smooth onboarding experience is a highly influential factor in a new employee's first impressions of a company.

- *Route to making it public.* The biggest soft-power play has been left until last. If people can buy into a future goal of making the handbook public, your company might even be as culturally prolific as GitLab. This could have significant effects such as attracting world-class candidates to your open roles, building trust with your customers so that they choose you over a competitor, and even attracting investment.

Even though creating a handbook is fundamentally about writing documentation, it means so much more than that. It can provide a significant cultural change that swings the balance of the centricity of information away from synchronous interactions in physical locations and toward asynchronous communication, which benefits remote workers. Never lose sight of this wider aim when you're trying your best to get others to keep their pages up to date. It's always worth the effort.

Fully Making the Shift

We hope you've enjoyed stepping through the process of putting your own handbook together and that you've had a chance to give it a go in your team. If you haven't, what are you waiting for?

Here's what we covered:

- We looked at the *GitLab handbook,* a public-facing repository for how the company runs its entire fully remote company. This was the inspiration for creating our own so that remote workers can more easily navigate their daily work.

- We looked at how to *create a handbook for your team.* We covered how to choose the right software, which information to include, how you can test what you create, and how to start encouraging others in your department to do the same.

- We explored what it might mean *if your whole company had a handbook,* and how that could make the lives of remote workers significantly better by increasing efficiency, solving common communication issues across departments, improving transparency, and enabling the democratization of data.

Although writing a team handbook might seem like a small thing, it can have an outsized impact, especially as—with your help, of course—the practice begins to spread to other teams. With a little effort, remote workers could have an index of links to everything that they need to know. You could save hundreds of hours of time spent searching for information and waiting for replies.

And remember, like most of what you've learned in this book, even though the main emphasis is on making the lives of remote workers better, it's actually bigger than that. Forming habits around high-quality documentation, discoverability, and transparency of information benefits all companies, regardless of how remote they actually are.

On the subject of how remote a company is: that's where we're going next. The following chapter looks at the spectrum of remoteness, from physically colocated to fully remote and everything in-between. We'll consider what it means for a company to make that choice, sometimes explicitly but often implicitly, and how that affects workers.

We are all now connected by the Internet, like neurons in a giant brain.

Stephen Hawking

CHAPTER 13

Becoming Fully Remote

You check your email. There's a message from the CEO.

Dear All,

Ahead of the company meeting later today, I thought that it would be best to inform you ahead of time about what we're going to be announcing.

We appreciate that the world has changed, and the way in which we wish to work and live our lives has changed also. We have been carefully listening to your feedback over the past 18 months, including your sentiment from the recent company survey.

We believe that we're now ready to make a decision.

As of the beginning of next year, we're going to be a fully remote company. This means that we'll be closing all of our offices and focusing all of our resources on making the experience of working remotely truly world class.

You, your colleagues, the executive team, and I will all be remote.

We appreciate that there are many of you who'll have different thoughts about this decision, so we'll be dedicating most of the company meeting to answering your questions after a short presentation. Please submit your questions by replying to this email, and we'll do our best to get through them all this afternoon.

I'm looking forward to speaking to you all later.

Kate

You feel a rush of excitement. Finally!

After reading countless articles about other companies becoming fully remote, and after weeks of questioning whether you'd need a new job to do it yourself, the company has actually done it for you. Whew! It seems like you've managed to catch a break after all.

You think of the possibilities. You'll never feel that guilt about working from home ever again. You won't have to have those awkward conversations in the kitchen. You certainly won't need to fight for space on the subway during rush hour. And most importantly, you can completely rethink what that down payment on a home can get you. All of a sudden, the future is looking quite different. It's looking brighter.

You take to your team chat channel to see what people are saying about the news.

```
[11:24] you: what do you think about the email?
[11:24] lara: at last! awesomeeee
[11:25] you: i know right?
[11:25] sarah: woohoo!
[11:26] tim: finally
[11:27] you: so happy!
```

You notice that Ben hasn't said anything, despite seeing the notification that he's typing. You send him a DM.

```
[11:28] you: is everything alright?
[11:28] ben: not really. i'm gutted
[11:29] you: really? what's up?
[11:29] ben: i love the office and hate working at home
[11:30] ben: might be time to look for something else :(
```

Uh-oh. This isn't what you wanted to hear from one of your best engineers.

```
[11:31] you: oh no! do you want to have a call?
[11:31] ben: in a bit. need some time to think.
```

Maybe the future isn't looking so bright after all.

During this journey together, we've been focusing on remote-centric tools and techniques that you can use regardless of exactly how your company implements its remote-work policy. If you're primarily working and communicating via your computer, which is likely the case, everything that you've learned so far can have a positive effect on your productivity and collaboration. Everyone is remote to us in some sense, even if they're in another office or even another floor of the same building.

However, the speed, extent, and desire of companies to fully embrace the tools and techniques of remote work is a function of their desire to make remote working as equal and inclusive as physically colocated working. As such, every company will have a different take on its current stance toward remote work and what its future plans are for it.

Some companies may see remote working as the exception rather than the norm and only allow its employees to be at home for one day a week; for all other days, they may be expected to be present in the office. Other companies may have more ambiguous stances, where some employees shift to become fully remote as their tenure increases, while there's still an expectation that new hires immerse themselves in the office culture. Some companies may not even have agreement within their leadership team as to what their official policy is. They may have differing opinions on how it will affect the morale of staff and worry that it may open multiple cans of worms about downsizing offices, finding budget for work-from-home stipends, and so on. It's complicated.

But the truth is that there are far more opportunities to be a remote worker than ever before. Understanding exactly where a company stands on remote work is critical both for employees and for companies themselves.

This is because of the following:

- *Employees need long-term guarantees about their employment situation.* People plan their lives around their work, from the location that they choose to live in to how they choose to spend their time with their families.

- *Companies need to define their culture and understand the effects of their choices.* There's a big difference between being an office-based company that supports remote work and a fully remote company. This difference manifests everywhere from how the company operates, such as in communication, budgeting, IT, development tools, and processes, to the necessary skills for human resources and legal staff and more. A company's approach to remote work runs deep through everything.

In this chapter we're going to explore the varying stances on remote work companies may have and fundamentally define what that means for you, whether you're an employee, a manager, or a company leader. Some feel there may be an eventual—or even inevitable—trend toward all companies becoming fully remote. But what does that mean, and is it truly what everyone wants? Is this a natural trend that will unfold with ease, or is it wrought with pitfalls?

Here's what we're going to cover:

- We'll look at the *spectrum of remoteness,* which covers physically colocated companies, fully remote companies, and everything in-between. We'll understand the implications of going fully remote and why it needs committed and considered leadership.

- We'll explore the *challenge of retrofitting a fully remote culture* into companies that currently aren't remote. We'll see why it's not as simple as *just doing it*, and explore what effect it may have on the workforce.

- We'll study the three-way trade-off dilemma represented by the *triangle of transition* that becomes apparent when planning and executing a companywide transition to remote working.

- We'll conclude by looking at some *notable, fully remote companies* you can research further to inspire yourself and others in your organization.

The Spectrum of Remoteness

Let's begin by understanding the different positions that companies can take on their support for remote working. And because the diagram worked so well earlier in the book, we're going to use a spectrum once again. Except this time it's a *spectrum of remoteness.*

But before we go any further, it's worth pointing out that, in reality, a company's classification may be somewhat fuzzy. Some companies may lie in-between each definition. Some may be at one end of the spectrum but regularly use practices from the other end. Everyone's mileage may vary. However, classification is useful to compare and contrast and understand how a transition may happen from one end to the other. This can sometimes happen through explicit choice ("We are now going fully remote!"), and sometimes it can happen through implicit emergent behaviors ("Did you notice that all of our senior staff are now hybrid workers?").

Here's the spectrum.

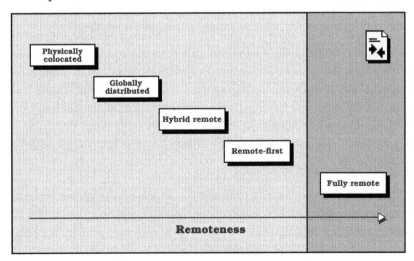

Let's read the spectrum from left to right. On the left we have a company setup that has no remote workers, and on the right we have a company that is fully remote. The classifications along the spectrum are as follows:

- *Physically colocated.* A company where all employees are working from the same physical location, which is typically an office

- *Globally distributed.* A company where employees are working from one of a number of offices, potentially distributed worldwide

- *Hybrid remote.* A company where some employees work from an office, or offices, and some work remotely and includes employees who split their time between working in the office and at home

- *Remote-first.* An extension of hybrid remote where remote work is the norm and office-based work is the exception

- *Fully remote.* A company where all employees are remote and there are no offices

Let's explore each of these classifications in more detail to understand how they can occur, with a focus on company growth and increasing allowances for employee flexibility.

Physically Colocated

The first classification is the simplest and one that many of us have experienced at some point in our working lives. Physically colocated companies operate from one office, and all workers are expected to be in that office when they're working. New staff are hired at this location. In fact, the office, and the workers being there every day, is a key part of the company's culture. Socialization both inside and outside of work is typically a key feature of this arrangement, allowing strong social bonds to form among workers.

Although collaborative software is used, the extent to which it's embedded in company culture may vary because workers may find it easier to talk to each other synchronously in person. Meetings occur in breakout spaces and in meeting rooms, which are designed around the physical presence of attendees. Outside parties may be expected to come to the office to do business, interview, and meet staff.

Physical colocation is a common situation for early-stage startups and more traditional companies, especially for those who aren't in the technology industry. It can also be a preferred choice for those who wish to have the clean separation that a commute provides between their work life and their home life, either for practical reasons (such as not having dedicated work space) or ideological reasons (such as treating the home as a sacred space free from work).

Globally Distributed

As companies grow, they often begin to branch out into multiple locations. Commercial opportunities around the world may mean that offices are opened near prospective clients in major cities to facilitate face-to-face meetings. Yet during a growth phase, a company's headquarters may see the most investment in terms of the quality of the office space and quantity of people who are being hired there, meaning that other offices can feel more like satellites.

The usage of collaborative software and the maturity of the practices we've learned in this book may vary. When there's no specific effort in forcing remote collaboration (e.g., by forming teams that cross different locations), there may be only a loose connection between offices. A typical pattern is to hire and place teams so that they're physically colocated, thus trying to maintain the culture of the physically colocated company pre-expansion.

Meetings are typically held in meeting rooms with audio-visual equipment, with people physically in them. In-person collaboration is still seen as the most effective way of communicating, with staff often traveling to one location for important events or project kick-offs.

Individual locations can begin to develop their own culture, so senior staff in each location have an important role to play in ensuring that new and existing staff feel a close bond to their physically colocated colleagues while also minimizing the cultural divide among other locations. This can be difficult for small offices that are geographically distant from the headquarters, especially when there's minimal time-zone overlap. Leadership must also ensure that equal opportunities for promotion and progression exist outside of the headquarters.

Due to the quantity of interactions with colleagues who aren't located in the same office, globally distributed companies may cautiously allow staff to work from home for a small portion of their time, such as every other Friday. Although, typically no additional provisions for home-office setups are available.

Hybrid Remote

Companies can be classified as hybrid remote when full-time remote working is acceptable, although the equality that remote workers have compared to office-based workers in this setup may vary greatly. Hybrid remote can be considered a gradual journey, from allowing a small number of remote workers to be part of the company, to the company consisting of a near-equal mix of office-based workers and remote workers.

This change can happen implicitly. For example, tenured workers who want to leave the company to relocate may be retained by being allowed to work remotely, which can then make the practice more acceptable and widespread with time ("If she's remote, why can't I be?"). It also may begin in response to job-market dynamics. If it becomes challenging to hire staff in the office locations, remote workers who are in the same country or state may be considered as well.

Having hybrid-remote employees can be difficult for companies because they need to provide something for everyone: both a great office experience and a great remote-working experience. This can be hard to do in practice. Offices require some baseline level of presence to provide the interactivity that office workers desire, yet remote workers don't want to feel like they're excluded from this.

Hybrid-remote companies that succeed follow the practices that you've learned in this book, such as treating everyone as remote. Those that don't risk introducing an inequitable experience for those who aren't working in the places where the leadership and the seniority of the company are located. This goes both ways: either manifesting in a poor remote-working experience (e.g., the leadership and senior staff are all office based) or in tumbleweed offices that are poorly equipped and supported (e.g., the leadership and senior staff are all remote).

Remote-First

When remote working is the norm and office working is the exception, these companies are remote-first. In theory it's still a flavor of hybrid remote. But there are typically important policy and cultural changes that have occurred to get to this point. For example, all new hires may be expected to be remote by default. Perks, benefits, and provisions are aligned around remote working, such as the provision of work-from-home stipends, explicitly treating everyone as remote as part of the culture, mindfully preventing office-based communication vacuums, and predominantly using asynchronous communication and collaborative software. It doesn't matter if you're at home or in the office, the playing field is exactly the same.

If a company has transitioned to remote-first, offices may have closed, downsized, or even converted to hot-desk arrangements. But this means that those who prefer working in offices may experience a severely diminished experience compared to when they first joined. The company isn't aligned to their preferences anymore. New hires will join remotely, and the company may be focusing HR effort on setting up legal entities in different countries to enable remote employment worldwide. Some remote-first companies may also hire anywhere in the world by allowing staff to be employed as contractors first, with an aim to convert into full-time employees once a legal entity is created in their country.

Fully Remote

Fully remote means just that: no offices and no physical locations. Staff typically work from home, and core hours may be flexible due to the geographical spread of employees.

Remote tools, techniques, and practices are part of the company's identity and culture, and the people who work for the company do so because they wish to be remote workers. Company leadership embraces and promotes remote working as a core cultural facet of what it means to be employed there.

Some fully remote companies may organize for staff to get together in one location, say, once per year. This allows workers to meet each other face to face, get to know each other better, defuse frustrations, discuss their work, and socialize. But some employees may never meet anyone else they work with, and that's perfectly normal.

Your Turn: The Present and Your Ideal

Consider your current company and the previous classifications.

- Where would you place your company on the spectrum? Did it end up there implicitly or explicitly? How?

- Is this the ideal situation that you would like to be in? If not, what sort of company would you like to work for?

- Think about what you might need to do to make your ideal situation a reality. Are you already in your ideal situation? Would getting there involve trying to influence your company to change? Or do you reckon that you might need to find a new job in the future?

The Challenge of Retrofitting Fully Remote Culture

If you look back at the spectrum-of-remoteness diagram, you'll notice that there's a vertical line separating the remote-first and fully remote configurations. This is because the transition between remote-first and fully remote can be challenging, and for some large companies, it may never even be possible. It may not even be desirable.

Therefore, it needs to be considered carefully, both from the perspective of companies that are wondering whether they should be making the transition and from employees who will be eagerly watching how their workplace is reacting to the needs of current and future employees and the direction of the industry in general.

If a company begins its life as fully remote, it avoids by default the issues that we cover in this section. Candidates who apply for jobs at fully remote companies already have an intuition about what the remote culture is like. If they didn't like remote work, they wouldn't have applied in the first place! At these companies, remote practices are present from the start. Operationally, everything is aligned toward supporting remote staff. The company budget will begin without line items for office rental and headcount for office managers and receptionists and will likely include stipends for getting staff set up properly at home.

However, a company that wishes to transition to fully remote—even if the leadership believes in it strongly—may find that there's too much to demolish before construction can begin again. Hybrid remote is like fighting a war on multiple fronts. Providing an excellent in-office experience is an entirely different game than providing an excellent remote experience. Giving up on the office may be the focusing of effort onto a single front that wins the morale war in the long term, but there may be casualties in the short term.

Transitioning to fully remote should not come lightly. In a hybrid organization, there will be a number of employees who prefer working in offices, and the company risks losing those employees in the transition. Many old habits and elements of the in-office or hybrid culture will need to be left behind for a fully remote configuration to work.

So what can we learn from others? As part of discussion and knowledge sharing with other companies in the industry, GitLab has compiled its advice on breaching that line and becoming fully remote.[1] It states that the specific path for companies making the transition will depend on the company size, number of offices, percentage of employees who already work remotely, existing tools and infrastructure for remote work, and the existing culture around communication and career mapping.

1.　https://about.gitlab.com/company/culture/all-remote/transition/

Assuming that a company is committed to becoming fully remote, the following actions are advised as part of the process:

- *Make the executive team remote.* This is one of the quickest ways to send a message about the commitment to a transition. The executive team will have to adapt to remote work themselves, which in turn will set the standard through the rest of the organization.

- *Establish remote infrastructure.* This can be initiated with a thought exercise: What would happen if everyone worked from home tomorrow? Companies should consider what possible information voids and confusion would appear, which issues with communication would arise, and where tools and practices are lacking. As many changes as possible should be put in place before making the transition.

- *Document the culture.* If there are no offices in which to observe company culture, it needs to be documented. What's the company's mission and vision? What are its values? What's the structure of the organization and how does it function? If nothing is written down, there's nothing for remote staff to discover, learn, and operate within.

- *Close the office.* Practicalities such as leases may need navigating, but another strong message is to close all or some of the offices. It makes the message about the fully remote transition concrete and is a clear signal everyone who works in the company is remote and equal to each other.

- *Equip and educate team members.* Not everyone will have worked remotely before, and even those who have may not have experienced what it's like to be part of a *good* remote culture. There must be a focus on training and education that's led by the company rather than letting employees work it out for themselves. The latter can cause disillusionment and attrition, especially when combined with the increased isolation of being at home.

- *Embrace iteration and transparency in transition.* The leadership of a company should be transparent in the same way that engineering teams are used to: work progresses in increments and requires continued testing, reviewing, and iteration to get it right. With the transition in mind, this involves proactive communication about progress, successes and failures, open discussions with all staff, collecting and processing of feedback, and so on.

If this is looking like a lot of work, that's because it is. If hybrid-remote companies are considering the transition, the additional overhead of doing so piled on top of the day-to-day running of the business can be too much for leaders, managers, and HR staff to manage.

Therefore, one suggestion is to hire a "head of remote" role who can then build a specialist team to assist with the transition.[2] One technical executive, Andreas Klinger, describes this role as "at the intersection of optimizing internal tooling, processes, transparency, collaboration, efficiency, inclusivity, onboarding, hiring, employer branding, culture, and communication overall."[3]

If you're speculating what direction your company may take, think about whether the executives would consider investing significant money into making this key hire and building out the head of remote's team. If this is something that you know the company would do without question, you're probably in a good place if it transitions. If pigs may fly sooner than that happens, any transition to remote work at your current employer may be challenging.

Here's what you should be looking out for:

- *As an employee, you should be thinking about what type of company you want to work for.* Think about the different configurations that we explored in this chapter, and try to understand what sort of working situation you want to optimize for in your life. This will be an important factor in determining how long you want to stay at your current company, or if you would be able to weather a transition period, or if you would prefer to make the jump and join a company that's already fully remote.

- *If you're a leader or manager in a company that's transitioning or considering it, do your research and commit fully.* Supporting remote work is a considered effort, and supporting hybrid remote can be harder than being fully remote. If you're in a position to influence these discussions and decisions in your company, take inspiration from the material that we've covered so you can encourage a better outcome for your company.

And here's one final thought: office-based work isn't to be looked down upon. Just because remote work is gaining in popularity, and just because it's likely you're invested in it, because you picked up this book, remember that office-based work is still entirely valid, workable, and the personal preference of many people. In the process of making remote workers not feel like outcasts, be sure not to encourage the inverse behavior.

---

2.   https://about.gitlab.com/company/culture/all-remote/head-of-remote/
3.   https://twitter.com/andreasklinger/status/1187841403381878785

The Triangle of Transition

When we walk through the spectrum of remoteness, we can make an observation: the company setups at both ends of the spectrum are a great deal simpler than the ones in the middle. Running a physically colocated company or a fully remote company is easier than any of the hybrid-remote configurations in-between. With hybrid remote, employees need to feel like part of the company whether they're at headquarters, a satellite office, or at home. This can be complicated and expensive to achieve.

Therefore, companies may want to transition further along the spectrum toward being remote-first, or even become fully remote. But the process of transitioning is not without constraints. In fact, these challenges can be represented in a similar way to the traditional project-management *iron triangle*, or triple constraints.[4]

When planning projects, there are typically trade-offs to be made among the iron triangle's scope, cost, and time. You can pick two, but you can't have all three. For example, if you want something fast and large in scope, the cost will be high. If you want it quick and cheap, it'll be limited in scope.

You can use this same triangle model to outline the *constraints* of a company transitioning along the spectrum of remoteness. Let's call it the *triangle of transition,* as shown in the following diagram.

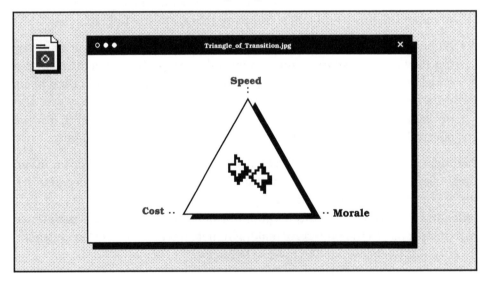

---

4.   https://en.wikipedia.org/wiki/Project_management_triangle

The three constraints are as follows:

- *Speed.* How quickly is the company progressing along the spectrum of remoteness? Is it doing so immediately, or in a sequence of phases over multiple years?

- *Cost.* How much money is a company willing to spend during the period of transition? Are purse strings tight, or is the company heavily investing in the initiative?

- *Morale.* How happy will staff be during the period of transition? Will there be contentment throughout, or will there be ups, downs, or departures?

The triangle dictates that you can only pick two of the three. Why is that?

- If a company wants to *transition quickly and do so cheaply,* it will likely create a negative effect on staff morale. Workers do not want to feel like they've been sent home unsupported to work in worse conditions than they had before.

- If the aim is to make a *fast transition while keeping staff morale high,* it probably will not be cheap to do so. Downsizing or closing offices, providing home-office equipment, and spending the time to train and educate all staff is no small feat, both in terms of time and money spent.

- If the goal is to *maintain a small budget while keeping staff morale high,* it'll likely result in a slow transition. If a company wants to go remote, it can't maintain the office status quo forever and hope that things change naturally. It needs to make proactive actions, typically by investing capital, that send clear signals about what the future will look like. And then it needs to go on that journey.

These trade-offs occur because transitioning along the spectrum of remoteness is a deliberate company initiative requiring a deliberate investment of resources. It's as deliberate an activity as the development of a flagship item on the product roadmap. It should have careful planning and research, and leadership should be accountable for its success.

All staff need education, training, managerial support, and money invested to ensure that they feel they're transitioning to a culture that's just as good, if not better, than what they had before. That's because the culture will be markedly different and requires deliberate changes in all aspects of running the company. It needs clear leadership and accountability. What does it mean for compensation? For hiring? For documentation and information sharing? For socialization? For tools, processes, and practices that need to change and those that don't? For office layouts, downsizes, or closures? For travel? For benefits and perks? Training and development? The list goes on.

Making a transition in a considered, transparent, and iterative manner has never been more important either. Doing it halfheartedly can result in a fractured culture that's worse than it was previously. The worrying corollary is that staff who have weathered a transition will have learned what they don't want from a remote company, and the number of other opportunities available to them in an increasingly remote industry is only increasing.

When considering the constraints, one could reason that the simplest solution is to spend more money on the transition. Hire a head of remote and let them build a team. Allow budget for top-tier home-office equipment and training. Ensure that pay doesn't change, or even increase it to be near the top of the market for each employee's location. Recycle the office budget to provide yearly staff retreats in beautiful locations. But it's likely that we've all been in situations where *just spending more money* is the answer—in hiring, in acquiring software licenses, and in staff compensation. It's hard to find it when you need it the most.

Those who have run companies before will understand how difficult it can be to embark on complex, long-term initiatives that are seemingly not directly related to shipping software faster. In fact, those same leaders may be expected by their boards to go faster and spend less money, and by comparison, a successful remote transition may never make the top of the company priority list.

Your Turn: Is Your Company Transitioning?

Reflect once again on your current company and previous companies that you've worked for:

- Have any of them embarked on a remote transition? Was it an explicit company initiative, or did it evolve over time? How do you think it was handled? What were some of the positive and negative aspects?

- In the triangle-of-transition diagram, where do you think that the constraints were being made in your workplace when the transition was occurring?

- Where's your current workplace with regard to its remote transition? Has it increased or decreased the likelihood that you want to stay at your company for the foreseeable future?

But here's why it's important. With time, other software companies that have managed to embark on successful remote transitions will be so far ahead in their remote processes, practices, and culture that they can never be caught up to. And when staff begin to leave to join these trendsetters, companies that didn't act quickly enough will wonder what on earth just hit them.

Learning from Trailblazers

At this point in the chapter, you may be thinking that the transition along the spectrum of remoteness is fraught with peril and hard work. And it is. But there's plenty of inspiration available from other companies that are at varying stages along the journey, and we can learn from them by what they've shared with the world.

Two of the influential early adopters of fully remote working culture that have also produced notable written works are Automattic (the creators of WordPress) and 37signals, which later changed its name to Basecamp, the creators of the software of the same name.

In 2013 Scott Berkun provided a behind-the-scenes look at early remote-working culture at Automattic, where he worked as a team leader, in his book *The Year Without Pants: WordPress.com and the Future of Work [Ber13]*. At the time he wrote it, Automattic was a company of around 120 people. It has now grown to more than 1,800 remote staff worldwide. If you or your company are interested in learning from an *in the trenches* approach to documenting remote culture, this book is a great place to start.

Automattic has refined its remote processes over the years.[5] It even developed P2, a tool that allows teams to share, discuss, and collaborate.[6] It's a great example of how an early mover attempted to solve the asynchronous communication challenge for other companies as well as for itself.

Also in 2013, Basecamp founders, Jason Fried and David Heinemeier Hansson, wrote *Remote: Office Not Required [HF13]*, which focuses less on stories and more on evangelizing the principle of remote working as the future of how we'll all work in the technology industry. It's a good companion piece to the previously mentioned book because it addresses what it means to be fully remote from the top down by those who were running the company. In addition, you can find a wealth of information on the Basecamp website[7] about

---

5. https://remote.co/company/automattic/
6. https://wordpress.com/p2/
7. https://basecamp.com/remote-resources

how it runs remotely. It shows how smaller companies can punch way above their size and attract top remote talent from around the world.

Buffer, which creates social media software, provides inspiration on transparency in combination with remote culture. In addition to being fully remote, the company publishes its salary information online,[8] which provides a unique insight into its approach for scaling pay based on a person's role and their cost of living. Additionally, Buffer was an early public advocate of regular company retreats, which it pays for so all employees can meet together in one place.[9]

GitLab's public handbook, which we covered in Chapter 12, Creating a Handbook, on page 237, demonstrates the benefits of a documentation-led remote culture.[10] Many of its pages are excellent templates for how you can produce your own company, department, and team documentation, and much can be learned about GitLab's processes, tools, mission, values, and goals. This again shows how small companies can become well known internationally through the strength of their remote culture.

Since the 2020 pandemic, many more companies have been making the transition to remote and have been sharing their journeys. Browsing their websites and culture pages can help you and your company plan your own transition along the spectrum of remoteness:

- Shopify has become remote-first, which means that employees can work from anywhere. The company writes about work being something that employees do rather than something that they come to the office for and how workers should be measured on their effectiveness and impact rather than the number of hours that they spend in the office.[11] To make remote collaboration more engaging and fun, Shopify built its own 3D world for employees to hang out, have meetings, and play games in.

- Reddit has transitioned to a hybrid workforce and has written about what that means in practice, compensation, and culture.[12]

- HubSpot has transitioned and outlines how employees choose from three options for how they wish to work: office based, flex, or at home.[13]

---

8.   https://buffer.com/salaries
9.   https://buffer.com/resources/inside-buffer-retreat/
10. https://about.gitlab.com/handbook/
11. https://newsroom.spotify.com/2021-02-12/distributed-first-is-the-future-of-work-at-spotify/
12. https://redditblog.com/2020/10/27/evolving-reddits-workforce/
13. https://www.hubspot.com/careers-blog/future-of-work-hybrid

- Coinbase transitioned to remote-first and shared its internal communication to its employees publicly when making that decision.[14]

- Dropbox transitioned to remote-first, stating that "remote work is now the primary experience for all employees and the day-to-day default for individual work."[15]

For further inspiration, GitLab has been maintaining a list of companies that have been transparently and publicly sharing their journeys.[16]

If you're involved in discussions about how your company is going to handle a transition, or are being consulted on your opinion on what type of remote-working culture your company should be providing, there's plenty of material out there that you can share with your colleagues and leaders to get a fuller picture of what it means and to find the inspiration that you need to make the change. Doing so transparently with the rest of the world presents an opportunity to increase the visibility of your company online, which has positive effects on internal accountability and responsibility and also on talent acquisition. Never underestimate how often employees pick up on companies that are being bold with their culture and their perks. See if you can help your company be bold too.

Now the Difficult Stuff

Whew. It turns out that transitioning a company to fully remote, or even just remote-first, is a serious endeavor that needs consideration, research, accountability, and ownership. Here's what we've covered:

- We looked at the *spectrum of remoteness*, considering what it means to be physically colocated, globally distributed, hybrid remote, remote-first, and fully remote.

- We understood how *retrofitting a fully remote culture* can be challenging, if not impossible, for some companies.

- The *triangle of transition* outlined the trade-offs that have to be faced when a company decides to fully support remote workers. It's not possible to get a speedy transition while maintaining cost-effectiveness and staff morale, so careful thought is required.

---

14. https://blog.coinbase.com/post-covid-19-coinbase-will-be-a-remote-first-company-cdac6e621df7
15. https://blog.dropbox.com/topics/company/dropbox-goes-virtual-first
16. https://about.gitlab.com/company/culture/all-remote/hybrid-remote/#blueprints-and-examples-of-companies-transitioning-to-hybrid-remote

- We concluded the chapter by outlining a number of companies that have been trailblazers in remote-working culture and some that are getting their own journeys underway. These can be used as inspiration for both yourself and the company that you work for.

We hope that you're leaving this chapter with a better idea of the configuration that you want to work in for your own career and are able to help others who you work with better plan whatever transition that they have in mind. And if they don't have anything in mind, make sure that you start bringing it up in conversation.

In the next chapter, we address the darker sides of working remotely: mental health, burnout, and isolation. Join us as we look at the hard parts.

To the edge of the universe and back. Endure and survive.

> *Ellie from The Last of Us*

CHAPTER 14

The Hard Parts

"Where's Ben?"

It's daily stand-up, and for the second day in a row he's missing.

"That's odd. Is he definitely not on vacation this week?"

You check the calendar. There's nothing in there of note. "Nope, he should be in this week. Has anyone heard from him?"

Sarah puts her hand on her chin and leans toward the camera. You can see lines of text whizzing by in the reflection on her glasses.

"You know what, I don't think I heard from him yesterday either. He hasn't said anything in chat since last week."

You look at recent changes to the codebase. "Hmm, there's nothing from him in the last five days. Not even a comment on a pull request."

This is a little worrying.

"When was the last time that we heard anything from him?" asks Mike.

You scroll back through your conversation history and your email inbox. You find something from him. "Looks like it was at the end of last week when I spoke to him after Kate announced that we were going fully remote," you say.

Sarah responds. "How did he react?"

"Not well. He said that he loves the office and hates working from home, and it might be time to look for something else."

"Oh, no! Did you get a chance to have a call with him?" asks Mike.

"I tried, but he declined, saying he needs some time to think," you reply. "After that it seems like he's gone totally off the radar."

"He's definitely not been himself over the last few weeks. He's been incredibly quiet other than getting the bare essentials of his work done," notes Sarah.

"Really? I had no idea," you reply.

"Yeah, he's been pretty checked out," says Mike.

"I'm going to try his phone," you say.

It rings and rings. Voicemail.

If you've ever spoken to somebody who doesn't work from home about your ability to do so, they may have reacted by saying that they, too, would like to do it. That's fair, since it has many benefits.

However, they may have also exclaimed that it sounds like a dream, or a way of doing less work, or that it's easy and relaxing, all while gesturing with their hands behind their head as if they're about to doze off. That judgment isn't fair. In fact, as many of us now know, it's just plain misguided. Working remotely has hard parts to navigate.

The grass always seems greener on the other side. It can take a significant event for the true reality of a situation to arise. Before most of our industry was forced to work from home due to the COVID-19 pandemic, our experiences with remote work were varied. Articles and studies would often focus more on the positive effects of working remotely, rather than the inverse.

A 2015 paper in the *Quarterly Journal of Economics* stated that about 10 percent of U.S. employees regularly worked from home at the time of writing, and that there was strong evidence from a Nasdaq-listed Chinese travel agency that allowing call-center workers to be remote led to a 13 percent performance increase and a 50 percent drop in employees quitting.[1] The authors believed that remote work was the future.

However, five years later, amid the pandemic, an interview with one of the authors of the original paper, a Stanford economist, revealed his hesitancy

---

1.   https://www.nber.org/papers/w18871

about an effective global rollout of remote working. He stated the difficulty of workers not having a proper home-office work space, the challenge of juggling childcare responsibilities, and bad experiences with videoconferencing.[2] As we've discovered in this book, the difference between working remotely and working remotely *effectively* can be significant.

As the 2020 mass remote-work social experiment unfolded, we began to learn more about the difficulties that lie beneath the surface. Articles and tweets extolling the benefits of a new world of remote work (featuring lunch-time yoga, raw-vegetable smoothies, and perfectly behaved children) stood shoulder to shoulder with worries about overwork, burnout, and our mental health.

Health institutions such as the National Health Service in the United Kingdom began to provide government-backed medical advice on staying healthy while working from home.[3] And the results of numerous surveys would show the harsh reality of what working remotely truly means for the masses rather than the few who actively chose that arrangement before 2020.

A 2021 survey by the Royal Society for Public Health in the United Kingdom revealed the following:[4]

- While 45 percent thought working from home was beneficial for their well-being, 29 percent thought it was worse.

- Negative health and well-being impacts included feeling less connected to colleagues (67 percent), getting less exercise (46 percent), and developing musculoskeletal problems (39 percent) and disturbed sleep (37 percent).

- Of those surveyed, 26 percent were working from inadequate spaces such as a sofa or a bedroom.

- Only 34 percent felt they had support from their employers for their mental health.

This chapter is about all of the hard parts of working remotely. These are the parts that we're only beginning to learn about in detail now that most of us in the technology industry have experienced a significant period of remote working for ourselves.

---

2.   https://news.stanford.edu/2020/03/30/productivity-pitfalls-working-home-age-covid-19/

3.   https://www.nhs.uk/every-mind-matters/coronavirus/simple-tips-to-tackle-working-from-home/

4.   https://www.rsph.org.uk/about-us/news/survey-reveals-the-mental-and-physical-health-impacts-of-home-working-during-covid-19.html

Here's what we're going to cover:

- We look in more detail at *what was written about remote working before and after the pandemic* to understand more about the darker side and why these concerns may or may not have been highlighted in the past.

- We look at some different *curve models* to understand why we've seen this changing narrative over time.

- We outline the *physical and mental issues* you need to be conscious of, both for yourself and your coworkers.

- We conclude by understanding *how to support others* in their physical and mental health.

Walking the Curves

When a disruptive idea such as a new technology becomes available, not everyone adopts it immediately. Often, small but vocal cohorts pick it up first and spread the message, allowing it to gradually gain traction among the wider population. We've seen this pattern play out over time with radio, television, the Internet, cryptocurrency, and electric cars.

A theory called the *diffusion of innovations* models the pattern of how the adoption of new ideas spreads within society.[5] It defines five categories of adopters, each of which has a different role to play within this diffusion of ideas:

- *Innovators.* These are people who are willing to take risks and have high social status, financial liquidity, and closest contact to others who are innovating. Their high-risk tolerance allows them to adopt ideas that may ultimately fail.

- *Early adopters.* These are individuals with the highest opinion leadership among the categories. They often have high social status, financial liquidity, and advanced education. They're judicious in their choices and use these choices to maintain their communication position.

- *Early majority.* These individuals have above-average social status and contact with early adopters. However, they seldom hold positions of opinion leadership.

- *Late majority.* These individuals are skeptical of innovations and typically adopt after the majority of society does.

---

5. https://en.wikipedia.org/wiki/Diffusion_of_innovations

- *Laggards.* These are the last individuals to adopt an innovation and are usually averse to change. They're typically focused on maintaining *traditions* rather than moving on to new trends.

These adopter categories can be plotted on a standard bell curve, as shown in the following image.

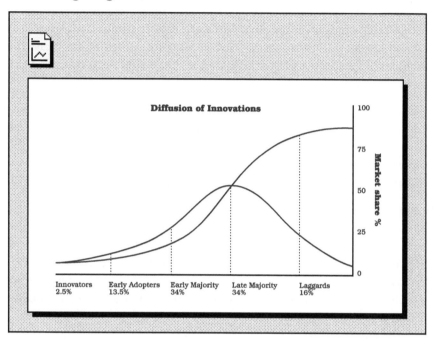

Remote working is an innovative idea to which we can apply this model. It may help us understand how the idea has been spreading and the motivations of those who have been spreading it.

Toward the end of the previous chapter, we noted how the early adopters of fully remote company culture also happened to be the influential individuals who are communicating these changes to the wider world. I changed this sentence around.

Now this makes sense. The early adopters are living up to the characteristics of their category. They use their judicious choice of remote working to maintain a communication position that makes them thought leaders in that space.

Wow. Who'd have thought?

The early adopters, due to their influential stance on remote working, hire individuals who showed similar traits as them: those who made the judicious choice to be remote workers and, therefore, actively chose positions at those companies. It makes sense, after all. They're in the same part of the adoption curve. They go after what they want.

However, it follows that the prepandemic literature on remote working has a bias because it's not imbued with the same skepticism and aversion to change that those in the later adoption categories carry. The virtues of remote working were communicated with far more enthusiasm than the hard parts that we're covering in this chapter. After all, if you were excited about early electric cars, you would be more likely to read, learn, and communicate about the break-throughs in technology and the reduction in emissions than you would about the environmental impact of lithium mining.

Now to the late majorities and laggards. When much of our industry was forced to work remotely during the 2020 pandemic, everybody, regardless of which adoption category they would be classified in, had to adopt the idea of remote working immediately. Those who were skeptical, adverse, and would not judiciously choose to adopt that idea had no choice.

Through our collective experiences and surveys, the harder parts of remote working became apparent. Issues such as ergonomics, diet, exercise, stress, burnout, isolation, depression, anxiety, and insomnia rose to the forefront of the conversation as core challenges that needed our collective attention and understanding. Financial uncertainty, such as whether employers would eventually consider cutting pay for staff based on their localized cost of living, contributed to their anxiety.

But this shouldn't put us off from a remote future. It may just be part of the normal process of change. If you're thinking that the outlook may be dire, there's another curve model that may instill some optimism as we spend time focusing on these difficult topics.

The productivity J-curve, shown in the diagram on page 279, is a pattern in data that shows that companies are often hesitant to adopt new technology because it requires significant investment of time and money due to the need to learn new tools and skills.[6] These investments lead to a drop in productivity while the adoption is taking place, even though in the long term the adoption will lead to a much higher level of productivity.

Talk of productivity in this book so far has been focused around the tools and techniques to make remote work a success. However, an even more important part of productivity over a long period of time is the health and well-being of employees.

---

6.   https://www.aeaweb.org/articles?id=10.1257/mac.20180386

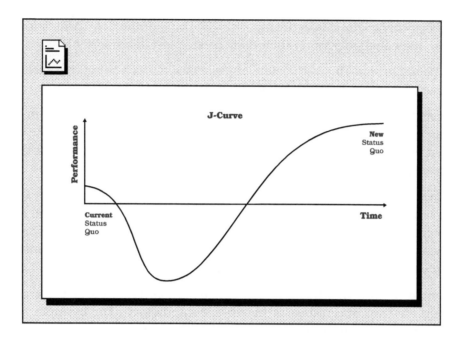

We need to look at it this way: in addition to the need for better tools and techniques to allow for effective remote working, increased knowledge and support is required for the physical and mental health issues that can come along with it. Whereas skepticism and aversion to change may have prevented mass adoption of remote working in the past, the pandemic made most of our industry forcibly move through the J-curve whether they liked it or not.[7]

Therefore, we could reason that the industry is now emerging and climbing out of the J-curve dip, on the upward trajectory toward greater productivity, flexibility, and employee happiness. By understanding the nature of physical and mental health so we can better discuss, identify, treat, and even prevent problems, we pave the way to a better remote-working experience for everyone, leading our industry toward a better future.

Are you with us?

The Physical and Mental Impact of Working Remotely

When we think about health, we could partition it into two dimensions that are worth considering separately:

---

7. https://www.tiktok.com/@planetmoney/video/6852010973117549830

- *Physical health.* This is the state of well-being of the body, which allows an individual to perform their daily tasks and live comfortably.

- *Mental health.* This is the state of psychological well-being that includes our ability to cope with stress and enjoy daily life.

Remote working means that we'll be spending more time away from our colleagues, who—no matter how much they may have annoyed you in the past by not refilling the coffee pot—do look out for us, ask after us, and notice how we're changing from day to day.

Some of us have families and friends who help us stay connected, but some remote workers may spend a majority of their time alone. Thus, we all have a responsibility to look after our own health and also look out for the health of those we work with. Even if all of our colleagues are at the end of email or video calls, they're still human beings, just like us.

Although we partition them in this chapter so we can look at them more closely, the two dimensions of health are interlinked.[8] For example, poor mental health is a risk factor for chronic physical conditions, and people with chronic physical conditions are at risk of developing poor mental health.

So as we work through some different facets of both physical and mental health, remember that a holistic, unified, good state of well-being is what we're all after. You need a little bit of everything to remain healthy and happy. Research in isolation; apply broadly.

Physical Health

Let's begin by looking at some different facets of physical health. We spend most of our days sitting at desks, so we need to look after our bodies.

Diet

What you're putting into your body makes a significant difference in your energy levels and your mood. In theory, working from home offers many more opportunities to eat well for less money than if you were going into the office. You've got access to your kitchen and—in theory, of course—you could be cooking yourself a nutritious breakfast, lunch, and dinner every single day.

You could even be preparing food in batches that you can easily store and access throughout the week without needing to carry food on the journey to and from the office. To those who have never worked from home before, having

---

8. https://ontario.cmha.ca/documents/connection-between-mental-and-physical-health/

access to the kitchen is a dream, one filled with breakfast bagels, healthy cooked noodle lunches, and early nutritious dinners.

However, in the same manner as when you spend a week of vacation at home and get ever lazier with showering, bad habits can begin to slip in. That dream of breakfast bagels can turn into one of sugary cereal, and instant ramen for lunch and a microwave dinner.

Similarly, easy access to your cupboards full of coffee and whatever sugary or caffeinated drinks you want can seem liberating, but it might just have you crashing hard in the afternoons or unable to sleep properly at night. You may end up eating because you're bored, stressed, or just snacking at the computer all day rather than eating balanced meals.

Before you know it, the professional has turned into the teenager. And if these habits continue for too long, a poor diet will lead to poor health.

When working remotely, you should do the following:

- *Have a plan for what you're going to eat during in the week.* Spending some time during the weekend to plan what you're going to have for breakfast, lunch, and dinner each day is beneficial for a number of reasons. Not only does it ensure that you'll have all of the groceries that you need ahead of time so that you're properly fueled, it completely removes the continual dilemma of "OK, so what am I going to eat later?"

- *Ensure that you've filled your kitchen with good snacks.* In addition to getting the groceries for the week, make sure that you also have healthy snacks such as fruit, cottage cheese, or yogurt with no added sugar that you can eat throughout the day with no guilt.

- *Reduce temptation by keeping bad foods outside of your home.* The easiest way to avoid eating a lot of chocolate is to not buy it in the first place. Although it's nice to stockpile treats for yourself as a reward, if you're anything like the author, you'll probably eat them all within two hours.

- *Track what you're eating, if it helps.* There are plenty of free applications that you can use to track the calories and macronutrient breakdowns of the foods that you're eating so that you can get a better picture of whether you're eating well. Just the act of tracking what you eat can make you more accountable for not straying from eating healthily.

- *Eat when you're hungry, not bored or stressed.* When that project deadline is looming, it can be easy to turn to sugar, caffeine, and carbohydrates for support. But this isn't going to do your health any good in the long term. Be mindful of your eating habits, and stick to a plan for what you're eating.

Your diet is the fuel that gets you through the day. The better the fuel, the better that every other aspect of your health is going to be. Ensure that you're eating a balanced diet and that you're getting the right amount of calories for your activity level. In addition to helping you maintain a healthy body weight, there's evidence that shows that good dietary choices can reduce the risk of heart disease, stroke, and some cancers.[9] However, this is easier said than done. There's a reason that dieting is a multibillion-dollar industry. But incremental changes, however small, compound over time.

The occasional bit of chocolate doesn't hurt, though. You've gotta live a little.

Repetitive Strain Injury

While not unique to remote working, repetitive strain injury (RSI) is a term used to describe pain in muscles, nerves, and tendons caused by repetitive movement and overuse.[10] For those of us who spend most of our time on computers, it typically affects the forearms, elbows, wrists, and hands and neck and shoulders.

Although it's easy to pass off aching, tenderness, stiffness, tingling, or numbness as normal when using the computer, it's important that you pay attention to the signals that your body is giving you. RSI can develop slowly over time, and mild issues can turn into severe ones that'll prevent you from using a keyboard or mouse at all.

The risk of RSI increases when you are

- Doing repetitive activities such as typing and using the mouse

- Performing these activities with high intensity for long periods of time without rest

- In a poor physical posture that does not adhere to good workplace ergonomics[11]

If that sounds like you, a change might be in order.

Given that you're likely to be unable to get away from using a mouse and keyboard, you should make sure that you're taking appropriate breaks from the computer throughout the day. Most importantly, however, is having good

---

9. https://www.nhs.uk/live-well/eat-well/
10. https://www.nhs.uk/conditions/repetitive-strain-injury-rsi/
11. https://www.mayoclinic.org/healthy-lifestyle/adult-health/in-depth/office-ergonomics/art-20046169

ergonomics. This is covered in more detail in Chapter 2, Getting Set Up, on page 13.

The key is that you should use your tools in the same way that a construction worker uses theirs. A circular saw is dangerous when used incorrectly, so workers use specific safety equipment and techniques to protect themselves. Additionally, the tool is regularly maintained so that it introduces less risk to the workers from it malfunctioning. Care is taken.

In the same way that you wouldn't expect a construction worker to use a circular saw one-handed while eating a sandwich and wearing no safety equipment, you shouldn't spend large portions of your day working on your laptop while lying down with your neck, arms, and hands at the wrong angles. It'll hurt you in the long run. Don't do it.

In addition to ensuring you have an ergonomically correct setup and you're taking regular breaks, you need to take action if you think that you're experiencing any of the symptoms of RSI mentioned previously. If you think that you are, speak to your employer to see if they can help you by improving your work space. If the symptoms continue in spite of that, see a doctor. It's better to work with more breaks now than to be unable to work at all.

Exercise

As wonderful as technology and computers are, they're making us do less physical activity as part of our work. Exercise is therefore essential for your physical health. It increases strength, develops your muscles and your cardiovascular system, and releases endorphins that make you feel better and reduce stress.[12]

Many people are put off from physical exercise because of bad past experiences. Feeling embarrassed at the gym, not knowing how to use weights or bizarre equipment, or being out of shape can create significant physical and mental barriers to feeling happy and confident in your own body. But the reality is that there are many ways to get the exercise that you need without needing to wear Lycra bodysuits or risk falling over in the middle of an exercise class.

Adults should aim to do the following:

- Do strengthening exercises that work the major muscle groups at least two times a week.

---

12. https://www.nhs.uk/live-well/exercise/

- Do at least 150 minutes of moderate-intensity activity a week or seventy-five minutes of vigorous-intensity activity a week.

- Reduce the amount of time that you spend not moving at all (e.g., sitting and lying down).

The good news is that moderate-intensity activity can include

- Brisk walking
- Riding a bike
- Hiking
- Cleaning your house
- Jumping rope

These are all things that you can do privately, away from thumping dance music and neon clothing. The same is true for more vigorous activities:

- Running
- Swimming
- Lifting weights
- Riding a bike fast or uphill
- Walking up stairs

There are plenty of options for activities, both alone and with others. The kinds of activities that count toward strengthening your muscles don't have to involve bench pressing a horse while somebody screams at you either. They can be

- Yoga
- Pilates
- Tai chi
- Resistance-band exercises
- Body-weight exercises such as push-ups and sit-ups

With a bit of thought, it's straightforward to be able to perform all of the exercise that you need with minimal equipment. You could get your vigorous exercise from running around your local park and doing a couple of sessions of body-weight exercises on the floor each week. None of these cost money, other than the initial purchase of some suitable clothing.

If you're after some inspiration for your fitness routine, you can find it for free online. For example, YouTube has yoga classes and body-weight routines that you can work out to, and it also has nutrition- and exercise-planning advice and pretty much anything else you can think of. We've come a long way from purchasing workout VHS tapes.

As you become more comfortable with exercising, you can work out what sort of exercises you enjoy doing most. Perhaps you could give high-intensity interval training (HIIT) a try if you're trying to optimize by using the least time possible for the biggest gains,[13] or maybe you could gradually explore your local area on a bicycle. Whatever you do, just make sure that you're enjoying it. That's what makes it become a habit.

Integrating daily exercise is important when working remotely because you may take for granted how much you were moving when you were going to the office. Those walks to the train, to the subway, and through the city at fast pace and all of those flights of stairs really add up.

Though you gain time from not commuting, finding the time to exercise can be difficult. We all lead busy lives, and when there are three high-priority things to do at home, exercise rarely trumps them at the top of the list. Experiment with times of the day and week that let you divide up that 150 minutes of moderate exercise among other activities that you're doing. Perhaps you could walk or cycle instead of taking the car. Maybe you could run for fifteen minutes at lunch while the rice cooker is preparing your food. Perhaps you could bookend your days with walks with the baby. Often there's a way even if there doesn't appear to be. It just requires some creativity.

Rest and Sleep

In addition to what you actively do for your health, there's one equally important activity that involves doing nothing. That's rest. It's crucial.

Although you may feel like the noble choice is to squeeze every ounce of productivity out of every single hour, regardless of how tired you actually are, the results are fundamentally counterproductive. We're not built for continuous functioning. Our bodies and minds need sufficient rest and recovery every day to perform at our best.

The term *rest* covers the times of the day in which we're not working and are partaking in relaxing leisure activities. There are no prescriptions here about what rest means for you. Some people enjoy reading books to switch off. Some like watching movies. Some find that cooking or playing with their children is the best way to disconnect from the stressors of the everyday. All physical and mental effort requires recovery.

---

13. https://en.wikipedia.org/wiki/High-intensity_interval_training

In the same way that software projects have scope creep, what we commit to every single day beyond the baseline of necessity can balloon out of proportion. Doing a full-time job is a significant undertaking. When you add errands and exercise into the mix, and family commitments, you can end up chasing a completeness and perfection in your life that's never achievable. This is a surefire way to burn out. As well as serving others, you need to serve yourself.

Active forms of rest include relaxation techniques such as yoga, meditation, and breathing exercises. Passive forms of rest include lying down and napping. You'll know what works for you, but you need rest. Try to ensure each day that you have periods of rest that act as bookends around activities. For example, eating a proper breakfast, lunch, and dinner allows you to break up the day and get away from the computer. At the end of the day, once you have some quiet, ensure that you dedicate some time to actively choosing to rest, perhaps by reading or watching television.

In addition to rest, you need sleep. It's essential for the health of your brain.[14] A lack of quality sleep impairs your attention span, concentration, reaction times, and emotions. Sleep is also crucial for keeping your heart healthy, your immune system strong, and your appetite under control.[15]

Additionally, as you sleep, short-term memories convert into long-term memories, helping you learn and see things more clearly. I'm sure we've all immediately solved a programming problem in the morning that seemed impossible at 5 p.m. the previous day.

Rest and sleep are intertwined. To set yourself up for good sleep, you need to create the conditions that you need through rest. To enjoy periods of rest, you need to have good sleep; otherwise, you'll be too tired to do any leisure activities.

You should try your best to sleep at regular times. By working toward a predictable bedtime and wake-up time, you program your brain with this routine. Once you know what time you're aiming to go to bed each night, you need to ensure that you wind down toward it.[16] There's growing evidence that poor sleep is linked to serious illness, so you should never push through tiredness, even if you feel that work demands it.[17]

---

14. https://www.sleep.org/resting-vs-sleeping/
15. https://www.bupa.co.uk/newsroom/ourviews/nine-benefits-good-night-sleep
16. https://www.nhs.uk/live-well/sleep-and-tiredness/how-to-get-to-sleep/
17. https://academic.oup.com/ehjdh/advance-article/doi/10.1093/ehjdh/ztab088/6423198

To help with this, you could do the following:

- *Try your best to leave all of your work communication behind at the end of the day.* If you have work email or notifications on your personal phone, mute them in the evening or put your phone somewhere else in your home, away from you.

- *Write down everything that you need to do the next day.* This allows you to not worry about forgetting something that you need to pick up later, for example. Once it's committed to paper, move on and begin relaxing.

- *Avoid using electronic devices for an hour or so before bed.* In addition to evidence that suggests that the light from device screens can have a negative impact on sleep, many applications are designed to be addictive and can provide too much stimulation when you should be relaxing.

- *Try some active relaxation.* You could try meditation or some breathing exercises or some light yoga stretches. In addition to the activities themselves relaxing you, doing them as part of your winding-down routine can help signal to your subconscious that it's time to relax.

- *Have a warm bath* to relax your muscles and change your body temperature to one that is ideal for resting.

- If you have difficulty with a restless mind once you're in bed, you could *try listening to a guided relaxation audio.* There are plenty of free guided breathing exercises and body-scan meditations online that are designed to help you fall asleep naturally at the end.

Like exercise, this advice is simple but not straightforward to implement. Remote working may make you feel like you're unable to switch off because the area where you work, and all of the unopened email contained within, is visible in the corner of the room. Spending the majority of your day in front of screens for business and pleasure may delay the release of melatonin and delay sleepiness. A little self-discipline around rest and sleep can go a long way toward making you feel better when you wake each morning, which also positively impacts your mental health.

Mental Health

Now that we've examined the elements of physical health, let's proceed to consider mental health. The topic of mental health is broad, so we'll limit our focus to some of the most commonly experienced mental-health issues in the workplace.

Your Turn: Audit Your Physical Health Routine

Take some time to reflect on the different aspects of physical health that we've covered and whether you currently feel that you're taking enough action toward them:

- Consider your diet. Are you eating nutritious food regularly, and are you ensuring that you stay hydrated? If it helps, keep a food journal for a week and write down everything that you eat and drink. What habits does it reveal about yourself? Would you like to change any of them?

- Spend a day being mindful of the feeling of your body while you're working. Do you feel any numbness, tingling, aches, or pains? Could these be caused by poor ergonomics? How could you improve this?

- Do you feel like you're currently getting enough vigorous exercise? If not, consider if there are simple ways that you can begin to incorporate it, such as bookending your day with fifteen minutes of brisk walking.

- What are your rest and sleep habits? If you aren't getting enough sleep, try to set a sleeping routine for yourself that includes a wind-down phase before bed.

Mental-health problems are real and they're serious. They should be considered and treated with the same care and attention that physical health problems are. If you believe that you're suffering from a mental-health problem, it's critical that you seek help. Your general health practitioner is a good place to start.

Another essential part of getting help is talking about how you feel. This can be with a friend, family member, or health professional. Depending on how you feel about it, you could seek help through your workplace by talking to your manager or HR department. They may have access to additional resources that you can use.

Just remember that whatever you may go through, you're not alone. According to the National Alliance on Mental Health, 20.6 percent of U.S. adults experienced mental illness in 2019.[18] The more we accept that mental illness is part of what it means to be human, and the more comfortable we become sharing our stories and feelings with each other, the better we can all become at coping with what's a natural part of the human condition.

Stress

All of us feel stress from time to time. If you work a busy job or have a hectic family schedule, stress is what you feel as you're trying to hit that deadline or call the dentist while trying to get screaming children ready for school.

---

18. https://www.nami.org/mhstats

In fact, sometimes stress can be beneficial. We can partition the feeling of stress into two categories:

- *Eustress.* From the Greek prefix *eu-*, meaning *good,* this literally means *good stress.* This occurs when the gap between what one has and what one wants is slightly stretched but not to the breaking point.[19] It's typically associated with desirable events, such as wanting to achieve a project milestone or get the family to the airport on time.

- *Distress.* This is persistent stress that's not resolved through coping or adaptation and may lead to anxiety, withdrawal, and depressive behavior. Often this occurs when uncontrollable events are happening and a person is unable to cope. It's typically associated with undesirable events.

Stressors on the body are taxing and require recovery. Physical symptoms of too much stress involve, but are not limited to, headaches and dizziness, muscle tension and pain, stomach problems, chest pains, and accelerated heartbeat. Mental symptoms include difficulty concentrating, inability to make clear decisions, feelings of overwhelm, constant worry, and forgetfulness.[20]

These symptoms may culminate in a person being irritable and snappy, sleeping and eating too much or too little, avoiding places and people, and drinking and smoking more. It's believed that the body can't tell whether a stressor has originated from distress or eustress, and to an extent, an individual's perception of a situation is what determines that categorization.

But regardless of the origin, too much stress can inhibit performance and make you ill. We need to try to keep stress at an optimal level. When checking in on your own stress, it's worth keeping in mind a model called the Yerkes-Dodson curve,[21] shown in the image on page 290, and where you've been on it over the preceding few days.

What the curve shows is that stress can increase performance to a point, but beyond that, higher levels of arousal lead to strong anxiety, which inhibits us. And given that periods of stress require periods of rest to recover from them, continual overarousal can begin to contribute to the other mental health problems that we describe in this chapter.

Being remote means that you have fewer opportunities to defuse stress within spontaneous interactions. Often an ad hoc chat in the corridor about how much of a pain that production issue has been can be cathartic. Often

---

19. https://en.wikipedia.org/wiki/Eustress
20. https://www.nhs.uk/mental-health/feelings-symptoms-behaviours/feelings-and-symptoms/stress/
21. https://hbr.org/2016/04/are-you-too-stressed-to-be-productive-or-not-stressed-enough

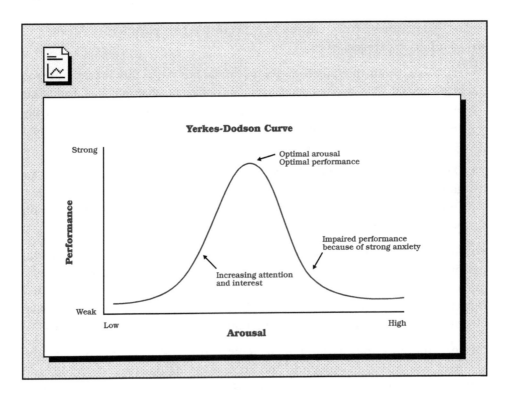

when we're stressed, we can turn inward rather than actively reaching out for help. And given that we have to actively reach out when remote, it can be easy to suffer in silence.

To manage your stress, you should try to do the following:

- *Regularly talk about how you feel* with a friend, family member, or colleague.

- *Exercise regularly* because it releases endorphins and disconnects you from the stressful situation.

- *Try calming techniques,* such as mindful breathing, meditation, or yoga. You should also ensure that you're sleeping properly and performing an evening wind-down routine.

- *Make a small step toward addressing the problem.* Even if it's overwhelming, taking action in a stressful situation, even if you feel like you can't and want to walk away, can build confidence that can see you through it. If writing that document is too overwhelming, try to get one paragraph done. If the presentation preparation is too much to handle, try to get one slide written.

- *Manage your time.* If you feel like everything is spinning out of control, you could use a method like the Pomodoro Technique,[22] which helps you focus your work into twenty-five-minute blocks with five-minute breaks in-between.

- It goes without saying, but *get help from a health professional* if you're unable to cope with your stress.

Low Mood, Sadness, and Depression

We've all had periods in our lives where our mood has been low, motivation has suffered, and it's hard to see the positive side of things. Experiencing a spectrum of emotions is normal. You may have experienced feeling sad, anxious, panicky, tired or unable to sleep, anger or frustration, or low confidence or self-esteem.[23]

Typically, these feelings pass after a few days, sometimes by changing something small in your life such as getting more sleep, being more active, or resolving an issue that's been bothering you. You could try any of the suggestions in the preceding section about managing stress to see if you can improve the situation yourself.

Where you need to be mindful is when a low mood begins to last for several weeks or more because it could be a sign of depression. Other symptoms of depression include not getting any enjoyment out of life, feeling hopeless, not being able to concentrate on everyday things, having suicidal thoughts or thoughts about harming yourself.

If you begin to identify with the symptoms of depression, it's important that you seek some assistance. If you're unsure of how you feel, you could try a self-assessment quiz to better understand it.[24]

The most critical thing to do if you feel that you're struggling is to talk to someone. If you categorize yourself as having a temporary low mood, ensure that you talk to friends, family, or your manager to get their support and advice.

However, if you can't cope with your low mood, or you identify more with the symptoms of depression, it's important you see a health professional. There are many ways they can offer support, such as by checking up on your general health, referring you to therapy, or suggesting medications that could help.

---

22. https://en.wikipedia.org/wiki/Pomodoro_Technique
23. https://www.nhs.uk/mental-health/feelings-symptoms-behaviours/feelings-and-symptoms/low-mood-sadness-depression/
24. https://www.nhs.uk/mental-health/self-help/guides-tools-and-activities/depression-anxiety-self-assessment-quiz/

In the context of remote working, there are some important things to know:

- *It's entirely normal to feel low or depressed, and there is help available.* Just ensure that you take some action, even if it's just talking to a friend. Do not suffer in silence.

- *Pretty much everyone goes through low moods and depression,* so connecting with others regularly about how they feel can be beneficial to see that you're not alone or abnormal.

- *You're likely spending more time physically distant from others,* so it's important that you're more proactive in understanding how you're feeling on a day-to-day basis. A daily mood journal can be helpful.[25]

- *Your colleagues may be going through similar situations too.* Make sure you check in on them. A simple "How are you feeling?" goes a long way.

Anxiety, Fear, and Panic

Like a low mood, it's completely normal to feel anxious and scared sometimes. However, when it's a feeling that persists and begins to affect you physically and mentally and how you behave, you may need some additional support.

Anxiety can manifest physically in faster heartbeats, lightheaded and dizzy feelings, headaches, chest pains, loss of appetite, sweating, breathlessness, and feeling hot and shaky.[26] Mentally, you may feel tense and unable to relax, continually worry about the past or future, or feel upset or unable to sleep or concentrate.

In addition to affecting your performance at work, it can mean that you're unable to enjoy your leisure time, you may not take good care of yourself or others around you, you're subject to compulsive behavior such as continually checking your phone or email, or you imagine that the worst is always going to happen.

When working remotely, there may be fewer people who are interacting with you from day to day, especially if you live alone. Without others noticing your mood, occasional behaviors may worsen if you aren't regularly taking time to reflect on how you're feeling.

When anxiety and fear happen intensely and suddenly, they may be the symptoms of a panic attack. This can be five to thirty minutes of feeling like you're losing control, overwhelmed with dread, and potentially nauseous.

---

25. https://www.healthline.com/health/how-to-keep-mood-journal
26. https://www.nhs.uk/mental-health/feelings-symptoms-behaviours/feelings-and-symptoms/anxiety-fear-panic/

Although these feelings are scary, they're not dangerous. Like all animals, we evolved with the fight, flight, or freeze response to protect us from danger.[27] Heightened anxiety and panic can make your brain feel like you're being chased by a bear when you're actually sitting in a quiet room looking at a screen.

If anxious symptoms persist and start to continually affect your life, you should seek help from a health professional. Again, similar to depression, anxiety may make you feel like you want to withdraw from interactions, which can be especially isolating when working remotely. Even though you may not feel like talking about it, it's critical that you do.

Anxiety is a different condition than depression, but they commonly occur together and have similar treatments.[28] Both usually improve with therapy, medication, or both. Improving all facets of your physical health, such as exercise, sleep, and diet, may help improve the situation.

Burnout

Closely linked with your job is burnout, a special kind of stress. Burnout is a state of physical or emotional exhaustion that includes a sense of reduced accomplishment and loss of personal identity.[29] It can affect your physical and mental health.

The Mayo Clinic offers some questions that you can ask yourself to see if you may be experiencing burnout:

- Have you become cynical or critical at work?
- Do you drag yourself to work and have trouble getting started?
- Have you become irritable or impatient with coworkers, customers, or clients?
- Do you lack the energy to be consistently productive?
- Do you find it hard to concentrate?
- Do you lack satisfaction from your achievements?
- Do you feel disillusioned about your job?
- Are you using food, drugs, or alcohol to feel better or to simply not feel?
- Have your sleep habits changed?
- Are you troubled by unexplained headaches, stomach problems, or other physical complaints?

If you answered yes to some of these questions, you may be suffering from burnout. Typically, you're at risk if you have a heavy workload and long hours,

---

27. https://www.mind.org.uk/information-support/types-of-mental-health-problems/anxiety-and-panic-attacks/about-anxiety/

28. https://www.mayoclinic.org/diseases-conditions/depression/expert-answers/depression-and-anxiety/faq-20057989

29. https://www.mayoclinic.org/healthy-lifestyle/adult-health/in-depth/burnout/art-20046642

are struggling with your work-life balance, or feel like you have little or no control over the work that you're doing. It could be seen as having no autonomy, mastery, or purpose.

Remote workers can suffer in silence with burnout, especially if companies aren't trying their hardest to ensure that employees are maintaining a healthy work-life balance. If you believe that it's affecting you, addressing burnout has two facets. The first is addressing your own physical and mental health and assess whether you need to make changes, seek help, or both.

The second facet is your work itself, which is causing you these problems. You should talk to your manager or HR partner to discuss how you're feeling and how it's affecting you. It may be that you could work on a different team or project or put a plan in place with your manager to track your work so you can confidently stop working at the end of each day with no guilt or worry.

If after working on it with your manager, the situation doesn't improve, you should consider your options. No job is worth undermining your health for. And remember, take all of your vacation days, even if you don't think you need them. You do.

Your Turn: Keep Track of Your Mental Health

When you're working remotely, the increased isolation can mean that you're less in tune with how you're feeling from day to day. Keeping a journal can be a simple way to stay in check with how you feel:

- Spend five minutes writing in a journal each day. It doesn't need to be a leather-bound notebook; it can be a text file on your computer.

- Take note of your thoughts, what you're feeling positive and negative about, and anything else that might be on your mind at the time.

- At the end of each week, look back over the journal. Did you have any concerns that didn't end up manifesting? Do you feel better mentally for having spent some time writing each day?

- If you haven't already, take the self-assessment quiz that we referenced earlier in this section on how you've been feeling recently. If you have any concerns about the results, seek some advice.

Supporting Others Remotely

When you're on a plane, you're told that in the event of an emergency, you should put your own oxygen mask on first before helping others with theirs.

Now that we've completed the previous section and covered the aspects of your physical and mental health, you can be mindful of how you feel and understand why. You also know how to take positive action that will benefit your body and your mind. But you also work with others who may not be as in tune with themselves.

What You Can Do

As we touched upon, remote work can be isolating. Even though we're physically distant, we need to be connected and supportive to ensure that we're looking out for others as well as ourselves. This is especially true for younger workers who rely on their workplaces to form their friendships and social groups. If you're older and have an established social group and family, make extra effort to interact with those who don't. They may need you more than you think.

Small efforts can make a big difference. Although it may be the case that you're not a healthcare professional and you haven't done any specific training, simply showing a vested interest in how others are feeling and creating the space for them to talk can go a long way.

Here are some things that you could try:

- *Ask after people in one-on-one and small group meetings.* The beginning of a meeting is a good time to spend a couple of minutes asking how everyone is feeling. If others seem hesitant to share at first, you can lead by example and make sure that you regularly share how you feel, whether it's good or bad.

- *Make sure that there's some social time for your team each week.* Blocking out the last hour of Friday afternoons to collectively chat, play some browser-based games together, and generally goof off strengthens the bonds among team members and builds the rapport that makes others more likely to share with each other how they feel.

- *Start a virtual exercise club.* Free fitness-tracking applications can allow users to form groups, and you could create one for your team. This way, you can cheer each other on as you do activities.

- *Share your recipes and creations.* Cooking and eating well is more fun when you're able to find, share, and discuss recipes. Starting a cooking channel on your company chat platform is a neat way for people to connect and discuss what they've been making.

- *Keep an eye out for colleagues who go quiet.* If there's somebody on your team who has become less visible over time, reach out and see how they're doing. Simply asking if they're alright because they've not spoken much recently is enough.

- *Regularly talk about the topics in this chapter.* Because of stigma around mental health, people may feel embarrassed to talk about it. But by encouraging conversation, we can help ourselves while also helping others and reduce the stigma.

Here are two specific tips for preventing overwork that could help your team:

- *Establish rules of engagement.* Being explicit about the expected reply times for different communication methods keeps people from getting stressed out if their email inbox is piling up with messages from staff in other time zones at the end of their day. They can get around to them in the morning.

- *Leave loudly at the end of the day.* This one is for managers especially. When you're done for the day, announce it explicitly. For example, "OK, I'm out—time for the school run. Speak to you tomorrow." Setting the example that there's an explicit time that work ends makes it easier for others to leave, too, and not overwork.

Listening, Not Judging or Fixing

As an engineer, you want to fix problems. After all, this mindset is what has created all of the incredible technology that we use every day.

However, we can't be as direct with judging and classifying the physical and mental-health problems of others, nor should we try to suggest fixes. What we have to do—in most cases—is just be present and listen. Ask questions. "How are you feeling?" is better than "You seem down today." It lets the other person share as much or as little as they like.

You're likely not a medical expert, so don't diagnose. If someone is talking to you about their feelings, let them take the lead, and ask questions and summarize back to them what they're saying. By demonstrating that you're listening and understanding, you're showing them respect for sharing with you how they feel.

If you feel that the problem is serious, encourage them to seek help. Otherwise, listening is a true show of kindness.

What Your Company Should Do

Although there's no harm in helping yourself and your colleagues through the hard parts of remote working, we should all expect that our companies are actively trying to assist us through one of the biggest workplace transitions in knowledge work for generations.

Similar to healthcare, there should be a focus on prevention of issues rather than treatment. There are a number of ways that companies can do this:

- *Create a safe space for us all to experiment, learn, and improve.* Many of us are doing this remote-working thing for the first time. It's inevitable we're going to stumble our way through as we experiment with what works and what doesn't in terms of working together and staying connected and informed as an entire company. Leaders should try things out and admit when they don't work, then iterate and improve. They should also frequently solicit feedback and suggestions from employees on how to make the company an increasingly better place to work.

- *Set and continually repeat the expectation of what hours staff will work each week.* Company leaders should lead by example by setting their working hours in their calendars, sticking to them, and repeating the message that this is what the company does. This reduces anxiety among remote workers who feel that they should keep checking messages outside of their working hours. It removes the guilt associated with switching off from work when colleagues in other parts of the world are still working.

- *Set aside budget for in-person meet-ups.* This doesn't need to require that all employees fly across the world to one location. Instead, staff can self-organize on a semi-regular basis meeting up with those who are close to them, and they can expense their travel and activities. This allows remote workers to have much-needed social time that enables them to get to know their colleagues better, do something fun, build trust and rapport, and most of all, do so on company time and money.

- *Be mindful of team composition so that collaboration is simpler.* Grouping teams so that people work with others in a similar time zone allows for more synchronous interactions such as pair programming and informal chats. A tiny window of synchronous interaction each day can be isolating and stressful.

- *Train HR teams so that they have the ability to support remote workers.* There is an increasing number of accredited courses for HR professionals that set them up with the knowledge and tools they need. Investment here pays back dividends.

If you feel that your company isn't doing much in this area, speak to your manager. What do they think about it? Is it possible for that situation to change, and is there anything they can do to help?

And Breathe ...

OK, that was some heavy stuff. Necessary, but heavy. Here's what we covered in this chapter:

- We looked at *what's written about the effects of remote working both before and after the pandemic.*

- We saw how the focus of the material changed as those experiencing remote work moved from the early adopters to the late majority by looking at some *curve models.*

- We explored the *physical and mental-health issues that we may all face* so we can be aware of their symptoms.

- We learned some strategies for *how we can support others* in their own physical and mental health.

We all need to look out for ourselves and each other. Even though you may be working remotely in reasonable conditions surrounded by friends and family, it's likely that many of your coworkers may not be, especially if they're younger and less tenured in their careers. They may have personal or environmental issues that are dragging them down. The first step is just talking about it.

By building rapport and trust with those you work with by being open and mindful of the topics in this chapter, you can have more of an effect than you may think. Check in on yourself, and check in on others. It might just change someone's week.

In the next chapter, we look at a critical topic in our industry: diversity and inclusion. Does remote working help or hinder our efforts to improve a systemic issue in the workplace? Come and find out.

Virtue can only flourish amongst equals.

Mary Wollstonecraft

CHAPTER 15

The Path to Equality Is Remote

Ding-dong!

A new project, a new team to meet, another video call. The grid populates with both new and familiar faces.

"Hey, how's it going? Nice to meet you."

"Hello!"

"What's up?"

The last participant joins the call and the meeting gets underway. Jen, the director of product, kicks it off.

"OK, so I figure that not everyone on this call has met before, given that we're about to connect together two parts of the product that have always been quite separate to the user."

You see everyone nodding in unison.

"I thought so. No problem. Let's take a minute to loop round and have everyone introduce themselves."

And the chain of introductions begins.

There are people on the call from Canada, America, United Kingdom, and Germany. Some people are living in cities and some are in relatively unknown rural locations. In the background, there are at least three babies and toddlers, one dog barking out of the window at a bird, and not an office in sight.

"Isn't this neat? I know we take it for granted, but it's so cool to be able to work with people from so many different places," you say.

"I know, right?" replies Jen. "I used to work in a startup in California that seemed to only employ white men that were aged somewhere between twenty-five and thirty-five with checked flannel shirts and beards. There was a craft-beer keg in the kitchen."

"I know I've never been cool enough for startups, but that story reminds me of my time at a big corporation in London in the 1990s," says Steve. "Have you seen that bit in *The Matrix* where there are hundreds of Agent Smiths standing out in the rain? That was like our fire drill in winter."

Jen smiles.

"Yeah, this is good," she says. "If I can help it, I'm never getting on that commuter train again."

Her toddler is trying to climb on her lap just off camera. You can see two little hands scrabbling around.

"I mean, how can I ever let the daycare staff be thoroughly terrorized by this little guy? They wouldn't know what hit them! OK, sharing my screen, just a second …"

So here we are: the final chapter of the book. Haven't we come a long way together? It won't be long until we part ways. But stay with it. This is an important chapter.

You've seen that as we began to reach the very depths of the book in *The Hard Parts*, we encountered some challenging topics. And now that we're in the final chapter, we're going to face some even harder realities about the industry that we work in. But first, let's remember what this industry is creating.

Technology has elevated humanity. We have a lot of knowledge at our fingertips. Anybody with an Internet connection can access Wikipedia for free—a source that's continually updated every single day, around the clock by volunteers. We're also closer to each other than ever before. We can stay in touch with family and friends no matter where they're located. As long as they have a reliable connection, we can have video calls. And if they don't have a reliable connection, there's always messages and email. Our progress has moved mountains.

Yet within the industry, there's a gloomy outlook. We have too many stories of prejudice, stereotypes, lack of diversity, pay imbalances, glass ceilings, inequality, poor working conditions, and harassment. It seems those who are speaking out are not being heard loudly enough. Scandals at big technology companies such as Google and Uber resulted in mass walkouts as workers felt that senior leadership was taking no action despite the evidence and may even have been protecting powerful men rather than delivering justice.[1]

And it wasn't just discriminatory matters that highlighted the void between workers and executives in big tech. As we endured the COVID-19 pandemic in 2021, companies worldwide began to consider their permanent approach to remote and hybrid work in a world that was starting to return back to normal. Many workers campaigned for remote-work arrangements to be made permanent or for their presence in offices to be only required for occasional gatherings.

Some of the biggest technology companies such as Twitter and Facebook agreed and declared that their employees would be able to work from home indefinitely. However, at the time of writing, thousands of employees at Apple were unhappy with a mandate to work at the office for at least three days a week, on set days, despite having worked remotely and performed normally for nearly two years.

In a plea written to the executive leadership,[2] workers noted that during the period of remote working, they had "developed two major versions of all our operating systems, organized two full WWDCs, introduced numerous new products, transitioned to our own chipsets, and supported our customers with the same level of care as before." So why were they not being heard?

Apple staff also noted that remote work had benefits for diversity and inclusion in retention and hiring by tearing down previously existing communication barriers, improving work-life balance, and better integrating existing remote workers with the rest of the company.

Could remote work therefore have a positive impact on some of the most systemic issues in our industry? It's possible. Could remote work even develop into something that could truly change the world? We think so. If we consider the issues that we're facing, we can see that remote working can be a catalyst for positive change for people all over the world. We can create safe virtual working environments, free from prejudice. We can work flexible hours. We can all have an equal chance at contribution and promotion, regardless of whether we're in California or rural France. And we may never have to

---

1. https://www.ft.com/content/3434a0ce-d97d-11e8-a854-33d6f82e62f8
2. https://www.theverge.com/2021/6/4/22491629/apple-employees-push-back-return-office-internal-letter-tim-cook

choose between work and our home lives again. Isn't this a situation worth fighting for?

In this chapter, we're going to see how remote working could provide the path to equality in our industry. Here's what we're going to cover:

- We look at *diversity and inclusion* in technology, which can include numerous characteristics of human beings such as age, gender, color, and socioeconomic background. We explore some industry statistics and highlight common concerns that prove that this is something we should all be aware of and proactive in tackling.

- We see how *remote work may be the path to equality* by understanding how it can begin to help address systemic diversity and inclusion issues.

- We'll close out the chapter, and the book, by exploring *how we're only just getting started.* There's a brighter, more exciting future out there for all of us because of remote working, and the technology that we have at our disposal is only going to get better and better.

So, for the final time, let's get going.

Diversity and Inclusion

A burning issue that's been facing the technology industry for decades is a lack of diversity and inclusion within our organizations. This isn't a superficial issue that's only as deep as the numbers themselves. It's a systemic issue that's arguably one of the root causes of many of the problems that we see in technology today.

Diversity and inclusion are separate issues, but they're interconnected. *Diversity* is about the individuals who make up your workforce. *Inclusion* is about how you encourage and enable a work environment that allows all employees to be psychologically safe and able to contribute equally.

When we talk about diversity in the workplace, we aren't just talking about one particular characteristic, such as gender. Diversity also applies to age, race, ethnicity, sexuality, education, background, religion, and so on. In theory, assuming that all routes into technology are fair and unbiased, a sample of the diversity of the general population shouldn't be too far off a sample of the diversity of the technology workforce. But we know that certainly isn't the case.

For example, let's look at gender. In 2021 the total percentage of women in the U.S. labor force was 47 percent, which is close to the total percentage of women in the United States (50.8 percent). However, the percentage of women in technology roles at big tech companies was quite different. At Facebook, Apple, Google, and Microsoft, the percentage of women doing these jobs was 24 percent, 24 percent, 25 percent, and 23 percent respectively.[3]

In fact, the lack of balanced female representation in the workplace only gets worse as we move up into leadership positions. Only 8 percent of Fortune 500 companies have female CEOs.[4] A study by McKinsey & Company shows that as workers climb the corporate ladder, the proportion of women present at subsequent levels shrinks.[5] In entry-level jobs, 47 percent of roles are female dominated, equaling the percentage of women in the workforce. However, this shrinks to 40 percent representation at the managerial level, 36 percent at director, 31 percent at vice president, and 25 percent at CEO. The *broken rungs* of the ladder compound. With only eighty-six women to every one hundred men being promoted at the first step into management, there are continually fewer women with the experience to keep progressing upward.

Diversity isn't just about gender, however. In fact, many diversity initiatives at large companies have been criticized for seemingly only caring about increasing the number of white women in the workforce,[6] without being aware that truly addressing diversity and inclusion means a focus on *intersectionality*,[7] where the identity categories such as gender, age, race, class, ability, background, and so on are all interrelated when it comes to compounding marginalization. And due to the aforementioned characteristics of those who are in charge at companies, combined with an innate human bias and lack of awareness, diversity and inclusion problems proliferate.

Again, it isn't all about numbers. We have every reason to focus our efforts on improving diversity and inclusion. Studies, including one published in *Innovation: Organization & Management [DGJ14]*, have shown that gender diversity within R&D teams improves radical innovation. Further studies reinforce the business case for gender, ethnic, and cultural diversity in corporate leadership and even show that the most diverse companies are now more likely than ever to outperform less diverse peers on profitability.[8] But we know this isn't all about profitability. This is about equality and fair treatment of human beings.

3. https://www.statista.com/chart/4467/female-employees-at-tech-companies/
4. https://www.statista.com/chart/13995/female-ceos-in-fortune-500-companies/
5. https://www.mckinsey.com/featured-insights/diversity-and-inclusion/women-in-the-workplace
6. https://techcrunch.com/2015/12/13/dear-white-people-you-suck-at-diversity/
7. https://medium.com/projectinclude/true-diversity-is-intersectional-2282b8da8882
8. https://www.mckinsey.com/featured-insights/diversity-and-inclusion/diversity-wins-how-inclusion-matters

It goes even further than that. Diversity and inclusion issues have also become implicitly encoded into the technology we're creating, and we may not have realized it. This may even be having an impact on the progress we're seeing in entire disciplines, such as artificial intelligence (AI).[9] Many of the technologies produced in the AI domain are the result of training models on huge quantities of existing data, which are often sourced by the teams that are developing these tools. For example, one popular open dataset of human faces called Labelled Faces in the Wild was assembled from pictures of celebrities in the media from the mid-2000s.[10]

Since many AI facial recognition models were trained on this data, numerous systems were noted to be unable to detect Black faces.[11] This may not be surprising when looking at the data that these systems were trained upon. Many of the photographs of celebrities in the dataset were of white people, thus implicitly encoding racial bias into the models. Diverse teams would likely have asked, "Why are all these pictures of white people?"

More recently, a U.S. government study confirmed that facial-recognition models that were developed in the United States were all consistently bad at matching Asian, Black, and Native American faces. Yet models developed in Asian countries produced very little difference in false positives between Asian and Caucasian faces.[12]

Diverse teams have a significant impact. The issues are real, and they need fixing, for good. But why do we see such a lack of representation in the industry for particular groups? Are they unable to progress in their careers? Are they not getting the top jobs in the first place? The answer is that it's a combination of both, and these issues are interconnected.

What's Going On?

If we think about the problem from first principles, to improve diversity statistics, we need to attract and retain talent from intersectionally diverse groups. We need to ensure that

- *There's a pipeline of diverse candidates* entering the industry from education and by cross-training from other disciplines.

---

9. https://venturebeat.com/2020/11/12/why-ai-cant-move-forward-without-diversity-equity-and-inclusion/
10. http://vis-www.cs.umass.edu/lfw/
11. https://www.youtube.com/watch?v=t4DT3tQqgRM
12. https://www.technologyreview.com/2019/12/20/79/ai-face-recognition-racist-us-government-nist-study/

- *Organizations are taking diversity and inclusion initiatives seriously* by eliminating bias in sourcing and hiring and having an inclusive and welcoming culture that ensures diverse employees stay for the long term.

You may have heard a colleague say, "But there just aren't that many nonwhite engineers out there" in response to the challenge of increasing diversity. This has been called the *pipeline problem*, a theory that diversity initiatives aren't working because there simply aren't enough people from underrepresented groups to hire.[13] However, this focuses on the pool rather than the process, which means not having to uncover the real issue: systemic bias.

A study by Kauffman Fellows in 2020 noted that the perceived ethnicity of startup executives was 79.2 percent white. However, the number of Latinx and Black Americans with degrees has risen 350 percent and 55 percent, respectively, over the past 25 years. But this hasn't translated into similarly higher levels of representation within startups. Even perceived ethnicity has a large impact on fundraising. The study notes that, when considered relatively, nonwhite founding teams raise less venture capital than their white counterparts. What gives?

Company reports on the gender pay gap required by recent legislation in the United Kingdom show the void between men and women. Branches of Siemens, Huawei, and Civica paid women 40 percent less than men between 2018 and 2019.[14]

One way to read this statistic is that women get paid less than men for the same roles. However, what's typically the case is that white males dramatically outnumber everyone else at the most senior and well-paid positions in companies. And looking at the previous statistics on the gender of startup executives, and how far fewer women progress to management, we can see one example of how this can happen. The diagram on page 306 shows how women aren't progressing into senior positions.[15]

Similar to the U.S. workforce statistics that we saw earlier, there's a near-equal balance of men and women at junior job levels. However, as seniority progresses, the rate of attrition for women far outweighs that of men. For career-driven women, simply having a child—a human right—can have a negative impact on their careers. A study showed that female job candidates who reported longer maternity leave periods on their resumes (e.g., twelve

---

13. https://www.gem.com/blog/diversity-hiring-pipeline-problem
14. https://www.theregister.com/2019/04/04/pay_gap_figures_201819/
15. https://yourlossbook.com/the-attrition-triangle-model-diagram/

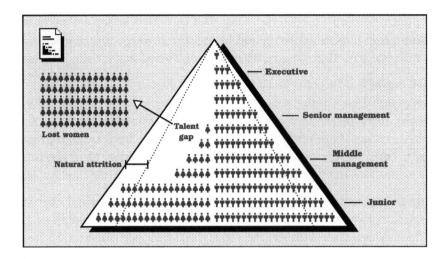

months) were perceived as less desirable candidates as those who took a shorter leave of one month.[16]

If you're part of an underrepresented group, it can feel like the odds are completely stacked against you.

Remote: The Great Leveler

But there's a reason to be hopeful. Back in *Treat Everyone as Remote*, we noted how the most important mindset to adopt when it comes to remote work is to do exactly what the title of the chapter suggests. Yet, even though it's a simple statement to comprehend, it's not entirely straightforward to implement.

This is because it not only covers practical changes to how we do our work, such as everyone joining meetings with their own cameras and microphones even if they're in the same building, it covers cultural changes to how we collaborate inside and outside of teams, across time zones, and on flexible schedules, where nobody is anything less than an equal contributor.

The good news is that if we're able to treat everyone as remote, and if we're able to master all of the topics that we've covered in this book, we'll begin to support a significant culture shift in how we think about—and go about—work:

- We can support people working *anywhere* in the world as long as they have a computer and an Internet connection.

- We can support people working on *flexible schedules* because we've shifted how we communicate and collaborate to support asynchronousness.

---

16. https://hbr.org/2018/09/do-longer-maternity-leaves-hurt-womens-careers

- We can ensure that as long as someone has a computer and an Internet connection, *they're an equal participant* with the same access to information, technology, and tools as everyone else.

Unpacking this further, remote working becomes much more than just a nice perk of working from home. It can enable people to significantly improve their lives.

Those who don't live in major cities—the places where the bulk of development jobs have always been—no longer have to face life choices such as whether to relocate to increase their opportunities to succeed in their careers. There's never been a good time for doing this. Earlier in life, you have less money and experience to fall back on. Later in life, it becomes harder to relocate due to families and all of life's commitments.

Instead, with remote work, hundreds of jobs are within the reach of anyone with a computer and an Internet connection. Flexibility around location becomes increasingly important as parents begin to age, which is something that this author has been acutely aware of recently. Whatever the situation, we can allow ourselves to be close to those who matter.

For people with young children, working remotely significantly increases the ability to be fully present and to make those challenging early years work, and even work well. As workplaces adopt increasing flexibility, and it becomes normal to be both parenting and working in a fluid rhythm, we get to see more babies on video calls. Otherwise, one parent might have to quit work because they couldn't lean on their families or afford childcare while they spent hours on trains to and from the office every day. No one should have to choose between family and work. With remote work we can have both.

With remote work we can begin to close the disability employment gap, which was at 53.7 percent compared to 82 percent for nondisabled people in the United Kingdom in 2020. Those who have disabilities have the opportunity to have comfortable, ergonomically correct home work spaces with any specialty equipment they may need to do their jobs to the best of their abilities. Those who were previously unable to make long and crowded journeys to company offices due to their condition need no longer feel like there are physical barriers between them and a world of career opportunities. Remember that *normal* life for disabled people can often mean being excluded.[17] Instead, disabled workers can have equally accessible careers via the Internet.

---

17. https://www.theguardian.com/commentisfree/2021/jun/02/remote-working-disabled-people-back-to-normal-disability-inclusion

Remote working means that there's never been a more exciting time to be in technology. Whether you're in a city, a small town, a bedroom, or even your parents' living room, you can build a career, learn new skills, and build the future while you're doing so. There no longer needs to be so much sacrifice. If you want to be near your family, you can. If you want to live a more peaceful and quiet life away from the city, you can. If you want to work with your child next to you, you can.

At the beginning of the book, in *Getting Set Up*, we opened the chapter by exploring the concept of the *workhome* in the Middle Ages, where people would intertwine their family and work lives. Sleeping and dining went hand in hand with crafts and creation.

We could be at the beginning of a cultural revolution that brings us back to a simpler way of living our lives, where we have ample time for work and also for ourselves and our families. We may no longer need to choose one over the other. They can all live under the same roof.

This is truly liberating and empowering.

This Is Just the Beginning

Those who were living in workhomes many hundreds of years ago wouldn't have been able to process the staggering progress that we've made in engineering, technology, medicine, and science since their time.

Not only does practically every home have electricity, heat, and running water, most of the global population now carries portable computers that allow them to communicate with anyone around the world and access any information that they need instantly.

We've come a long way.

And when we're talking about technology specifically, that statement holds true even over a relatively short period of time. The World Wide Web was only beginning to become a working reality on Tim Berners-Lee's CERN computer in 1990, after all. Even he probably didn't realize how fast we would progress in the decades to come. Very little is out of reach when we all stand on the shoulders of giants.

We've seen personal computers, dial-up modems, compact discs containing free trials of Internet-service providers on magazine covers, chat rooms, email, online gaming, broadband, Wi-Fi, smartphones, virtual and augmented reality.

It has all happened in a flash. Once something has potential, it gains focus from the smartest minds around the world, like you. And when that happens, anything is possible.

In ten years' time, the tools that you're using today to collaborate remotely will seem primitive. It wasn't long ago that we had to listen to nearly a minute's worth of garbled pips and squeaks from our 33.6K modems to get online; whereas, now we have an exponentially faster Internet connection almost anywhere, wirelessly over the air, via our phones. Given the rate of progress we've observed, we can see that when there's something for engineers to be interested in—and remote work is one of those things—improvements come forth in leaps and bounds.

So what does the future hold? Will we all have home offices where we're joined by holograms of our colleagues? Will we all meet and collaborate together in an immersive, 3D, online world via virtual-reality headsets? Will computers even look like they do today, or will we have progressed to brain-computer interfaces or implants? We can only imagine. Will we still be fixing null pointer exceptions? Probably.

But it goes even further. Perhaps mass remote working will bring more people together where they live. Local hubs of like-minded engineers can help bring their skills to the next generation and show them that there's a world of opportunity at their fingertips. There will be no more people left behind because of where they grew up or were educated. If the pen is mightier than the sword, a computer with an Internet connection is an entire army.

In a way we hope that this book ages quickly. Why? We hope that we can make remote work such an integral part of our lives that everything in this book becomes as obvious and second nature as typing on a keyboard or using a mouse. It feels like this is a true step change for our lives and our careers.

We hope that the times that working parents had to choose between their children and their careers are over, because they can have both. We hope that we can choose to be near our families when they need us the most. We hope that people all over the world take the opportunity to work in this incredible industry where almost anything is possible. We hope that a child born in a remote community can grow up to realize that the dream of making their own ding in the world isn't a fantasy reserved for the few lucky ones.

Because all it takes is a single *click*.

And That's It

We've made it to the end of the book. But before we part ways, let's review what we covered in this chapter:

- We went deep into *diversity and inclusion* to understand how there's still a long way to go to make our industry fair, equitable, and free of bias. These are issues that we should all be proactive in discussing, preventing, and educating others about.

- We saw how there's a possibility that remote work can forge *a path to equality* by beginning to help tackle some of the systemic diversity and inclusion issues that we highlighted previously.

- We took a step back and considered how fast technology is moving, and when it comes to remote working, *we're only just getting started.* The future is bright for all of us.

Back in the *Introduction*, we said that a significant hurdle for many companies committing to remote-working initiatives was that they hadn't yet learned the skills. Workers spent decades commuting to and from open-plan offices, relying primarily on synchronous interactions. We saw that companies needed to adapt their culture and practices to support being happy, healthy, and effective while remote.

Now that we've made it to the end, we hope that the possibility of a remote future is something that fills you with excitement. You now have the tools to do your job more effectively in the present moment, but most importantly, you're standing there at dawn with your surfboard ready to ride the wave as soon as it appears. Remote work can have an incredible impact on our society: more flexibility, more family time, more balance, more possibility, more routes into our industry, and more amazing ideas that we can all build together, no matter where we are.

It's now time that we part ways. It's been an absolute pleasure sharing this journey with you, and we're grateful that you decided to pick up this book.

If you stop by again in the future to remind yourself of some of the ideas, or to show a friend or colleague, we'll see you then. But until then, from one like-minded human to another—wherever you are in the world—I hope that remote working opens countless doors for you. Good luck. You've got this.

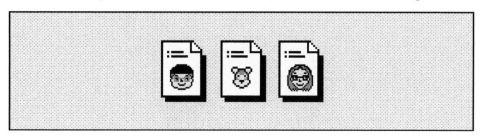

Bibliography

[Ayr05]   Robert U. Ayres Katalin Martinás. *On the Reappraisal of Microeconomics: Economic Growth and Change in a Material World*. Cengage Learning, Cheltenham, UK, 2005.

[Ber13]   Scott Berkun. *The Year Without Pants: WordPress.com and the Future of Work*. Jossey-Bass Inc., San Francisco, CA, 2013.

[Bro95]   Frederick P. Brooks Jr. *The Mythical Man-Month: Essays on Software Engineering*. Addison-Wesley, Boston, MA, Anniversary, 1995.

[DGJ14]   Cristina Díaz-García, Angela González-Moreno, and Francisco Jose Sáez-Martínez. Gender Diversity Within R&D Teams: Its Impact on Radicalness of Innovation. *Innovation: Organization & Management*. 2014, Dec.

[Gra09]   Paul Graham. Maker's Schedule, Manager's Schedule. *Essays by Paul Graham*. 2009, July.

[Gro95]   Andrew S. Grove. *High Output Management*. Vintage Books, New York, NY, 1995.

[Hal13]   Tim Hale. *Smarter Investing*. Edward Elgar Publishing, Boston, MA, 2013.

[HF13]   David H. Hanssen and Jason Fried. *Remote: Office Not Required*. Vermilion Books, London, UK, 2013.

[Pin09]   Daniel H. Pink. *Drive: The Surprising Truth About What Motivates Us*. Riverhead Books, New York, NY, 2009.

[Sta20]   James Stanier. *Become an Effective Software Engineering Manager*. The Pragmatic Bookshelf, Raleigh, NC, 2020.

[UXBB13] Iboro Udomon, Chuyee Xiong, Ryan Berns, Kathleen Best, and Nicole Vike. Visual, Audio, and Kinesthetic Effects on Memory Retention and Recall. *Journal of Advanced Student Science.* 2013.

[Wil98] James R. Williams. Guidelines for the Use of Multimedia in Instruction. *Proceedings of the Human Factors and Ergonomics Society Annual Meeting.* 1998.

[Won14] Linda Wong. *Essential Study Skills.* Edward Elgar Publishing, Boston, MA, 2014.

[Zie98] Martina Ziefle. Effects of Display Resolution on Visual Performance. *Human Factors: The Journal of the Human Factors and Ergonomics Society.* 1998.

Index

Thank you!

We hope you enjoyed this book and that you're already thinking about what you want to learn next. To help make that decision easier, we're offering you this gift.

Head on over to https://pragprog.com right now, and use the coupon code BUYANOTHER2022 to save 30% on your next ebook. Offer is void where prohibited or restricted. This offer does not apply to any edition of the *The Pragmatic Programmer* ebook.

And if you'd like to share your own expertise with the world, why not propose a writing idea to us? After all, many of our best authors started off as our readers, just like you. With a 50% royalty, world-class editorial services, and a name you trust, there's nothing to lose. Visit https://pragprog.com/become-an-author/ today to learn more and to get started.

We thank you for your continued support, and we hope to hear from you again soon!

The Pragmatic Bookshelf

SAVE 30%!
Use coupon code
BUYANOTHER2022

Become an Effective Software Engineering Manager

Software startups make global headlines every day. As technology companies succeed and grow, so do their engineering departments. In your career, you'll may suddenly get the opportunity to lead teams: to become a manager. But this is often uncharted territory. How do you decide whether this career move is right for you? And if you do, what do you need to learn to succeed? Where do you start? How do you know that you're doing it right? What does "it" even mean? And isn't management a dirty word? This book will share the secrets you need to know to manage engineers successfully.

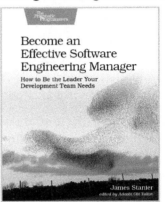

James Stanier
(396 pages) ISBN: 9781680507249. $45.95
https://pragprog.com/book/jsengman

Go Brain Teasers

This book contains 25 short programs that will challenge your understanding of Go. Like any big project, the Go developers had to make some design decisions that at times seem surprising. This book uses those quirks as a teaching opportunity. By understanding the gaps in your knowledge, you'll become better at what you do. Some of the teasers are from the author's experience shipping bugs to production, and some from others doing the same. Teasers and puzzles are fun, and learning how to solve them can teach you to avoid programming mistakes and maybe even impress your colleagues and future employers.

Miki Tebeka
(110 pages) ISBN: 9781680508994. $18.95
https://pragprog.com/book/d-gobrain

Competing with Unicorns

Today's tech unicorns develop software differently. They've developed a way of working that lets them scale like an enterprise while working like a startup. These techniques can be learned. This book takes you behind the scenes and shows you how companies like Google, Facebook, and Spotify do it. Leverage their insights, so your teams can work better together, ship higher-quality product faster, innovate more quickly, and compete with the unicorns.

Jonathan Rasmusson
(138 pages) ISBN: 9781680507232. $26.95
https://pragprog.com/book/jragile

Fixing Your Scrum

Broken Scrum practices limit your organization's ability to take full advantage of the agility Scrum should bring: The development team isn't cross-functional or self-organizing, the product owner doesn't get value for their investment, and stakeholders and customers are left wondering when something—anything—will get delivered. Learn how experienced Scrum masters balance the demands of these three levels of servant leadership, while removing organizational impediments and helping Scrum teams deliver real-world value. Discover how to visualize your work, resolve impediments, and empower your teams to self-organize and deliver using advanced coaching and facilitation techniques that honor and support the Scrum values and agile principles.

Ryan Ripley and Todd Miller
(240 pages) ISBN: 9781680506976. $45.95
https://pragprog.com/book/rrscrum

Software Estimation Without Guessing

Developers hate estimation, and most managers fear disappointment with the results, but there is hope for both. You'll have to give up some widely held misconceptions: let go of the notion that "an estimate is an estimate," and estimate for your particular need. Realize that estimates have a limited shelf-life, and re-estimate frequently as needed. When reality differs from your estimate, don't lament; mine that disappointment for the gold that can be the longer-term jackpot. We'll show you how.

George Dinwiddie
(246 pages) ISBN: 9781680506983. $29.95
https://pragprog.com/book/gdestimate

Real-World Kanban

Your team is stressed; priorities are unclear. You're not sure what your teammates are working on, and management isn't helping. If your team is struggling with any of these symptoms, these four case studies will guide you to project success. See how Kanban was used to significantly improve time to market and to create a shared focus across marketing, IT, and operations. Each case study comes with illustrations of the Kanban board and diagrams and graphs to help you see behind the scenes.

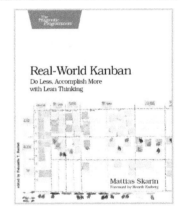

Mattias Skarin
(138 pages) ISBN: 9781680500776. $28
https://pragprog.com/book/mskanban

Rust Brain Teasers

The Rust programming language is consistent and does its best to avoid surprising the programmer. Like all languages, though, Rust still has its quirks. But these quirks present a teaching opportunity. In this book, you'll work through a series of brain teasers that will challenge your understanding of Rust. By understanding the gaps in your knowledge, you can become better at what you do and avoid mistakes. Many of the teasers in this book come from the author's own experience creating software. Others derive from commonly asked questions in the Rust community. Regardless of their origin, these brain teasers are fun, and let's face it: who doesn't love a good puzzle, right?

Herbert Wolverson
(138 pages) ISBN: 9781680509175. $18.95
https://pragprog.com/book/hwrustbrain

Hands-on Rust

Rust is an exciting new programming language combining the power of C with memory safety, fearless concurrency, and productivity boosters—and what better way to learn than by making games. Each chapter in this book presents hands-on, practical projects ranging from "Hello, World" to building a full dungeon crawler game. With this book, you'll learn game development skills applicable to other engines, including Unity and Unreal.

Herbert Wolverson
(342 pages) ISBN: 9781680508161. $47.95
https://pragprog.com/book/hwrust

The Pragmatic Bookshelf

The Pragmatic Bookshelf features books written by professional developers for professional developers. The titles continue the well-known Pragmatic Programmer style and continue to garner awards and rave reviews. As development gets more and more difficult, the Pragmatic Programmers will be there with more titles and products to help you stay on top of your game.

Visit Us Online

This Book's Home Page
https://pragprog.com/book/jsrw
Source code from this book, errata, and other resources. Come give us feedback, too!

Keep Up to Date
https://pragprog.com
Join our announcement mailing list (low volume) or follow us on twitter @pragprog for new titles, sales, coupons, hot tips, and more.

New and Noteworthy
https://pragprog.com/news
Check out the latest pragmatic developments, new titles and other offerings.

Save on the ebook

Save on the ebook versions of this title. Owning the paper version of this book entitles you to purchase the electronic versions at a terrific discount.

PDFs are great for carrying around on your laptop—they are hyperlinked, have color, and are fully searchable. Most titles are also available for the iPhone and iPod touch, Amazon Kindle, and other popular e-book readers.

Send a copy of your receipt to support@pragprog.com and we'll provide you with a discount coupon.

Contact Us

Online Orders:	*https://pragprog.com/catalog*
Customer Service:	*support@pragprog.com*
International Rights:	*translations@pragprog.com*
Academic Use:	*academic@pragprog.com*
Write for Us:	*http://write-for-us.pragprog.com*
Or Call:	+1 800-699-7764

CPSIA information can be obtained
at www.ICGtesting.com
Printed in the USA
BVHW011334060422
633570BV00006B/30